DATE DUE	
NOV 17 2009	

BRODART   Cat. No. 23-221

Flamenco

Conflicting Histories
of the Dance

MICHELLE HEFFNER HAYES

McFarland & Company, Inc., Publishers
Jefferson, North Carolina, and London

Portions of Chapter 4 originally appeared in "Blood Wedding: Traditions and Innovation in Contemporary Flamenco" in *Dancing Bodies, Living Histories: New Writings on Dance and Culture*, Lisa Doolittle and Anne Flynn, eds. (Banff, Alberta: Banff Centre Press, 2000).

Portions of Chapter 6 originally appeared in "Reading Improvisation in Flamenco and Postmodern Dance" in *Taken By Surprise: A Dance Improvisation Reader*, David Gere and Ann Cooper Albright, eds. (Middletown, CT: Wesleyan University Press, 2003).

LIBRARY OF CONGRESS CATALOGUING-IN-PUBLICATION DATA

Hayes, Michelle Heffner.
    Flamenco : conflicting histories of the dance / Michelle Heffner Hayes.
        p.   cm.
    Includes bibliographical references and index.

    ISBN 978-0-7864-3923-2
    softcover : 50# alkaline paper ∞

    1. Flamenco—History.   I. Title.
GV1796.F55H39   2009
793.3'19468—dc22   2009000730

British Library cataloguing data are available

On the cover: Pilar Andujar and Zenon Ramos in *Carmen: El Baile* (Photograph by Lois Greenfield)

Manufactured in the United States of America

McFarland & Company, Inc., Publishers
    Box 611, Jefferson, North Carolina 28640
    www.mcfarlandpub.com

For my mother,
Laraine, *la Reina* (the Queen)

Acknowledgments

The creation of a book requires a cast of thousands to support its production. This work, in particular, has benefited from the generosity of many people from disparate places on the globe. My mentors Marta Savigliano, Susan Foster, and Susan Rose helped to shape the research that led to this book. They taught me to think, read, and write critically, but most importantly, they taught me to trust my vision, and for that I will always be grateful. Linda Tomko provided me with the methodology for traditional dance history, a lesson I resisted, but for which I thank her every day. My teachers in flamenco deserve any credit for the veracity of what I write, and none of the blame for my errors: Armando Neri, Antonia Rojas, Katherine Thomas, Niurca Márquez, Omayra Amaya, Inmaculada Aguilar, Ángeles Gabaldón, Nelida Tirado and Pastora Galván. Carlota Santana and Eva Enciñias-Sandoval offered the wisdom gleaned from their years preserving flamenco in the United States. Without the expertise and friendship of Niurca Márquez and José Luis Rodriguez, none of my field work in Spain would have been possible. Pastora Galván and Belén Maya shared the gift of their creativity and candor in interviews that I will treasure forever. Photographers Liliam Dominguez and Paco Sánchez deserve to earn a great deal of money for their artistry, but they offered up the use of their images for this book out of our shared love for the art. The New York Public Library for the Performing Arts, under the peerless, impossibly elegant leadership of Jacqueline Z. Davis, is a national treasure. This book would not be possible without the resources of the Dance Collection, especially the people who work there. Pat Rader and Charles Perrier were invaluable guides in the process of acquiring the historic images that appear in this book. Kansas photographer Amy Lahr helped me bring all these photographs to print. Computer guru Brian Heffner, a most excellent brother, saved the text from the ether a number of times. Funding from the Kansas University Center for Research, in the form of a New Faculty General Research Fund Award, as well as a Hall Center for the Humanities Travel Grant, and an International Travel Grant from the Office of International Programs supported the final phases of work that led to the completion of this book.

Table of Contents

Introduction: Flamenco's Exotic Currency

Flamenco music and dance emerged in nineteenth-century Andalusia, a fusion of cultural influences from two major migrations of the *Roma*, an 800-year Moorish occupation, an entrenched Jewish Sephardic tradition, and the regional forms of the Spanish South. During the twentieth century, flamenco became one of the most visible symbols of Spanish national identity in the international community, largely due to the attraction of the tourist-oriented spectacles in Spain and abroad. Despite the continuing popularity of the exotic stereotype of the Spanish South, flamenco has also served as a counter-culture site of youthful resistance against the Franco regime, a forum for Gypsy civil rights activism within Spain, a means of asserting regional identities in a country often treated as a single, monolithic culture, and more recently, a state-sponsored and state-regulated art form.

My fascination with flamenco began with a textbook scenario of tourist exoticism. In 1975, not long after the death of Franco, my grandparents traveled to Spain on holiday. They collected several souvenirs as gifts for members of the family. I received a plastic flamenco doll in a fuchsia skirt trimmed with gold and lace, and a tambourine with the painted image of two flamenco dancers on its surface. As my grandmother carefully unwrapped the tissue paper surrounding them, she told me of the flamenco dancers' performance in the *tablaos* (nightclubs). She still recalls this experience, with an emphasis on the highlight of the performance, the moment in which the sweat from the dancers' brows flew from their bodies into the audience. Her description planted the seeds of exotic fascination in me, a desire predicated by difference and, simultaneously, self-identification. Tearing around the yard thumping on my tambourine in sweaty abandon, I could be someone else. In my mind, the flamenco doll did not have to pull up knee socks, stay silent and still in Mass, walk in single file, or wash her face and hands. In a childhood filled with blonde dolls and golden fairy-tale heroines, the flamenco doll reflected a dark-haired image back at me. She represented an unruly femininity, full of possibilities.

Early in my flamenco research, I spent hours watching performances. I felt compelled to "see" as much dance as I could access, and by any means necessary: live performance, video, film, documentaries, accounts in histories, scholarly articles, travel diaries, and popular fiction. I sought out any reference to flamenco in commercial films and music videos, and corresponded with other, similarly obsessed aficionados (amateur flamenco experts) through a listserv on the nascent internet. As I consumed these images, I started seeing predictable, discernable patterns in the representations of flamenco as an art form, and the flamenco dancing body as a site at which social and political forces collide.

I was seduced by the ways in which those tensions were masked by grand concepts like passion, femininity, beauty, love, and death. It was as if someone were trying to convince me that the particulars of the representations I was viewing were not tied to real people who lived in a world shaped by colonialism, class, race, regional competition for resources, repressive gender and sexual codes, and the international struggle for power. Instead, these dancing bodies expressed some essential characteristics of the human condition, beyond analysis. The intoxication I experienced as a viewer was compelling, but disturbing. I didn't want to complicate, or possibly ruin, such breathtaking beauty. Like so many of the students I teach at the university, I just wanted to enjoy my experience of visual pleasure. Why did I have to analyze how my assumptions about beauty were culturally constructed? Why couldn't I just "let it be"? As I became invested in the tradition as a scholar and practitioner, I realized that I was implicated in perpetuating assumptions that had a material impact on the artists I admired and the tradition I loved. So I had to direct a scrutinizing gaze inward and beneath the surface of those romantic narratives.

For example: the cable-access television show *Eye on Dance*, hosted and produced by Celia Ipiotis and broadcast in New York, served as a proxy for presence at live performances prior to the days of YouTube and streaming video. During the opening credits for a 1991 episode of the series, Ipiotis introduces her topic to the audience: "The mention of Spanish dance perfumes the air with sensuous and exotic images...."[1] With this sound byte she convinces viewers to stay where they are—don't touch that dial!—and promises to deliver images borne, like a scent, upon the air. Ipiotis directly addresses the underlying assumptions held by most American spectators as they view Spanish, and particularly flamenco, dances. Stereotypical images of flamenco portray the form and its practitioners as passionate, fiery, seductive, potentially violent, sensuous, and exotic. The flamenco dancer signifies an enviable and intimidating capacity for passion, both desirable and fearsome.

Witness the popular currency of the flamenco stereotype in U.S. music videos of that time, like Bryan Adams's "Have You Ever Loved a Woman?" (1995) in which the singer, dressed in a Cordoban hat, croons as the flamenco legend Paco de Lucía strums a guitar. Female flamenco dancers in polka-dotted dresses parade in the background. The song (from the soundtrack for the film of the same year, *Don Juan de Marco*) expresses the excessive love habits of the disturbed leading man, who envisions himself as the quintessential Latin Lover. Adams, a blond Canadian rocker, is endowed with a dark, romantic *machismo* through the presence of the flamenco performers. The effect is further supported by intercutting scenes from the film: an image of the American actor Johnny Depp is juxtaposed on top of the silhouette of the singer Adams. The dark-haired Depp is dressed in a costume undoubtedly resurrected from the wardrobe of another Hollywood Latin exotic, Zorro the Gay Blade. The proximity of the flamenco dancers and musicians in the background places Adams in a fictional exotic landscape. The Cordoban hat on his head and the filmic illusion of his interchangeability with Depp's character, Don Juan de Marco, persuade the viewer that Adams possesses the passionate qualities of the Latin Lover.

The popularity of the film and music video demonstrates the American enthusiasm for an image of flamenco carefully constructed for sale in a global marketplace. This particular configuration of the flamenco stereotype, the dark, brooding Latin Lover, requires the presence of the dancers in order to make it intelligible as a sign of passion, excess and exoticism. This process is seamless; it requires the mere presence of a few visual and audio signifiers to communicate a flood of associations. More recently, in the fourth season of Fox's television show *So You Think You Can Dance?* Los Angeles flamenco Timo Nuñez appeared as a guest artist in a bare-chested solo (well, he wore a vest, unbuttoned) reminiscent of Joaquin Cortes's early solos of the 1990s. The singer, guitarist, and footwork of the dancer were inaudible above the constant screaming of the audience through the entire piece. No other performance of the season elicited such a response. The history of flamenco provides a colorful template from which artists all over the world borrow in order to represent the "darker" side of human nature, from the nineteenth century to the present.

The tensions of colonialism, class, race, regional competition for resources, repressive gender and sexual codes, and the international struggle for power invest the image of the dancer with several layers of meaning. Even as they titillate the audience, these tensions fuel heated debates among flamenco practitioners and aficionados. These curators of a tradition struggle to preserve and promote an art form that is, on the one hand, visually appealing and highly accessible for audiences unfamiliar with the form and its history, and on the other hand, constantly in danger of being replaced by the "tourist-oriented" version of flamenco that has spurred a highly profitable market interest across the globe. The question of flamenco's identity, past, present and future, understandably concerns those who have devoted their lives to the pursuit of the art. What emerges in the discussions is not a single, concrete definition of flamenco. Rather, in the attempts to account for flamenco's history, conflicting perspectives emerge: dancers, guitarists, vocalists, teachers, and historians each will tell you a different story of the origin, development, great personalities, and "pure" forms of flamenco. The differences between the stories betray the agenda behind each narrative and the anxieties those narratives encompass.

Anxiety and the perception of difference predicate the formation of stereotypes, and stereotypes emulate the patterns of fear and desire that produce them. That is, stereotypes are specific, but never rigid. According to Sander L. Gilman,

> Stereotypes are a crude set of mental representations of the world. They are palimpsests on which the initial bipolar representations are still vaguely legible. They perpetuate a needed sense of difference between the "self" and the "object," which becomes the "Other." Because there is no real line between self and Other, an imaginary line must be drawn; and so that the illusion of an absolute difference between self and Other is never troubled, this line is as dynamic in its ability to alter itself as is the self.[2]

The conflicting narratives of flamenco's history reflect the struggles for power among differently aligned participants in a global culture. Although the flamenco stereotype retains enough consistent qualities to be intelligible, its overall characteristics shift according to the specific context. Correspondingly, the historical narratives that shape stereotypes contract and expand, fall out of order and develop "black-out spells" to accommodate disruptions in the distribution of power. Gilman explains,

> The models we employ to shape the stereotype are themselves protean. As we seek to project the source of our anxiety onto objects in the world, we select models from the social world in which we function. The models are thus neither "random" nor "archetypal."... Every social group has a set vocabulary of images for this externalized Other. These images are the product of history and of a culture that perpetuates them.[3]

The shape of the history depends upon the authorial voice, the "authority" of the voice that speaks or writes it. There is no single, monumental history of flamenco. Instead, different representations of history and the versions of the flamenco stereotype they produce form an entire field of meaning, embedded in and constitutive of a specific culture. An analysis of the historical development of the flamenco stereotype must account for the varied and changing components of that field, which makes the "discovery" of a definitive history impossible.

I am interested in the configuration of many flamencos within the traditionally accepted "history" of flamenco, the narrative techniques that constitute the authority of each text, the "authenticity" of the version of flamenco presented in each context, and the transformation of the flamenco stereotype at different historical moments. My purpose is to analyze the different representations of the dancer and of flamenco as a practice produced by flamencophiles during the course of the twentieth century through the present moment, and to examine the ways in which social tensions surrounding the production of each history inform its structure and content. This particular project, the exploration of the conflicting stories that compose the history of flamenco, searches for and grapples with representations of flamenco dance and images of the dancer in literature, formal histories, popular magazine and newspaper articles, flamenco journals, film, and contemporary performance. These representations of flamenco performance refer to artists, audiences, cultural stereotypes, political movements, and flamenco as a tradition from various vantage points at specific historic intervals.

I use the term "representation" with caution and deliberateness. Each "text," whether it is a literary description of a fictional character or a photograph from a playbill, carries with it a certain amount of weight; a claim, by virtue of its intelligibility, to "speaking of" or "speaking for" flamenco. Gayatri Chakravorty Spivak in her pivotal essay, "Can the Subaltern Speak?," presents an argument, articulately spun around an etymological dissection of the Marxist terms *darstellen* and *vertreten*, which points to the differences and similarities between two interpretations of the word "representation." To paraphrase, *darstellen* might be loosely translated as "re-presentation," in the sense of writing, a "reiteration." This meaning is different from *vertreten*, which indicates political "representation," an act of substitution on behalf of another. In my mind, at least, she describes a process of slippage between the two definitions and provokes a question: For whom do I speak when I re-present the events of the past? To whom, or to what, am I accountable? Spivak's response to her own questions led to an analysis of the Western subject in postcolonial discourse and some theories as to how the process of representation, in both senses, supported by a complex political and social history of colonialism in India, prevents the subaltern woman from "speaking." The final paragraph of the essay reads:

The subaltern woman cannot speak. There is no virtue in global laundry lists with "woman" as a pious term. Representation has not withered away. The female intellectual as intellectual has a circumscribed task which she must not disown with a flourish.[4]

Spivak insists that representation enacts its violence through the demarcation of difference. Since any form of representation, "speaking of" or "speaking for" another, necessarily involves the casting of a mute subject, the discussion of representation within a discourse cannot erase what Jacques Derrida refers to as "the violence of the letter."[5] Spivak squelches all hopes of innocence and, more pointedly, piety in the resistant writer, particularly in the work of the feminist scholar. She challenges the female intellectual to rigorously examine her role within an ideological apparatus that allows her the privilege of the authorial voice and the luxury of writing. Stories, by virtue of their "writing," compose subaltern bodies. That is, these bodies are necessary terrain to be traversed—and I invoke the full colonial history of that statement—for the foregrounding of the authorial voice. Without the demarcation of difference in relationship to a "selfsame," there is no field of reference, no priority of information to allow for the formulation of meaning. That this system is hierarchized, and assigns to the position of the speaker or writer a privilege matched only by the muteness of the narrative's object, is no accident. Systems of representation, as in Spivak's analysis, echo the models simultaneously produced by and reproducing unequal distributions of power. However, rather than mourning the complicity of the female intellectual in the silencing of the subaltern subject, Spivak suggests "a circumscribed task": specificity, the asking of questions, a willingness to surrender to the possibility that there is no single answer, and the delimitation of those areas where one can and cannot speak for or of others.

Here the question arises, how do I dare to write about flamenco from the position of the foreign flamencophile? Am I not just another privileged outsider who is doomed to misunderstand and misrepresent flamenco and flamencos, perhaps at great cost to the artists and the art form? These questions plagued me for several years in my research. An adequate answer would be difficult to contain within a sentence, an introduction, or even a book. However, the structure of my analysis is designed to approach the problem of my authorial position as I attempt to explain, for those readers who do not have access to the flamenco texts written in Spanish, as well as those scholars who do, how the position of the outsider has shaped the way audiences and artists view flamenco, especially the dance. This book borrows from film theory, feminism and postcolonial theory tools to discuss how the "spectatorial gaze" of the foreign flamencophile participates in a complex dialogue across boundaries, nations and bodies to alternately reify and disrupt the stereotypes associated with the form.

The casting of the subaltern in this moment slips in terms of its fixity. Perhaps the flamenco subject has always "spoken" from the margins, through lyrics, musical ornaments and dance steps, but now more than ever, flamencos are "speaking"—generating new work, performing across the globe, talking about their work and the ideas that inspire them, so that the question of who has access to the "authority" of the "authorial voice" no longer assumes the muteness of the flamenco performer as the object of the colonial gaze. Further, the silencing of my individual authorial voice does not stop the uncomplicated perpetuation of these problematic stereotypes across many different discourses on a daily basis. To be sure, most flamencos I know find the expectations of audiences whose experience is limited to tourist venues extremely confining, parochial and sentimental. In dialogue with these artists over the years, this point, this hesitancy to "speak for" the artists and the art form, has elicited the response (to paraphrase in English): Work hard, pay your respects and try not to be so annoyingly American about it. *Venga.*

My relationship to flamenco and flamencos became more complex when I made the transition from performer and teacher to arts presenter. After I finished my graduate degree at the University of California, Riverside, I cobbled together as many teaching and performance opportunities as I could find as I waited to land the "dream job" in academia. Like many artists, I struggled to support myself, counting tips to pay my electric bill, rationing frozen chicken breasts until the next paycheck. To supplement my income, I started working in arts administration on a contract basis, doing grant writing, organizing artist residencies, handling publicity for dance companies and presenters, working in box offices, helping support capital campaigns, freelance dance criticism—you name it, I did it. It wasn't long before the need for health insurance inverted my priorities of art and life. In 1997, I became a full-time arts presenter who taught dance and performed in her free time. I continued my research and training in flamenco, but my life and income were structured around the commissioning and touring of new work and supporting extended artist residencies across the disciplines of dance, music and theatre.

As the Artistic Director of the Colorado Dance Festival and then the Executive Director of Cultural Affairs at Miami Dade College, I learned about the economic structures that support the performing arts from the perspective of the arts presenter. Most people, even the most seasoned participants in the arts, do not necessarily understand what an arts presenter actually does. In a nutshell, an arts presenter is usually part of a non-profit organization that assumes the financial risk for the success of an artist's work in a community, cultivating the funding to support artist fees and production costs. I had the incredible good fortune to be supported in this work by private foundations like the Lila-Wallace/Reader's Digest Funds, now the Wallace Foundation, the Ford Foundation, the Knight Foundation and the Rockefeller Foundation, as well as the National Endowment for the Arts, Arts International, and arts agencies at the local, state, regional, national and international levels. My six years of experience as a Hub Site for the National Dance Project, administered by the New England Foundation for the Arts, opened my eyes to the complex matrices that support professional dance in the United States and the touring of work internationally.

Miami Dade College's *Cultura del Lobo* (Culture of the Wolf) Performance Series and the Center for Cultural Collaborations International allowed me to play a curatorial and financial management role in bringing Spanish flamenco artists to the United States and to commission new work for South Florida flamenco artists like Duende Ballet Español and Bailes Ferrer. In 2002, we brought *cantaor* Miguel Poveda, his sister, dancer Sonia Poveda, and guitarist Chicuelo with other musicians to perform at the Lincoln Theater in Miami Beach. In 2004, Miami Dade College and Bailes Ferrer, in conjunction with FUNDarte, presented *Íntimo*, a collaboration between choreographer/dancer Belén Maya, guitarist José Luis Rodriguez,

Belén Maya performs in *Íntimo* as part of Flamenco in the Sun 2004 at the Lincoln Theater in Miami Beach, Florida. Photograph by Liliam Dominguez, used with permission.

and percussionist Sudhi Rajagopal, under the artistic direction of Rodriguez, for the Flamenco in the Sun Festival. Joining forces with the Broward Center for the Performing Arts, the partners co-produced the Festival in 2005 with workshops in guitar, dance, and song and performances by Son de la Frontera, Pastora Galván, D.C.-based *bailaor* Edwin Aparicio, and choreography for Bailes Ferrer by Andres Marín and Belén Maya. By 2006, the festival brought *Dos Hermanos,* a work by Israel and Pastora Galván, to South Florida and in 2007 commissioned an international flamenco collaboration between Cuban, Spanish, and U.S. artists called *Alfonsina, La Mujer en el Mar.* The festival continues each year.

These experiences illuminated previously invisible barriers to the widespread performance activity and touring of flamenco artists in U.S. and Spain. Flamenco artists in the United States tend to be community-based and self-produce their performances in affordable venues. Regional touring efforts are supported by state arts agencies, but the funding, and therefore the activity, is limited. Notable exceptions to this model are companies like Flamenco Vivo Carlota Santana, a company that tours annually in the United States, and Noche Flamenca, a Spanish flamenco company under the artistic direction of Martín Santangelo and Soledad Barrio that tours internationally, including in the U.S. However, most Spanish flamenco companies perform within Spain as part of the "flamenco circuit" and at festivals in Europe and Japan. The reasons are multiple. In recent years, the process of obtaining visas for foreign artists in the U.S. has become prohibitively expensive and labor-intensive, and the strength of the Euro compared to the U.S. dollar, combined with the respectable salaries working flamenco artists can command in their home country, make the widespread booking of Spanish companies, or even individual artists, nearly impossible in the United States.

However, Miguel Marín, an arts entrepreneur based in the U.S. and Spain, has created a working model for the international touring of Spanish artists that brings several artists of renown to select cities in the U.S. under the umbrella of Flamenco Festival USA. His production company also creates touring opportunities for Spanish flamenco artists in Canada, England, France, China, Japan and Australia. Flamenco is an art form, a culture, an aesthetic, a tradition, and an industry. The demands of the marketplace play a key role in determining which artists receive support, the extent of this support and the kind of work that is produced in different venues. Flamenco audiences have curiously strong opinions about what they expect to see onstage, whether they are aficionados or uninitiated to the art form. These expectations are conditioned through a host of cultural practices. This account of flamenco privileges the elements of the production behind the production, the material circumstances that create the art form, even (or especially) the ugly realities of commercialism.

With these priorities, then, I am compelled to address, but perhaps not resolve, certain questions with respect to flamenco history. Where does this particular "representation" of flamenco history fit into the larger spectrum of flamenco history? This is a history of "representations" that complicates "speaking of" and "speaking for" the flamenco subject. I am interested in the hidden subject behind the function of the author—not just the writer or choreographer or filmmaker, but the host of social and cultural practices that construct the flamenco body, and the desire of the viewer, through representations.

In Chapter 1, "Desiring Narratives: Flamenco in History and Film," I present theoretical discussions that serve as a foundation for future chapters. This chapter provides an overview of flamenco history and outlines the debates that characterize the established canon. I examine the assumptions that define pivotal concepts within the timeline of flamenco history: the racial origin of flamenco as a tradition, the role of outsiders in articulating the image of the flamenco dancer, the aesthetic peak of flamenco as an art form,

Raúl Rodríguez accompanies Pepe Torres in a performance by Son de la Frontera as part of Flamenco in the Sun 2005 at the Gusman Center for the Arts in Miami, Florida. Photograph by Liliam Dominguez, used with permission.

Dancer Edwin Aparicio performs in *Espejos del Alma* at Flamenco in the Sun 2005 at the Broward Center for the Performing Arts in Fort Lauderdale, Florida. Photograph by Liliam Dominguez, used with permission.

the role of tourism, and the means of maintaining flamenco for future generations. Then, I create connections between these assumptions and the markings of race, gender, class and national identity that give rise to the different representations of the flamenco stereotype.

For my purposes, it is most important to recognize that representations, as signs, are not *synonymous* with their referents, however much the signs may *resemble* their referents. The striking image on the poster that advertises a 1942 performance by "The Human Vesuvius," Carmen Amaya, at Carnegie Hall, represents the expectations of her audience as much as her presence on the stage. As Bill Nichols explains in his analysis of representational images on film, "An image is not what it represents, for in making its referent present again it does so despite the referent's absence, its actual location elsewhere."[6] Historical records and even films of flamenco performance tell a story, but that story must not be confused with reality. These "texts" re-present events already lost in the moment of performance.

Having acknowledged the impossibility of recapturing the "reality" of a moment, I am intrigued by the conflicting stories of that fleeting instantiation of presence. This is not to deny the constructive potential of these stories as a kind of discourse. The stories themselves, and my discussion of them, have a material and lasting effect on flamenco as a tradition, and the people involved in that tradition. But this impact occurs across a host of social regulatory practices, and not only in this particular "representation" of flamenco history. As Judith Butler writes of representations and their functions: "To claim that discourse is formative is not to claim that it originates, causes, or exhaustively composes that which it concedes; rather it is to claim that there is no reference to a pure body which is not at the same time a further formation of that body."[7] Stories of flamenco refer to and construct material bodies in a myriad of ways. My participation in the process of "representation" necessarily involves a recognition of the ways in which writing about dance and dancing bodies has an effect on the lived experience of flamenco. Writing and dancing the history of another culture from a position of relative privilege, I am simultaneously outside and inside, named and not named. And so I vacillate back and forth, trying to capture and name the slippage that endows representation with a simultaneous emptiness and plenitude.

I use as resources for this necessarily impossible task works produced mainly by authors outside Spain. American and British flamencophiles, in particular, have contributed to the exotic images of the flamenco dancer that pervade texts written in English. However, this exotic image did not originate in twentieth-century histories produced by American flamencophiles. In the mid–nineteenth century, Prosper Mérimée created the character of Carmen, a French Romantic exotic incarnation of duplicity and femininity that first galvanized the attributes of the highly sexualized and potentially dangerous Hispanic Other. In the second half of the nineteenth century, Spaniards created an internal brand of exoticism called *costumbrismo* that celebrated the forms of the Spanish South. But, within the twentieth century and continuing into the present, the United States, as an economic and political world power (sometimes capriciously and always in its own interest), enacted its policies of representation on bodies rendered Other in the process. The popular perception of the flamenco dancer in the United States has been framed by the relationship of the nation to other world powers.

The second half of Chapter 1, "The Ideology of Flamenco Histories," deals with the emergence of authority in history and film. Key relationships are charted here: each historical account vies for the position of speaking the "truth"; the persuasiveness of the historical account depends on the ways in which the overall structure of meaning adheres to a basic set of values determined by the cultural context of the reader. I rely on the work of Louis Althusser to define that relationship between the subject and ideology, and apply his theories to the task of historiography. The discussion of the reader in the context of history then provides a model for the consideration of the viewer and film. In historiography and film theory, the subject gains access to meaning via the establishment of difference and entry into the realm of desire. One of the most powerful ideologies that has informed the development of the flamenco stereotype has been the rhetoric of colonialism. The position of the author in flamenco histories and the role of the viewer in films emulate the part of the colonial gaze in the spectacle of European and American imperialism. This omniscient presence assumes the responsibility of "speaking for" that which it attempts to control. The object of desire, the Exotic Other, becomes the focus of the narrative, drawing the attention away from the operation of power and the production of meaning.

In Chapter 2, "Purism, Tourism and Lost Innocence," I analyze three pivotal flamenco histories generated outside Spain during the twentieth century and how they portray the dance, as opposed to the guitar or song components. Representations of the flamenco dancer, particularly the female flamenco dancer, consolidate the anxieties surrounding the dancing body at each historic interval. These tensions emerge through naturalized assumptions about bodies and how they construct meaning. From the perspective of foreign flamencophiles, the dance represents a dangerously attractive spectacle of exoticism that threatens the "essence" of "pure" flamenco. The reconstruction of flamenco history and the reification of "purity" within the tradition disguise the social tensions that led to the marginalization of

Dancer Niurca Márquez of Bailes Ferrer performs in Belén Maya's *Madre Tierra* at Flamenco in the Sun 2005 at the Broward Center for the Performing Arts in Fort Lauderdale, Florida. Photograph by Liliam Dominguez, used with permission.

flamencos within Andalusian and Spanish culture, and the hierarchized relationship between Spain and other countries.

Chapter 3, "Imagining Andalusia," deals with the scholarship by foreign academics who describe the renaissance in flamenco at the end of the Franco regime and the years of resurgence in global enthusiasm for flamenco from the 1980s through the present. Using different methodologies borrowed from fields like history, sociology, anthropology and cultural studies, these narratives critique the cultural bias and scholarly rigor of previous works, but still grapple with the difficulty of representing the dancing body within the history of flamenco. These works shed light on the cultural conditions that produce flamenco and offer theories of how gender is constructed within the tradition, but in each case, the analysis halts when it approaches the concept of the body and its intelligibility beyond titillation. Pedestrian movements and social bodies achieve meaning in these texts, but dancing presents the eternal problem of sensuality and sexual taboos. However, these histories provide a framework for an entry into the discussion of the dance as a rich component of flamenco's history, equal in its profundity to the components of song and guitar.

In each flamenco story, whether it is the anecdote of my childhood introduction to flamenco or the texts I examine in chapters two and three, as the narrative takes shape, certain gendered and racial markings coalesce to produce a representation of flamenco. However much they may shift in an individual context, three elements are consistently present in the larger narrative of flamenco history. First, flamenco as a practice always points to the marginalized position of the gypsies and lower-class Andalusians in Spanish society. Even as authors attempt to downplay the contribution of gypsies to the tradition, or locate its origin elsewhere, the practitioners and their art form are always associated with the Other. Second, flamenco dancers, whether they are men or women, are feminized in relationship to the gaze of the viewer. The gendered markings of flamenco performers in each discussion lend insight to the ways in which hierarchies of power are given masculine and feminine qualities. And finally, the flamenco dancer is always sexualized. The hyper-sexual qualities associated with flamenco dance stem from several different sources, among them the European history of the female body as spectacle, the dance's problematic proximity to the body, the feminized position of the Other who provokes anxiety and must be controlled within the legitimate forces of law and writing, and the material circumstances of many female flamenco dancers who performed the desire of the viewer's gaze through the dance and prostitution. The feminized qualities of the Other always speak to the masculine desire of the viewing subject in a heterosexualized dynamic of domination and submission.

The position of the American flamencophile is based on such a desire to see a dark part of the self mirrored back at the viewer or listener. The "dark continent" of female sexuality resonates here, threatening and titillating. The American flamencophile enjoys all the privileges of the stereotypical Western subject: couched in the ideology of the ruling or privileged classes, American flamencophiles locate something essential and lost in the flamenco tradition. The most famous of the American flamencophiles was Donn Pohren, a guitarist and historian whose life in Spain among flamencos yielded three respected books on flamenco. His *finca* (ranch) in Morón served as a gathering place for non–Spanish flamencos who traveled to Spain to study and financially sustained more than a few Spanish and gypsy flamenco artists who performed there. His works detail the flamenco "way of life," chart the historical lineage of artists, and establish values for "pure" performance. These values have been adopted by many American flamencos, rendering the aficionados curiously more parochial and rigid than many Spanish or gypsy artists in the tradition. Inasmuch as their philosophy rules out the possibility of a "pure" American flamenco artist and condemns the role of American tourists in the "popularization" of the art form, these American purists form a curious fraternity of experts in the flamenco community. They are informal anthropologists—they learn the language, spend time among the "natives," perform scholarly research, and study with respected figures within the tradition. American flamencophiles treat the label of aficionado very seriously; they love and practice flamenco, and they guard against any possible threat posed to the integrity of the tradition. The effect of such efforts is a much-idealized portrait of flamenco, a Romantic projection of passion. I write about American flamencophiles as "they," when perhaps I should choose the pronoun "we," because I am one of them. I occasionally provoke the anger and distrust of my colleagues through my embrace of choreographic innovation and experimentation, but I am as attached to the preservation of the tradition as they. We are all family.

My analysis of flamenco history focuses mainly on three kinds of "texts": formal histories, representations of flamenco on film, and live performances. The histories I have chosen for close readings and analysis compose the canon of historical texts available in English. U.S. flamenco aficionados, especially those who do not have reading competency in Spanish, rely upon these books as preliminary sources. These representations of flamenco crystallize certain elements of the artists and the practice into specific, and relatively static, forms. Unless he or she has the resources to travel regularly to Spain, the American aficionado experiences flamenco through the occasional live performance, infrequent classes and *juergas,* and most often through audio recordings, histories, film, and now, with the availability of high-speed internet access, through video online. The published words of flamenco scholars and the celluloid or digital bodies flickering across the screen take on a ritual function. We repeat the words *verbatim*, imitate the contours of the choreography to reconjure the presence of something that exists only through the process of its reproduction, its re-presentation. These histories and films are textual artifacts of the American flamencophile's education. They trace an inconstant history of representation and re-presentation: the development of the flamenco stereotype.

Chapters 1, 2 and 3 lay the necessary groundwork for an analysis of flamenco historiography and link the process of representation in history to the semiotics of film. These chapters provide a theoretical discussion of the authorial voice and the function of desire in narrative, and then construct a field of meaning that informs representations of the flamenco dancer from the perspective of the American flamencophile. However, as I point out in each instance, the dancing body continually evades the authors of flamenco histories. Films, and also video, as visual media populated by deceptively realistic bodies, provide an opportunity for the discussion of dancing bodies in more specific terms. In Chapter 4, "Fatal Filmic Flamencas," I compare the tropes used to establish the flamenco stereotype in twentieth century history to images of the female flamenco dancer in films by Luis Buñuel, Carlos Saura, and Antonio Gades. I focus on detailed movement descriptions in these readings as a way of decoding the process by which dancing bodies achieve intelligibility, and to propose a theory as to the choreographic function of the camera's eye. This analysis points to the different mechanisms for representation in history and film, as well as the consistent field of meaning that informs both media. Saura and Gades, as Spanish artists producing dance films after Franco's regime, disrupt and reinforce the stereotypes described in texts by non–Spanish flamencophiles.

The discussions in Chapters 3 and 4 depend upon a certain amount of familiarity with the story of Mérimée's *Carmen* and the historical development of the flamenco stereotype in an international context, which I will provide here. Despite attempts by artists and historians to downplay the significance of the mythical, and often degrading, stereotypes of Southern Spain, flamenco scholars cannot ignore their presence. In fact, the analysis of the Hispanic Orientalist Exotic serves as a unique opportunity to examine the effects of colonizing discourses in a transnational context. The stereotype of Carmen, the gypsy dancer, has illuminated representations of Spain, in various configurations, for more than a century. Meaning accumulates in and transforms the stereotype in each historical context. Carmen, as a representation of Southern Spain, consolidates the qualities attributed to the Other through colonial discourse: a sexual vibrancy combined with a moral purity that can be traced to her racial, class and gendered markings.

It seems, at first, a theoretical leap to posit the image of the gypsy dancer as a colonial stereotype; after all, Spain was once a colonial power among European nations. However, Spain's Golden Age had long since passed when, in 1845, Prosper Mérimée published a fictional account of "a scholarly, amateur French archaeologist [who] has gone to Spain to locate the real battlefield of Munda, the location where Caesar finally defeated the Republican forces in the Roman Civil War."[8] The site of this victory marks the beginning of Caesar's legacy of imperial authority. The story, published alongside other non-fiction accounts from travel diaries and scholarly articles in *La Revue des deux mondes*, attested to "the desire to rediscover the truths of the past, to place France at the head of a continuum of scientific progress, to assert its supremacy over lesser cultures."[9] In effect, *Carmen* provided the basic plotline for the narrative of colonialism. The mythic figure of Carmen came to represent, in Mérimée's story, the threat of the unruly, exotic, and distinctly female Other. The Frenchman sketched out a colonial narrative in which "[t]he battlefield itself, the territory that obsesses the text, is none other than her body, as the text continually raises the question of who shall own it while describing those who are fighting over it."[10]

Mérimée's Carmen is a lush figure from an Orientalist fantasy. She is all flesh, sexuality, and violence. She tempts the otherwise sane man, Don José, into the oblivion of desire and, ultimately, murder. Her lure? The undulation of her hips, as she grasps the folds of her skirt in fists, baring her thighs, and moves with weighted steps toward her victim. When he reaches out to touch her, she laughs, tosses her black hair and turns abruptly away from him. Her choreography, borrowed from Andalusian dance but then injected with the narrator's desire so that it exceeds the boundaries of her body and threatens to engulf him, also corresponds with portrayals of harem girls from Orientalist texts of the nineteenth century:

> [T]hese women stand for the east itself: veiled in mystery but finally penetrable by the Western desire to know and possess. The East as a whole became "feminized," understood as sensual, static, irrational and nonproductive, though fertile with resources and ripe for plunder.[11]

The depiction of Carmen draws upon the resonance of Muslim culture in Andalusia, and the suspected "Oriental" origins of the gypsies who settled in Southern Spain. So, although the narrator is located in a European country, he is transported to the mystical East, and the Hispanic Exotic becomes interchangeable with the Orientalist Exotic. The contested body of the gypsy dancer incorporates a moment of confrontation between Western

Photograph of a dancer named Carmencita, c. 1900 by Napoleon Sarony. Collection of Carte de Visite and Cabinet Card Photographs (Jerome Robbins Dance Division, New York Public Library for the Performing Arts, Astor, Lenox and Tilden Foundations).

institutions of power and the resistant Orientalist Other. The character of Carmen defies all laws: she attacks another woman and slashes her face, she escapes from jail, she seduces her captor and leads him to a life of crime, and finally, she betrays the lover who has abandoned legitimate structures (his military regiment, his family, his intended marriage) to pursue her. In the end, she can only be contained through murder. What's more, Carmen appears to invite her own domination through her threatening excess: her hair escapes the confines of pins, her dress slips away to reveal shoulders, cleavage, thighs, and her movements undulate through the forbidden zones of her body.

Librettists Ludovic Halévy and Henri Meilhac adapted Merimée's story for Georges Bizet's famous opera, *Carmen*, originally presented at the Paris Opéra-Comique in 1875. According to musicologist Susan McClary, *Carmen* was not the first opera by Bizet to capitalize on the appeal of the Orientalist Exotic, nor was it his first experiment with the character of the *femme fatale*.[12] *Au contraire*, French artists had been tapping the Orientalist imagination for

Originally released in Germany in 1918, the film *Carmen,* directed by Ernst Lubitsch and starring Polish actress Pola Negri, was released in the U.S. as *Gypsy Blood* in 1921 (Jerome Robbins Dance Division, New York Public Library for the Performing Arts, Astor, Lenox and Tilden Foundations).

subject matter from the early part of the nineteenth century. Viscount Chateaubriand, in *Les Aventures de Dernier Abencerage* (1826), Victor Hugo, in *Les Orientales* (1829), and Théophile Gautier, in *Voyage en Espagne* (1841), described a countryside and characters that animated the Orientalist landscape, a mountainous, white-walled affair with Moorish arches, a terrain in which descriptions of languid gypsies, rich food and heady wine convinced the French reader that he could return to a "primitive innocence" that so contrasted with his own "modern, civilized" country. Even within Spain, during the mid–nineteenth century, *costumbristas* produced auto-exotic portraits of Andalusian life, complete with "bullfighting, gypsy dancing, grape harvests, *majos* (cocks-of-the-walk), [and] *bandoleros* (bandits)."[13]

By the twentieth century, the fantasy of the Exotic who invites her own domination was to become a major icon of early Hollywood film in the United States. Between 1910 and 1929, seven film versions of *Carmen* had been released for American audiences. Three of the seven were released in 1915; they included starring performances by Charlie Chaplin, Theda Bara, and Geraldine Ferrar. Alfred Charles Richard, Jr., author of *The Hispanic Image on the Silver Screen*, provides interesting details concerning the public response to these films, and to the portrayals of Carmen. Of Fox's production, he mentions,

> Although Variety considered Raoul Walsh's directorial effort just shy of being a "masterpiece," they felt that Theda Bara lacked the "physical allurement of the Spanish cigarette girl." While they were satisfied with all other Hispanic characterizations, all of them played by Anglos, Miss Bara's eyes and body were not enough to portray what they considered to be the "standard characterization" of Carmen as, "a slow-moving, lazy, listless, shambling, warm-blooded girl, concealing beneath a phlegmatic exterior an intensity of passion only fanned to life by jealousy ... the Spanish make up is merely one of the mechanics with which any actress [must be] familiar.[14]

The critical response to Theda Bara's performance of Carmen reveals the aspects of the stereotype that had already become a "standard characterization" by 1915. The qualities attributed to Carmen's character match the stereotypes of other Latin Hollywood exotics, particularly the duplicitous combination of laziness and intense passion. What's more, the commentary by critics demonstrates the ways in which the "mechanics" of performing Spanish identity had been absorbed in the array of techniques expected of a professional actress. The desire for an Anglicized, tempered Exotic speaks from the subtext, perhaps only to be fulfilled by Margarita Cansino (Rita Hayworth) in Columbia's *The Loves of Carmen*, in 1948.

In 1941, the gypsy flamenco sensation Carmen Amaya fascinated the American public with her fiery, cross-dressed performance of the masculine

Modern dance pioneers Ruth St. Denis and Ted Shawn capitalized on the appeal of the Hispanic Exotic in their work *Cuadro Flamenco* in 1923. Photograph attributed to White Studio, New York, New York (Jerome Robbins Dance Division, New York Public Library for the Performing Arts, Astor, Lenox and Tilden Foundations).

Spanish dances. Her popularity coincided with the public's attention to its Latin American neighbors and the anti-fascist sentiment of a country at war. The Orientalist stereotype of Mérimée's Carmen transformed to represent a different kind of aberrant female, still a *femme fatale*, but more coarse and threatening in her potential for violence and true disruption of the order of power. Hollywood *femme fatales*, like Hayworth's Carmen, allayed the American cultural anxiety produced by the conflicts with Latin America and fascist Spain.

Franco's victory within Spain and the subsequent defeat of the Axis powers placed the dictator in a subordinate position to the United States in the global power order. In an attempt to rebuild Spain in the wake of a devastating civil war, Franco appealed to the stereotypical associations with flamenco in the American and European cultural imaginations. The version of flamenco tailored to "tourist" performances emphasized a charming but nonthreatening portrait of Spain. These productions toured the United States and were recorded in several Hollywood films. Franco's shrewd manipulation of the flamenco stereotype simultaneously generated a lucrative tourist industry and served to reiterate an internal order of power that placed gypsies and Andalusians at the lowest rungs of the social ladder.

In the 1970s, near the end of Franco's regime, leftist Spanish artists produced performances and images of flamenco that articulated an anti–Franco political stance. These performances celebrated the particularly Andalucían aspects of flamenco and emphasized the role of gypsy practitioners. Filmmakers like Luis Buñuel, in *That Obscure Object of Desire* (1976), and later Carlos Saura, in the "flamenco trilogy" created with choreographer Antonio Gades, reinvented the stereotype of the flamenco dancer. Their manipulations of the female gypsy dancer, however self-conscious of the ways in which the European stereotype of

This undated photograph (c. 1950s) of Carmen Amaya portrays her in a posture of emotional abandon, displaying the quality of intense passion that audiences sought in her performances (Jerome Robbins Dance Division, New York Public Library for the Performing Arts, Astor, Lenox and Tilden Foundations).

Carmen has informed the Spanish cultural ethos, did not significantly disrupt the firmly entrenched "Otherness" of the *bailaora* (female flamenco dancer).

In Chapter 5, "Realism Reinvented," William Washabaugh's work on documentary films of flamenco in the late 1970s provides insight to the forms of representation employed by Saura and Gades in their epic films of the 1980s. Saura's return to the documentary format in his films of 1992 and 1995, *Sevillanas* and *Flamenco*, suggests a reinvention of those techniques used to undermine the homogenizing influence of *franquismo* in earlier years. Saura's transition from epic film narrative to a very stylized documentary format marks a transition in the point of view constructed by the camera's eye and the perspective of the director. While his collaborations with Antonio Gades introduced the conflicted stereotype of the flamenco dancer through the eyes of two prominent Spanish artists to an international audience, the intent stands in marked contrast to the documentary-like format of *Sevillanas* and *Flamenco*. By recuperating the strategies of leftist artists from the decline of the Franco era, Saura assembles a different kind of educational tool. Instead of examining the perspective of the individual artist and his process, like the protagonist/choreographer Gades in *Bodas de Sangre* and *Carmen*, Saura's recent films deal with flamencos as a community. Within this community, he emphasizes the vast spectrum of regional artists, traditional, popular, amateur, professional, old and young, male and female. This shift in perspective from one to many voices, inclusive of previously underrepresented artists, parallels the recent developments in flamenco scholarship and contemporary performance.

The development of the Hispanic Orientalist Exotic underpins the close readings of flamenco on film and allows a point of re-entry into the discussion of the authorial voice and the representational image in Chapter 6, "Reinterpreting the Exotic." Here I reconsider key concepts presented in preceding chapters in the context of contemporary Spain as a re-emerging world power and within flamenco as a global tradition. The cartography of the Exotic developed in flamenco histories and films of the twentieth century traces the transformation of the flamenco stereotype from Spain's fall as a European power after the Spanish-American War to its recent reassertion as a member of the European economic community. Among many other social, political, and cultural developments, the reappropriation of the flamenco stereotype has coincided with Spain's favorable change in status among "First World" nations.

Theorists of globalization, like Jonathan Xavier Inda and Renato Rosaldo, refer to this process as de/territorialization. In their words, "The term captures at once the lifting of cultural subjects and objects from fixed spatial locations and their relocalization in new cultural settings."[15] The flow of flamenco as a cultural product in a global marketplace at many different moments in history, not only today, has allowed for the entry of multiple meanings into the process of representation. Flamenco artists have been remarkably adept at manipulating the expectations of their audiences, inserting irony and critique into their performances. Those moments frequently involve a dialogue with the image of the Hispanic Exotic and the expectations of audiences who long for the reassertion of the qualities she represents. The performances frequently challenge or reconfigure the stereotype so that it serves the needs of the individual performer.

As an example of the flamenco artist's role in the recuperation of the stereotype, I use the fragmented history of Carmen Amaya's rise to fame at the outset of the Spanish Civil War through the 1950s. Interviews and scholarly articles form a portrait of Amaya that is contradictory, both complicit in and resistant to the media attempts to represent her as a twentieth-century incarnation of Mérimée's Carmen. I locate Amaya's subversion of the codes intended to contain her, as a Gypsy woman and as a flamenco Exotic, in her choreographic choices and the practice of improvisation.

Amaya's much-debated cross-dressed performances simultaneously threatened the established codes for flamenco and injected them with a new life. She reconfigured the role of the female dancer in the tradition of flamenco, a dangerous innovation made safe by her undeniable skill in *zapateado* as well as her status as an undisputed "authentic" gypsy. I use her choreographic innovation and reliance upon improvisation as a model for a theory of flamenco's transformation during the twentieth century. While scholarship in musicology, especially work on the *cante,* has provided an important foundation for a consideration of the dancing body in flamenco's history, a choreographic analysis of the flamenco stereotype must necessarily account for movement on a number of levels. Improvisation, as a structured negotiation of culturally determined codes, offers a theoretical framework for a dialogue that includes multiple participants in continually changing roles of performing, viewing and evaluating the dance.

During the course of the twentieth and twenty-first centuries, the flamenco stereotype has been reconfigured and reproduced in many distinct yet familiar forms. At the same time, the changes in flamenco as a practice and the representation of its history chart a realignment of nations in a postcolonial context. Without a doubt, flamenco has become a global practice that speaks to the cultural positioning of several ethnic, class, and national groups. Flamenco's varied strains of hybrid forms represent a dialogue that has shifted from the colonial model of the desiring gaze and its exotic object to a multilayered negotiation of constantly changing points of view embedded in specific cultural and historical contexts.

In Chapter 7, "'Somos Anti-Guapas'—Against Beauty in Contemporary Flamenco" the performances of three different artists, Belén Maya, Pastora Galván, and Rocío Molina, demonstrate the ways in which contemporary female flamenco dancers negotiate the flamenco stereotype of Carmen as well as the return of an idealized Spanish feminine that pervades "traditional" flamenco. These readings are situated between comments shared in interviews I conducted with some of the artists and the remarks of different flamenco critics about the work. The dialogue that results reveals the ways in which contemporary *flamencas* speak very pointedly to the representations of their exoticism and their struggle to create a space for "authority" in the narratives that contain or constrain their performance. I do not claim a naïve space of innocence for the contemporary moment in flamenco history. My purpose in analyzing the development of the flamenco stereotype is to show the ways in which flamenco has always exceeded any attempts to represent it and the particular challenges presented by the dancing body. However, I do believe that the work of contemporary artists relies upon a rigorously informed recognition of the role of the stereotype in the continuing development of flamenco, but they also critique the category of "appropriate" femininity that serves as Carmen's alter-ego, La Guapa. I look with optimism to the future of flamenco as a tradition equipped, by virtue of its choreographic conventions, its penchant for debate, and its insistence upon historical preservation, to not merely survive, but thrive in the new millennium.

That naïve hope is nurtured by the multiplicity of voices present in flamenco today, as well as a vibrant internet marketplace. Flamenco scholarship in Spain has exploded within the past ten years, with new graduate degree programs, certification and *titulación* in performance, the proliferation of flamenco journals like *Candil* and *Acórdes de flamenco*, increased provincial support of flamenco artists, and a thriving tourist economy based around the festival circuit. Websites like *www.flamenco-world.com* and *www.esflamenco.com* provide news, reviews, photos and video of performance. They also sell new and historic books on flamenco produced by peñas, universities, and commercial presses, as well as clothing, shoes, DVDs and CDs. These books have changed in terms of the scope of their research. For example, the flamenco critic Silvia Calado, frequently featured on *www.flamenco-world.com*, recently released a bilingual (English and Spanish) overview of flamenco called *All About Flamenco* (2006). Gerhard Steingress, a postmodern scholar at the University of Seville, has produced works on a number of different themes within flamenco history, including *Sociología del cante flamenco/The Sociology of Flamenco Song* (1993, 2006), *Flamenco y el Nacionalismo/Flamenco and Nationalism* (1998) and *Carmen se fue a Paris:*

un estudio sobre la construcción artística de género flamenco (1833–1865)/Carmen Went to Paris: A Study of the Construction of the Artistic Genre of Flamenco (1833–1865) (2006). Cristina Cruces Roldán, from the University of Seville, has written several titles on flamenco, like *Más allá de la Música, Antropología y Flamenco I and II/Beyond the Music, Anthropology and Flamenco, Volumes I and II* (2002, 2003). Many meticulously researched scholarly efforts, particularly those published by smaller presses within Spain, never reach the internet marketplace, but bookstores in Spain carry titles that deal with the development of a single *palo* in a specific region, if one is willing to spend time searching the shelves. These scholarly efforts are balanced by journalistic criticism and the contributions of the performing artists through the multiple media accessible via the internet.

This book developed partially from my own need to define the role of the foreign flamencophile in the history of flamenco, perhaps as a means of carving out a space for myself as a dancer "outside" but in dialogue with the tradition. It is not intended as an exhaustive history of flamenco, particularly with respect to the *cante* or the *toque*. Less a history than a historiography of absence, this work privileges the exotic representation of the dancing body in its consideration. Over the years, several artists and students in the United States have lamented the relative lack of information (especially in history but also references for terminology and musical structures) on flamenco in English. Instructors and students frequently ask me if I have a source, one source, that they could read to provide them all the answers. There are some basic histories, like Calado's bilingual overview, or Barbara Thiel-Cramér's *Flamenco: The Art of Flamenco, its History and Development Until Our Days* (1991), but no single volume encompasses the universe of flamenco. In the words of a late friend and mentor, Gregory Bredbeck, "That's not the problem, that's the point." It doesn't exist that way for a reason. At least some of the conditions that contribute to the impossibility of such a volume are the subject of this book. Despite the efforts over the centuries to reduce flamenco to its most convenient, consumable "essence," the artists *y el arte* maintain their complexity, and the form continues to evolve. *¡Que siga la tradición!*

1

Desiring Narratives:
Flamenco in History and Film

This chapter first deals with the debates within flamenco history, and second, examines how history and film function as ideological structures within these debates. Third, the discussion shows how history and film demonstrate the role of narrative in the representation of desire, specifically a desire for the Other. These theoretical models provide a foundation for the analysis of the flamenco dancer as the icon of the exotic imagination in future chapters.

Conflicting Histories

As an oral tradition, flamenco history suffers from the uncertainty of its "chain of evidence," to borrow a legal term. Almost all flamenco historians describe their written accounts as "approximate" or "uncertain," because so little about the history of the art form has been written down. What's more, the stories kept alive by the surviving elders in the tradition have a way of contradicting one another, and themselves, and take on the character of the author, complete with prejudices and biases. For example, if a well-intentioned investigator interviews a flamenco from Granada, the informant will almost certainly report that Granada is "the birthplace of flamenco." However, the interviewer is likely to receive the same claim from a flamenco in Jeréz de la Frontera or Seville, because each of these cities has played an important role in the development of flamenco at different times. Regional pride pervades flamenco history, distinct even among the practitioners from different cities in Andalusia.

Regionalisms in flamenco result from the genesis of song forms from different cities in Andalusia. Flamenco is divided into different *palos*, or song forms, and these are grouped into different song families. Some families use the rhythmic meter as a point of classification, like *tangos* (4/4 time), which is both a *palo* and a family that includes the *palos* of *tientos*, *tangos* and *tan-*

The "absent" figure of the dancer in many flamenco histories. Guitarist Antonio Souza performs in Flamenco in the Sun 2005 at the Broward Center for the Performing Arts in Fort Lauderdale, Florida. Photograph by Liliam Dominguez, used with permission.

guillos. Flamenco *tangos* bear the same name, but little other resemblance, to the Argentine tango. Others are grouped by virtue of their development, like the *cantes de ida y vuelta,* or "songs of coming and going," which include *colombianas* and *guajiras,* song forms that emerged as hybrids between Spanish and Latin American or Caribbean styles.

As if the situation were not sufficiently complicated, then different styles developed among the *palos.* For example, folklore links *soleá* to Cádiz or Seville, but there are several kinds of *soleares* specific to neighborhoods in Seville (*soleares* de Triana, the gypsy quarter of Seville) or to different cities in Spain (*soleares* de Alcalá, de Jeréz, de Cádiz, de Lebrija, de Utrera). As a result, there are hundreds of song styles in flamenco, because variants developed within specific communities or were popularized by individuals. So the singer who insists that Huelva is the birthplace of flamenco is technically correct, as Huelva produced *fandangos de Huelva.* However, this book does not deal with the development of the different *palos* in flamenco. Certainly, there is a wealth of sources in both Spanish and English that attempt to do so. But relatively few attempt to trace the development of the ephemeral *baile,* and it is the evaporating presence of the dance that concerns this history. However, to address the conspicuous absence of the dance in these accounts, one must map a field of information.

Scholarly debates in flamenco history erupt around (at least) three major issues: the origin of flamenco, the transformation of the practice from social settings to the concert stage, and the definition of "pure" flamenco. These issues are entangled as threads in a large, living textile. Pulling at one end of a single skein will result in changes to the whole. The problem is exacerbated by the three separate, but interrelated (impossibly entangled, to continue the metaphor) components of flamenco: *cante*, *toque*, and *baile*, or song, guitar, and dance. Traditionally, flamenco history is traced through the *cante*, or singing, the oldest of the forms. References to the guitar accompaniment to the singing can be found in sources dating back to the seventeenth century, but the design of the flamenco guitar as we know it became defined during the mid–nineteenth century. The dancing, according to most narratives, came last, and what we now recognize as flamenco dancing emerged during the late nineteenth century, largely due its role in the spectacles of the *cafés cantantes*. However, if one examines the scholarly accounts of flamenco history, the problems of representing the dancing body become immediately apparent. The dancing body in performance carries with it the weight of corporeality. Dance cannot be divorced from the bodies that perform it.

In the interest of narrative coherence, these debates, and the cascade of implications that follows them, are presented according to the model provided by the historical chronology. In short, the tale begins at the beginning. However, plotting the beginning of a story determines the shape of the narrative, excluding certain possibilities and revealing new paths. Be forewarned, flamenco history has a way of rewriting itself, and talking back, as the story unfolds.

Origin Points

The genre that most musicologists, flamencologists, aficionados, and practitioners recognize as flamenco song and dance emerged during the mid– to late nineteenth century as a hybrid product of Andalusian and gypsy cultures. However, theories of flamenco's ancient antecedents provoke questions about the racial origin and contemporary cultural ownership of the art form. If, for example, it were possible to locate a "pure" bloodline, gypsy or Andalusian, within Spain's long history of occupation by any number of conquerors and conquered populations, then it might be possible to assign the role of primary innovator in flamenco to a specific culture. When considering the debates in flamenco, it is imperative that one recognize the distinction between the categories of Spanish, Andalusian, and gypsy. A Spaniard could hail from any region of Spain, but an Andalusian comes from the South of Spain. And while Andalusians and gypsies have shared the same soil for centuries, the two groups are regarded as racially and socially distinct from one another. Historically, gypsies have been considered the lowest social class, ranked below even the most impoverished Andalusians.[1] So even as some scholars point to the dubious "purity" of either bloodline, the social perception of cultural difference between Andalusians and Spaniards carries an important weight within these debates. For example, if gypsies "invented" flamenco, then the practice that has come to represent Spanish national identity as a whole actually bears the mark of Spain's lowest classes.

By contrast, stories of flamenco's Andalusian origins provide a bizarre coherence to the mixture of classes and cultures that have occupied the region. Flamenco, as an Andalusian cultural product, unifies and streamlines the history of Andalusia. In effect, the image of the flamenco dancer gives Andalusian regional identity a recognizable symbol. By extension and through a similar elision of the boundaries that determine difference, the stereotype of flamenco serves as a sign for Spanish national identity. In the second half of the twentieth century, viewed through a global lens filtered by history, politics, and commercialism, flamenco came to represent Spain.

Now, that effortless jump from the image of a polka-dotted skirt to an association with a nation of vastly different cultures, each with its own, and shared, convoluted histories, did not happen in a single moment, or within one sector of Spanish society. To trace the evolution of flamenco, some concessions must be made to argument in order to move forward. The compromise is this: Most historians agree that, until the late nineteenth and early twentieth centuries, flamenco was practiced among gypsies and lower-class Andalusians as a social dance form and only occasionally in commercial settings for upper-class Spaniards or tourists.[2] The end of the nineteenth century brought with it the commercialism of flamenco as a popular art form in the *cafés cantantes* in several major cities of Spain. As the "singing cafés" increased in popularity, several different Andalusian and gypsy song forms were incorporated into the flamenco repertory. The patrons of these establishments, upper class playboys (*señoritos*) and foreign tourists, also sponsored private flamenco parties (*juergas*), where flamenco artists performed for money. As the market for professional flamenco performance increased during the twentieth century, larger numbers of non-gypsy artists joined the ranks of the flamenco "working class." Regardless of their racial or regional origin, flamenco performers were still regarded as members of a lower class.

The gypsy origin of flamenco continues to carry weight in terms of the degree of perceived authenticity of a given performance. In several flamenco histories, dancers are described as pure-blooded gypsies who practice a more

Carmen Amaya dancing among gypsies in the 1940s. (Jerome Robbins Dance Division, New York Public Library for the Performing Arts, Astor, Lenox and Tilden Foundations).

"authentic" version of flamenco than *payos*,[3] or non-gypsies. Along the same lines, exceptional non-gypsy dancers are lauded for their abilities, their sense of "authenticity," despite the fact that they are not of gypsy lineage. One of the highest compliments offered to a performer during a solo is the spoken or shouted *jaleo*, "¡Qué gitano!" ("Very gypsy!")

Vicente Redondo Saavedra, "El Pecas," *cantaor* and gypsy activist of Huelva, Spain, performing in Flamenco in the Sun 2005 at the Broward Center for the Performing Arts in Fort Lauderdale, Florida. Photograph by Liliam Dominguez, used with permission.

But the histories of the gypsies in Europe make it difficult to pin down a specific ethnic or cultural heritage for any given community. The *Rom* in diaspora reveal a diverse array of cultural markings, suggesting that, as they have traveled across the Middle East and Europe, gypsies have adopted the cultural practices of the areas through which they have passed.[4] Their nomadic wanderings, combined with the popular prejudice that gypsies are thieves, contribute to the paradoxical notion that, while a stereotypical idea of "pure" gypsy blood exists, there is no such thing as "original" gypsy culture. The conclusion, then, is that flamenco developed from elements of a culture already established in Andalusia prior to their arrival.

One example of this "Andalusianist" perspective can be seen in the scholarly attempt to trace the antecedents of Andalusian culture and flamenco as far back as the Muslim invasion and occupation of Southern Spain from 711 to 1492. Depending largely on scholarship by musicologists, these authors trace similarities between the *zajal* (ancient Arab poetry/song forms) and the flamenco *coplas* (rhythm and verse forms).[5] These narratives resurrect the power and wealth of the Muslim civilization that once ruled Andalusia, perhaps the poorest and least industrially developed region of contemporary

Spain. The tradition of flamenco, then, emerges as evidence of the past glory of an ancient civilization preserved in the culture of Andalusia. The "Oriental" aspects of Muslim culture underpin this association and endow flamenco with the mysterious qualities attributed to the "East."

Similar attempts have been made to align the musical structures of flamenco with the Sephardic Jewish chants of Southern Spain. During Muslim rule, Judaism was solidly established in Andalusian culture. In fact, the term "Sephardic" refers to the specific cultural group of Jews from the Iberian peninsula, a presence that is reported to predate the Roman occupation of Spain.[6] The Inquisition and the rule of the Catholic princes led to the forced conversion of all non–Christians and the expulsion of Muslims, Jews, and gypsies. Some scholars speculate that this shared exile forged the unique sound of flamenco song.

Hearkening back even further, some authors posit the beginnings of flamenco dance as occurring with the popularity of performances by temple prostitute dancers in the city of Gades, now Cádiz, during the time of the Greek occupation of Andalusia from 500 to 250 B.C., a practice that reportedly continued into the years of Roman rule from 250 B.C. to 475 A.D.[7] Cádiz, a city founded by the Phoenicians, was known among its Greek and Roman occupants for the charms of its dancing women, the *puellae Gaditanae*. One author, Allen Josephs, seeking a link between temple prostitute dancers dedicated to Astarte, the *puellae Gaditanae*, and flamenco *bailaoras*, first emphasizes the shared "Oriental" characteristics of the dance descriptions by figures like Martial, Juvenal and Petronius and then compares them to the accounts of *bailaoras* in the writings of travelers like Richard Ford.[8] An analysis of Josephs's history of flamenco dance appears in Chapter 2. However, this theory is significant in the context of the debates concerning the gypsy origin of flamenco because it attributes the genesis of flamenco to a time prior to the gypsy presence in Andalusia, supporting the contention that flamenco is primarily Andalusian in origin, though it was popularized by the gypsies in the nineteenth and twentieth centuries.

While the attribution of early flamenco's roots to the Greek and Roman employ of temple prostitute dancers disassociates the art of flamenco from the taint of low-class Gypsy origin, it also suggests a connection between the dance and prostitution. During the twentieth century, practitioners and historians alike attempted to downplay flamenco's association with prostitution, a problem that encompasses nineteenth century European travelers' perception of the female dancer's sexualized exoticism, the embarrassing economic reality of the patronage of flamenco by upper-class *señoritos*, and the institutionalized practice of prostitution in the flamenco *tablaos* (nightclubs) of Franco's regime. The choice to align the temple prostitute dancers with flamenco *bailaoras* curiously renders the highly commodified sexual appeal of the female flamenco dancer divine, rather than human, in origin.

Other scholars emphasize the gypsy influence in the creation of flamenco and call attention to the similarities between flamenco dance and classical Indian dance, particularly *kathak*. Donn Pohren, the most famous foreign flamenco aficionado, in his *Lives and Legends of Flamenco*, in the section "Dance," immediately links the *baile flamenco* to "traditional Hindu classical dance."[9] He then lists the schools from which flamenco dancing "may well have evolved": *bharata natyam*, *kathak*, and *kathakali*. Contemporary dance historians might question how all these forms might have led to the development of flamenco, since each tradition has a distinct regional origin and context for performance. It seems highly unlikely that any single cultural group, even the itinerant *Roma*, would be able to travel through the entirety of India and master forms that are usually imparted through intensive, lifelong study with a guru. For example, *kathakali*, from the southwest region of India (Kerala), is performed mainly by men and involves elaborate makeup and costumes more akin to Japanese kabuki than to flamenco, including the performance of female roles by men. Like Allen Josephs, Pohren suggests that the Hindu dances reached Spain through the port city of Gades, or Cádiz, with the introduction of professional Indian dancers during the time of the Greeks or Romans.[10] Recent findings among geneticists suggest that the *Roma* descend from a "founder population" among the lower-castes of India,[11] disputing the once-popular perception that gypsies hailed from Egypt and lending credence to the connection with *kathak*, which has its origins in northern India, in what is known as the Indus-Gangetic belt.[12] Since so little is known about the origins of the *Roma*, or the development of dances from these ancient practices to the present, it is unclear how directly to attribute flamenco's antecedents to Indian classical dance. However, the correlation between the development of flamenco and the history of classical Indian dances within these historical narratives calls attention to the simultaneously religious and sexual "origins" of certain forms, like *bharatha natyam*, and the caste of *nautsch* dancers or dancing courtesans in the history of *kathak*.[13] Further, this assertion borrows from *bharatha natyam* the newfound respectability established for the dance and its practitioners by upper-class Brahmins in the twentieth century. Rukmini Devi's appropriation of the *devadasi* tradition and recuperation of Balasaraswati as a descendent of the *devadasi* made the performance of the *nautsch* dances respectable for upper-class women.[14] Flamencologists who claim the art form's origin in Indian classical dance account for both the gypsy influence in the development of the form and its close ties to prostitution, but emphasize the "classical" categorization of *kathak* and *bharatha natyam* in an attempt to recuperate flamenco as a "respectable" icon of contemporary Spain.

More recent research among American dance history scholars links previous scholarship in the history of the *cante*, or the migrations of the gypsies, to an analysis of the structure of the dance forms. Miriam S. Phillips, in a 1991 presentation before the Society of Dance History Scholars, compares the formal conventions of the North Indian classical form *kathak* and flamenco dance:

> Commonly shared features can be observed in kathak and flamenco on a dance motific level—such as, how the body is used in space, specific movement techniques and positions of body parts (as in, hands, arms, feet, whole body positions, turns). Similarities can also be seen on a structural level— that is, how individual movement motifs and patterns are organized into larger sections or parts of a dance (such as, sections emphasizing upper body carriage, footwork, or integrated full body movements).[15]

This repositioning of the gypsy contribution to the development of flamenco creates a link between the origin and development of *kathak* and flamenco traditions, suggesting, at least for scholars like Phillips, that gypsies and *kathakas* shared a similar cultural context, if not the same one. The reconfiguration of the divine dancer from antiquity plays into an Orientalist exoticism of both the *nautsch* dancer and the *bailaora* that emphasizes the feminine dancing role as the focal point of examination. This theory allows scholars to downplay the associations between contemporary flamenco performance and the prostitution of twentieth-century gypsy and Andalusian women for upper-class Spanish or foreign men. In this historical re-imagining of the divine purpose for the dance, the figure of the female dancer becomes a convenient site for the collision of complex international and class tensions. She is reduced to an icon, and her image signifies the contested space of legitimacy and "First World" status denied to both post-colonial India and Andalusian culture in the early twentieth century.

In each case, the retrospective assignment of an origin point several centuries before the emergence of what is generally recognized as "flamenco" reflects the ethnic and class tensions between Andalusians and gypsies, the region of Andalusia and the rest of Spain, as well as Spain and the "more economically developed" countries of the world during the twentieth century. These representational strategies continually recreate the practice of flamenco, and particularly the image of the flamenco dancer, as a commodity that can be owned by a specific group and reconfigured so that it serves as an emblematic practice representative of that group.

Romantic Excursions

Few written accounts of flamenco performance survive from the disputed origin points until the nineteenth century. Interestingly, most accounts
of gypsy dance before 1865 can be found in travel diaries and literature outside Spain. Lord Byron, a primary voice of English Romanticism, passed
through Andalusia in 1809, perhaps gathering notes for his work *Don Juan*
(1819), set in Cádiz. The writer George Borrow published two works based
upon his travels in Spain among the gypsies, *The Zincali: An Account of the
Gypsies in Spain* (1841) and *The Bible in Spain* (1842). The most famous of
the English wanderers through Spain is Richard Ford, whose *Gatherings from
Spain* was first published in England in 1845 as a handbook for travelers.
Ford's work is considered, among flamenco scholars, one of the few "realistic" portrayals of Spain from this period. His descriptions of the dancing
women of Spain focus on the persuasive charms bestowed upon them by
nature:

> The ladies, who seem to have no bones, resolve the problem of perpetual
> motion, their feet having comparatively a sinecure, as the whole person per-
> forms a pantomime, and trembles like an aspen leaf; the flexible form and
> Terpsichore figure of a young Andalusian girl—be she gypsy or not—is said
> by the learned, to have been designed by nature as the fit frame for her volup-
> tuous imagination.[16]

Exotic representations of flamenco dance and dancers such as this one
were widely circulated during the early nineteenth century by a series of
artists from France. The landscape and people of Andalusia represented, for
the French Romantics, the setting and characters in an Orientalist fantasy.
In Spain, they found a land untouched by time and progress, and a people
who possessed "grace, libidinal freedom and self-expression."[17] Among the
French Romantics, Viscount Chateaubriand chose Granada as the setting for
his 1826 work *Les Aventures du Dernier Abencerage*, and Victor Hugo set his
impressions of the Moorish palace, the Alhambra, to verse in his epic *Les Orientales* of 1829. The dance enthusiast Théophile Gautier recorded several
descriptions of the dancing women of Andalusia in his *Voyage en Espagne* of
1841. But the most famous and enduring representation of the Spanish dancer
was presented in 1847 by Prosper Merimée in his short novel, *Carmen*. Merimée's gypsy tale served as the structure for Bizet's production at the Paris
Opéra Comique (Salle Favart) in 1875. By the mid–nineteenth century, "The
dancing gypsy girl was to be, alongside the bullfighter, the infinitely repeated
and infinitely debased symbol of the Spanish South."[18]

The exoticism of the flamenco dancer fueled a commercial industry that
transplanted the practice from *juergas* and small tourist venues to the stages

of the *cafés cantantes* (flamenco bars). During this period (roughly 1847–1936) flamenco performance was elevated to a platform and presented before tourists and Spaniards alike in the cities of Seville, Jeréz de la Frontera, Granada, Córdoba, Madrid, and Barcelona. Some of the most famous figures in flamenco history performed at these venues, particularly during the Golden Age of this era, 1881–1900: La Macarrona, Salud Rodríguez, La Malena, La Paloma, and numerous others.[19]

La Edad de Oro/The Golden Age

The turn of the twentieth century functions as the highest point in most flamenco histories. Scholars of the *cante*, in particular, place the Golden Age after the decline of the *cafés cantantes*, around the time of the Festival de Cante Jondo hosted by Manuel de Falla in 1922, prior to the Spanish Civil War. However, very much in the same way that scholars debate the actual years of the Middle Ages, for example, there are slipping dates for "Golden Age." The appellation may also differ according to region. However, the standards for excellence in flamenco attributed to this period serve as the ideal for purists in each area of performance: guitar, song and dance. According to many contemporary historians, each element was featured equally in performance, and the art was marked more by simplicity and expressiveness than by technical display of virtuosity. But at the same time, the conventions that came to characterize flamenco dance after the Golden Age, a period of deterioration, emerged during the era of the *cafés cantantes*: complex, rapid footwork (*zapateado*) and the use of castanets (*castañuelas*).

After the turn of the century, many flamenco artists formed touring companies and traveled through Europe, the United States, and South America. Non-Spaniards such as Antonia Mercé, "La Argentina," and Leonide Massine received international acclaim in their performances of the dance/dramas *El Amor Brujo* (1916) and *El Sombrero de Tres Picos* (1919), composed by Manuel de Falla. He also collaborated with the poet Federico García Lorca to hold a festival devoted to the Andalusian song form *cante jondo* (deep song), generally regarded as the sacred prototype of flamenco, in Granada in 1922.

Lorca wrote two famous cycles of poems devoted to Andalusian and gypsy cultures: *Poema del Cante Jondo* (1921) and *Romancero Gitano* (1928).[20] In these works, the image of the gypsy dancer played an important role, shattering the more accessible stereotypes circulated in commercial flamenco circles. According to flamenco scholar Félix Grande, the poems of Lorca "did not narrate flamenco, they palpated it. They did not describe what could be seen, they translated what could be felt."[21]

Important to the reinvention of the Golden Age among flamenco purists is the concept of *duende*. But to call *duende* a concept is to negate the essence of Lorca's definition of the term. In his essay "Theory and Function of the Duende," Lorca describes *duende* as a "struggle and not a concept." For Lorca, the supernatural force of the *duende* enters human beings and possesses them as they create inspired, deeply moving work. The *duende* "will not appear if it sees no possibility of death."[22] *Duende* can be compared to Dionysian passion, a trial by fire. It is this essence that is lost in commercial performance, according to flamenco purists. The sense of loss and danger implied in the invocation of *duende* resonates within the narratives of Lorca's life, which discuss his struggle as a homosexual, his identification with the gypsies, his anti-fascist activities and ultimately his assassination at the onset of the Spanish Civil War. He was murdered in a mass execution by the *Guardia Civil* in Granada in 1936.

Transformation Abroad and Tourism at Home

Some flamencos chose to emigrate rather than remain in Spain when Civil War broke out in 1936. While flamenco flourished in foreign countries, particularly in the cities of Paris and New York, flamenco activity in Spain very nearly halted during the war and in the early years of Franco's regime. The decade of the 1950s was marked by a period of resurgence in flamenco activity facilitated by the intervention of Hollywood producers, who recorded on film the legends of the time: Carmen Amaya, José Greco, Rosario and Antonio, Pilar López, and La Chunguita. For many flamenco scholars, this period represents the compromise of the art to meet the demands of commercialism. The dance moved to the forefront, pushing the arts of guitar and song into subordinate positions. The popularity of the dance among foreign audiences changed the conventions of its performance: Dancers became prone to acrobatic displays of footwork, and they incorporated balletic leaps and turns into their routines. Worse, for purists, the costuming and presentation of the spectacle appealed to the popular, stereotypical conceptions of flamenco and Spain. According to flamenco scholar Madeleine Claus, "Commercial productions ... use 'flamenco' to display the charms of frenzied, coquettish, plastic, imitation 'Carmens.'"[23]

After the decade of the 1950s, flamenco became a major component in Franco's plan to develop Spain through revenue accrued from the tourist industry. American military bases were established in Spain, and several *tablaos* were created to cater to the desires of the new clientele. The period from the sixties to the seventies stands out as the all-time low period for the art among flamenco scholars. Flamenco and prostitution became synonymous, and the performance conventions sank to the level of the burlesque. At the same time, Franco's government circulated the image of the flamenco dancer to promote Progressive Spain.

Purity and Preservation

Since the 1970s, a sense of outrage against the commercialization of the art has developed among flamencos within and outside of Spain. The revitalization of flamenco within Spain in the last years of Franco's regime incorporated a coded sense of rebellion against the dictator and a criticism of his repressive policies, felt keenly by Andalusians and gypsies. However, these revolutionary ideas were deeply embedded in the codes of flamenco, through song lyrics, introduced suddenly after years of singing the traditional song verses. The movement toward purism in flamenco flourished through the end of the century and continues to buoy conversations among "traditionalists." Many aficionados have devoted themselves to the preservation of the *cante* and the development of flamenco guitar performance to the exclusion of the dance. Among flamenco historians such as James Woodall, who laments the marginalization of the song and guitar elements of the art among popular audiences, the potential for the vulgarization of the dance lays inherent in its proximity to the body: "Such is the nature of dance—visual, physically stirring, in the case of flamenco palpably erotic. The possibilities for immediate sensual response are paraded before one—and flamenco, bad though it often is, is always hard to resist."[24]

It is generally understood among flamenco dance enthusiasts that even today "real" flamenco is not performed at the *tablaos;* it can sometimes be found in the classroom of a very old teacher, but more likely in the company of other aficionados, at a *juerga* (jam session) sponsored by a private flamenco club *(peña)*.[25] These flamencophiles attempt to reenact the early days of the *cafés cantantes*. The conventions of performance attributed to that time serve as the standard by which the authenticity of the flamenco is measured. Musicians, dancers, and guitarists all play equal roles in performance, although it should be noted that many *peñas* focus exclusively on the *cante*. The dividing line between audience and performers is completely blurred. In the context of a *juerga*, everyone who is present is a participant in the performance. As they watch and listen, participants play *palmas* (hand-clapping accompaniment to the song or dance) and encourage other performers through *jaleo* (spoken or shouted comments). Dancers, if they are featured, perform as soloists in a limited amount of space, contrasting the stage conventions of the *tablaos*, where several dancers, usually women, may execute spatial patterns in unison.

During the late 1970s and 1980s, a hybrid mix of flamenco and Spanish classical dance traditions called *baile teatral* emerged as the contemporary vehicle for flamenco dance outside the *tablaos* and the *peñas*. Professional ballet companies, including the National Ballet of Spain, resurrected the early flamenco theatrical dance works by Manuel de Falla. Perhaps the most influential contemporary choreographer to have worked in this genre was Antonio Gades, whose film collaborations with director Carlos Saura received international acclaim. *Bodas de Sangre* (1981), an adaptation of Lorca's play of 1933, began a trilogy of flamenco ballets designed for film. In 1984, the two collaborated on a contemporary flamenco version of Mérimée's *Carmen*, and in 1986 they created a new incarnation of de Falla's *El Amor Brujo*. Sadly, Gades died in 2004. Since their famous collaboration, Saura has contributed several Andalusian/flamenco films to his existing repertory, *Sevillanas* (1992), *Flamenco* (1995), *Salomé* (2002), and *Ibéria* (2005).

While Gades's film works include some flamenco choreography and deal with Andalusian/gypsy themes, he incorporates ballet, modern dance, *escuela bolera*, and pantomime into the dance vocabularies performed by classically trained dancers. Nearly every contemporary scholar of flamenco discusses the contributions of Antonio Gades. However, he is often considered by purists to be a choreographer of Spanish ballets, not traditional flamenco dance. According to Madeleine Claus:

> His international fame rests mainly on his impeccable staging and the almost scientifically geometric precision of his choreography: Nothing is overlooked, from the raising of an eye to the color of shoes. This results in a show of such incomparable quality that one almost forgets that the purpose, flamenco dancing, is so tightly controlled that almost nothing of it remains. [26]

The concern seems to be that the innovations in contemporary flamenco, which are a welcome change for many flamencos from the tourist-oriented productions in the *tablaos*, also threaten to eradicate traditional flamenco by introducing new vocabularies into the choreography. Innovation brings with it the power of contagion, very much like the contamination of the flamenco body through commercialism and prostitution. As dancers trained in traditional flamenco perform in tourist productions or experiment with hybrid forms, purists insist upon the preservation of the tradition. To fend off the threat of losing flamenco's past glory, aficionados publish memoirs and other historical research on the figures of the Golden Age and codify traditional vocabularies in texts such as the *Dictionary of Spanish Dance* by Matteo and Carola Goya (1991).

The debates surrounding the development of flamenco are concerned with the disputed origins of flamenco, which inevitably lead to arguments involving the cultural "ownership" of the tradition. The professionalization of flamenco and the effects of international commercialism provoke anxiety among flamenco scholars who mourn the "loss" of an "originary" practice and are enraged by the literal and figurative "prostitution" of the art form. Attempts to "reinvent" the "purity" of "true" flamenco spark debates regarding authenticity. These debates, in turn, influence the efforts of those who wish to codify and preserve "traditional" flamenco for future generations. As flamenco increasingly becomes a global practice, issues of cultural appropriation and contamination re-emerge, calling into question the role of flamenco as representative of a specific ethnic, class, or national identity.

The Ideology of Flamenco Histories

The debates in twentieth-century flamenco history reveal the potential for narrative to be bent to fit a specific ideological agenda. However, the ways in which history as a form of representation functions as a part of an ideological apparatus deserve further development. Historical accounts do not merely differ in the mapping of flamenco's evolution; each narrative uses specific conventions to claim access to the "truth." History promises to make ordered and meaningful the events of the past so they may resonate in the present. In the words of Walter Benjamin, "History is the subject of a structure whose site is not homogeneous, empty time, but time filled by the presence of the now [*Jetztzeit*]."[27] That is, the frame of the history, its organization and structural conventions, places the reader in a specific position in relationship to the "reality" represented by historical discourse. History, as a form of representation, constitutes the reader as a subject of ideology. This process depends on the formation and immediate repression of the relationships between ideology and the subject, ideology and history, and finally, history and the subject.

Louis Althusser's essay "Ideology and Ideological State Apparatuses" (1971) discusses the function of ideology in the constitution of the subject. He begins with Marx's definition of ideology as the representation of the imaginary relation of "man" to the conditions of his existence, and develops this idea to show a tautological relationship between ideology and the subject. He says,

> ...the category of the subject is constitutive of all ideology, but at the same time and immediately I add that *the category of the subject is only constitutive of all ideology insofar as all ideology has the function (which defines it) of "constituting" concrete individuals as subjects.*[28]

Ideology is the process by which the individual locates him or herself in a field of relationships, including the family, religion, law, and culture. This process of location creates the subject as an entity. Once formed, this relationship must be repressed, for

> the peculiarity of ideology is that it is endowed with a structure and functioning such as to make it a non-historical reality, i.e. an *omni-historical* reality, in the sense in which that structure and functioning are immutable, present in the same form throughout what we can call history....[29]

Ideology determines what is true and meaningful for the subject, and places the subject in relationship to those ideas. These truths, and the existence of the subject, appear to be constant and unchanging, removed from the workings of time and the conditions of material existence. Due to this curious process of production and erasure, Althusser ironically states, "Ideology has no history."[30]

Upon closer examination, Ideology, the function, can be seen as ideologies—different schematic representations of truth and meaning in a given historical context, and History, the chronological occurrence of events in time, can be seen as histories—narrative representations of past events and their significance. While Ideology has no History, ideologies are represented in histories, and histories express ideologies. For Althusser and Marx, this relationship has everything to do with class positions, the hierarchy of power and the unequal distribution of wealth. In light of these ideas, it is not surprising that the history of flamenco, economically and socially rooted in class struggle, should be characterized by competing ideological agendas. History, as a form of representation expressive of ideology, is an effect of power and desire, and it must deny the operation of those forces in its production to claim the status of "truth." History must erase its own writing, and the authorship of "the subject," to appear as an assemblage of "facts."

The relationship of the subject to history, or histories, has to do with the imaginary relationship of the individual to his/her material circumstances, and to the function of ideology. The compulsion to locate the subject in ideology through the historical account is prompted by danger, which gives way to desire. In his "Theses on the Philosophy of History" (1969), Walter Benjamin states:

> To articulate the past historically does not mean to recognize it "the way it really was" (Ranke).[31] It means to seize hold of a memory as it flashes up at a moment of danger. Historical materialism wishes to retain that image of the past which unexpectedly appears to man singled out by history at a moment of danger. The danger affects both the content of the tradition and its receivers.[32]

The "moment of danger," in flamenco history, takes many forms. In the plotting of origin points, the dangers are the embarrassing associations of gypsy lower class status and prostitution with what has come to be the icon of Spanish identity in an international context. As historians recount the effects of commercialism, the danger is the loss of an originary practice, and the circumstances of political repression under the dictatorship of Franco. The move toward *flamenco puro*, pure flamenco, is motivated by the threat of cultural appropriation in a global market and the loss of control in the preservation of an art form. The desire that follows is the desire to control, through narrative, the representation of flamenco history and flamencos, as well as Andalusian, gypsy, and Spanish identities. The anxiety can be contained, and the desire enacted, through narrative. But narrative demands an author, a disclosure of the subject in ideology as s/he constructs his/her imaginary relationship to these circumstances and the danger they present. And history, like science, must appear as if it is the transparent revelation of preexisting "facts" if it is to be authoritative.

The Desiring Subject

Ironically, the authority of a given history depends upon the seamless deployment of those elements that characterize good storytelling. The unfolding of events must appear effortless, uncontrived, while at the same time adhering to the conventions of the compelling story. "Good storytelling" allows the reader/listener to become a part of the story as the omniscient observer, and the opportunity to identify with some aspect of the landscape described. Perhaps flamenco's most powerful testament to the enduring appeal of "good storytelling" is Mérimée's *Carmen*. In fact, it was published alongside actual travel diaries and mistaken as a ethnographic account of a linguist's interaction with Spaniards and gypsies.[33] In it, a masterful authoritative presence relates his encounter with a fallen man and the man's beloved nemesis, an exotic and dangerous gypsy girl. The reader has access to the protagonist's thoughts and considerable insight, and can vicariously witness the tragedy of Don José's obsession and Carmen's murder. The momentary suspension of disbelief, termed "suture" in contemporary film theory, allows the viewer/reader to be absorbed in the diegesis of the story, transported from outside observer to participant in the spectacle.

Persuasive histories work along similar lines. Like stories, historical representations present events as real rather than imaginary through the structures of narrative. The paradox of history rests in its demand for scrutiny as scientific discourse, while at the same time persuading the reader that: "[t]he authority of the historical narrative is the authority of reality itself; the historical account endows this reality with form and thereby makes it desirable by the imposition upon its processes of the formal coherency only stories possess."[34] The narrative structures that frame the "facts" of a specific historical account mean to convince the reader of an immanent truth. But the frame is not adherent to, or merely surrounding, the "truth" represented in the text; it constitutes the very notion of "reality." And it is the danger, the crisis of accounting for the "now," that predicates the desire to narrate and make significant the events of the past so they endow the present moment with a fullness that locates the subject in relationship to other things in a field of meaning.

So it is with the eagerness of the storyteller's audience that the reader engages with the historical text: a child opening her eyes to a Viewmaster, the voyeur at the keyhole, the narcissist before the mirror. In "Narrativity in the Representation of Reality," Hayden White argues that the relationship between the historical text and the reader is one of desire—"we can comprehend the appeal of historical discourse by recognizing the extent to which it makes the real desirable, makes the real into an object of desire, and does so by its imposition, upon events that are represented as real, of the formal coherency that stories possess."[35] The techniques used to convince the reader of the legitimacy of a single account among many others reveal a specific construction of the desirable real. This construction depends upon and supports a host of other discursive realms—processes that govern gender, race, family, and class, to name only a few—in its claim to authenticity.

Within the history of flamenco dance, several different forms of historical discourse compete for the position of speaking "the authority of reality itself," and each has an investment in a particular construction of that authority. Technique manuals, memoirs, written dance histories, oral histories and travel diaries describe events through specific narrative structures. Authority and reality are represented differently in each context. Technique manuals detail expert manipulations of bodily codes learned by practitioners. The systemic mapping of an encoded vocabulary indicates a comprehensive knowledge of a field of possibilities. The steps are presented in a specific order, demonstrating the process by which they are learned by students and suggesting the syntax of their combination in performance. The structure of the technique manual approximates "realness" through its emulation of the classroom experience. In the case of flamenco, a tradition only recently standardized according to the model of the "classical" dance training method, the presentation of the vocabulary in a developmental sequence invokes the "legitimacy" of forms like ballet and Spanish classical dance. The ordering of steps provides flamenco the status of "Western" concert dance, distinguishing it as an art form and not "merely" a folk practice.

Memoirs and biographies attest to the authority of direct experience within the flamenco community. Since the standardization of the flamenco vocabulary is a recent invention, memoirs imitate the more informal method of transferring information from elders to their disciples through anecdotes from everyday life. Usually, these texts deal with the lives of flamenco legends and offer an "insider's account" of the flamenco "way of life." Memoirs have a mythical quality about them, as if through reading about these personalities, one can touch their greatness and channel their genius. Unlike technique manuals, memoirs and biographies support the practice of flamenco as a folk form by locating the reader in a social environment rather than a classroom setting. Since this landscape is always located in the past, memoirs often support the purists' contention that flamenco has "lost" something in its contemporary incarnation.

Written dance histories call upon the legitimacy of scientific discourse and the collection of evidence to support a hypothesis. Very often, they are compiled by scholars who scrupulously research archives for "artifacts" of flamenco's past and subject them to rigorous analysis supported by a "legitimate" scholarly theoretical framework. The object is to confirm "what really happened" through the assemblage of "facts" in a chronological narrative structure, but they are not simply objective sequences. These are "proper histories" as Hayden White defines them:

> ...the account must manifest a proper concern for the judicious handling of evidence, and it must honor the chronological order of the original occurrence of the events of which it treats as a baseline not to be transgressed in the classification of any given event as either a cause or an effect. But by common consent, it is not enough that an historical account deal in real, rather than merely imaginary events; and it is not enough that the account represents events in its order of discourse according to the chronological sequence in which they originally occurred. The events must be not only registered within the chronological framework of their original occurrence but narrated as well, that is to say, revealed as possessing a structure, an order of meaning, that they do not possess as mere sequence.[36]

White's definition points to the narrative strategy of the "proper history": the author must not overtly propose a series of causes and effects within the narrative, instead s/he must arrange the events so they appear to have an intrinsic logic already present in "real life." The influence of the authorial perspective is masked by the weight of the evidence and the revelation of pertinent events through an academic argumentative structure.

Oral histories, like memoirs, depend on the authority of experience, but emphasize the generational model of pedagogy. The information gleaned from interviews and classroom settings claims to represent not only the experiences of a single person, but those who preceded him/her within a tradition. The early recording on vinyl, audio and video, or transcriptions of them, do not appear to be mediated and deliberately organized in the manner of the history or technique manual. Instead, the questions posed by the interviewer and the responses of the artist suggest a conversation, or even the structure of an improvisation. The staged "informality" of this model evokes a "real-life presence," which, in the history of flamenco, characterizes the purist ideal of a lost tradition, open to chance and to the visitation of the *duende*.

Travel diaries construct an "outsider" space that benefits from a certain distance and clarity of perspective not available to the practitioners of the art, while at the same time maintaining a privileged proximity to the object of study, the "insider's story." The authorial voice in travel diaries usually belongs to a foreigner who manages to insert him/herself into a space reserved for native practitioners. Like Mérimée's fictional travel account, these diaries take the form of amateur anthropological studies. The educated "Westerner" spends time in a remote gypsy village and records events s/he is privileged to witness. Travel diaries communicate these experiences in accessible terms to other interested "outsiders."

As the notion of authority is constructed differently within these examples of historical narrative, the image or idea of flamenco is transformed. The performance of flamenco, an object of study within a discourse of desire, is subjected to those discursive strategies that support and reproduce a specific configuration of the desirable real. Each history examines the development of flamenco from a distinct perspective, endows the dance with a specific origin, a chronology of important events, periods of ascendancy and deterioration, choreographic conventions and aesthetic standards. In each case, an invisible authorial presence reveals the characteristics that constitute "real" flamenco according to his/her ideological affiliations. Through this process, flamenco emerges as both the product and the process of its representation, not a stable entity that can be immobilized and dissected. As such, any discussion of flamenco further participates in its construction and details the process of that construction by focusing on the apparatus involved.

A Choreographic In(ter)vention

The posture of the historian, eyes cast behind her as she stumbles forward, leads her to believe that meaning is located *back there*, underlying the evidence. Using a detective's methods, she searches for the truth hidden under layers of mystery and subterfuge. The attitude is retrospective: unearth and reassign significance to previous events. However, the project of the historian is significantly changed if she chooses to invert the equation. What if, instead of truth giving rise to facts and reality leading to representation, the operation were reversed? What if the notion of a fact, spoken in the voice of authority and mantled in the robes of legitimacy, constitutes the truth? What if the codes of representation give rise not only to reality, but the idea that reality precedes representation? Such an inversion changes the analysis of the historian. Her project, then, is not to discover the truth, but the means by which the notion of *the truth* is constructed in each context.

Film Narrative as a Discourse of Desire

If historical narratives, through their chronological structure and their re-presentation of the "facts," represent reality persuasively by means of the compelling story, then film narratives further exploit the relationship of the subject to ideology through their mimetic reenactment of "real" action over time. As film theorist Bill Nichols states, "The cinema is a strongly representational art: it presents us with recognizable figures or objects whose lifelikeness is sometimes uncanny."[37] Films, like historical narratives, function as apparatuses of ideology by virtue of their claims to represent "reality." The relationship of the subject to the visual codes, or images, signified on film—the ways in which the subject identifies with these images—is intensified by the realistic appearance of these signs. An individual interprets written language as a symbolic system that may not resemble its referents, a field of arbitrary signs. However, the viewer recognizes filmic images due to their iconic resemblance to the material world. Film, like history, constitutes a particular kind of subject through its representation of reality. While this relationship is expressive of the same kinds of relationships to power and class positioning as history through the use of cultural codes, the language that theorists use to describe that relationship focuses on the formation of the self and desire for the Other.

Althusser's concept of the subject constituted within ideology has an analogous counterpart within film theory. In the Lacanian model of psychoanalysis, the "Mirror Stage" occurs somewhere between the ages of six and eighteen months of childhood development. At this point, the child makes a realization that he is a separate entity from the world that surrounds him. Lacan uses this example to link the perception of self and difference to the anxiety provoked by this realization, and to the mechanisms used to allay that anxiety. The "Mirror Stage" is important to the formulation of a theory of a film subject because it focuses on the relationship of the individual to a field of signs, and the processes of perception involved in recognizing or "reading" those signs. As in historical narrative, the intelligibility of films relies upon the formation and immediate repression of key relationships between ideology and the subject, ideology and the image, and the filmic image and the subject.

This primary relationship between the self and the other marks a moment of entry into the world of ideology. That moment of perception of difference produces anxiety, for the image of the Other appears to have complete mastery over its surroundings, and the mirror image of the child appears as an impossibly coherent ideal. According to Nichols,

> The consequences of this are vast. The self-as-subject or ego will be precisely a term in a relationship; the subject comes to define itself in a relationship of opposition to, and identity with, the other. (We speak of our own identity but forget to ask with what—for Lacan, our identity is identity with the other, the image of perfection apparently denied us.)[38]

Nichols creates a link between Lacan's theory of the formation of the self in childhood development and Althusser's concept of the subject constituted in ideology. This link allows for a theory of the film's viewer, an audience transfixed by the camera's eye:

> The camera, like a magician, appears to read our mind, and our own act of reading, our necessary act of collaboration in this deceit, goes unnoticed and unnoted. Photographic realism, then, works to naturalize comprehension; it hides the work of perceiving meaning behind the mask of a "naturally, obviously" meaningful image.[39]

The naturalization of the production of meaning in films parallels the erasure of the authorial voice in histories. Both forms of representation employ narrative to provoke and then contain desire for the Other, all the while masking the role of the Subject.

Here, the analysis of flamenco on film concentrates mainly on the works of Carlos Saura and Antonio Gades. During the decade of the 1980s, the Spanish director and choreographer resurrected flamenco myths through their collaborations on film. *Bodas de Sangre* (1981) rescripted Federico García Lorca's gypsy tragedy as a flamenco ballet. *Carmen* (1983) set Bizet's opera and Merimée's story to flamenco rhythms, and *El Amor Brujo* (1986) revived Manuel de Falla's flamenco ballet of 1915. These films used epic narratives to both reconfigure and reproduce the stereotypes of flamenco history for international audiences. The "flamenco trilogy" offered accessible images of the Spanish South and fed a renewed interest in flamenco across the globe. However, these films also posited a critique of flamenco dance as an icon of Spanish identity. According to film scholar Marvin D'Lugo, the films of Saura and Gades explore the paradoxical relationship of the Spaniard to the cultural stereotypes of "Spanishness":

Ultimately, it is not the outward, clichéd trappings of Andalusianism that we come to see as the unifying element of the trilogy, but rather Saura's characteristic impulse toward a lucidity about the familiar cultural artifacts that construct social and personal identity. For that reason, the centerpiece of all three films is the figure of *performance*: dancers playing the part of fictional characters who are bound inextricably to fatalistic scenarios; individuals whose identity as dancers is itself the result of a willed submission to a cluster of artistic and social mythologies; finally, the figure of the Spaniard as performer of a cultural ethos to which his own identity appears irrevocably bound.[40]

In D'Lugo's assessment, the coded markings of the flamenco dancer— the posture, the costuming, the danced vocabulary—are assumed in two senses of the word: They exist as "artifacts" of exoticism, cultural assumptions; and they are taken on as aspects of performance, as one might assume a character. He asserts that these markings have significance for the artist, not merely as reflections of how the spectatorial, colonizing gaze constructs the stereotype of the Spaniard, but also how the Spanish artist views himself. D'Lugo goes on to point out that this double way of seeing is not a new or radical thought among Spaniards. The philosopher José Ortega y Gasset wrote, in a 1927 essay called "Theory of Andalusia,"

This propensity of the Andalusians to play act and mimic themselves reveals a surprising collective narcissism. The only people who can imitate themselves are those who are capable of becoming spectators of themselves, of contemplating and delighting at their figure and being.[41]

Ortega y Gasset's "Theory of Andalusia" carries its own assumptions concerning the difference between Andalusians and other Spaniards, a difference scripted along the lines of regional tensions, class and race. Flamenco provides a spectacle for the performance of exoticism between Spaniards, creating the categories of gypsy and lower class Andalusian as strange and different from the upper class Andalusian or foreigner in a hierarchy of power and meaning. Ortega y Gasset's evaluation of the performance of these roles suggests they are not only assigned to Spain by other nations and cultures, but also internalized and outwardly performed by Spaniards themselves. Carlos Saura and Antonio Gades, as two specific examples of artists who deal with the notions of individual and communal identity in their collaborative work, use flamenco as a means of exploring the split spectatorship of the Spaniard as exoticized object.

Every author of texts concerning flamenco operates within a complex set of tensions of ethnicity, class, gender, national identity, and international power relations at specific historical moments. In the chapters that follow, the purpose is to analyze the different configurations of the flamenco dancer and the practice of flamenco produced by flamencophiles during the course of the twentieth and early twenty-first centuries and to analyze how the social tensions surrounding the production of each history inform its content. The work focuses on histories of flamenco written by non–Spaniards, Spanish films released for international audiences, and contemporary performances by female flamenco dancers. These texts allow for an examination of the flamenco stereotype from the position of the "Western" gaze that constructs the Other as a spectacle of exoticism. This particular history of flamenco is no more removed from the stage of the spectacle than any other. Why? Because the history of flamenco is inextricably entangled with the legacy of colonialism, in which the terrain of the "dark continent" of female sexuality is constructed as an icon of Otherness, and that image is the flamenco dancer. There is no way to discuss the stereotype of the flamenco Exotic without further participating in the construction of the same, but hopefully, in the process of this discussion, a previously invisible presence will be made at least intelligible, the subject who gazes upon the Other and produces her as an object of desire. Once visible, the agent of the colonizing gaze no longer occupies the same position of power; s/he becomes the object of scrutiny, subordinate to the demands of desire and narrative.

2

Purism, Tourism and Lost Innocence

Flamenco Bodies: Essence or Effect?

Within the larger rubric of flamenco studies—particularly among works published in English—discussions of the dance component are far outnumbered by works devoted to the song and guitar elements. As a result of this imbalance in the scholarly work surrounding flamenco as an art form, researchers of the dance frequently rely on sources that privilege the song forms as the "core" of flamenco and relegate the dance and guitar elements to subsidiary positions. There are a number of considerations to account for the relative absence of discussion surrounding dance in flamenco history. To begin: Flamenco as a tradition has been associated with the lower classes. The persecution of gypsies in the history of Europe, and particularly in Spain, attests to the marginalization of their cultural practices. Further, according to Loren Chuse, a scholar of the *cante*, and anthropologist William Washabaugh before her, "Along with gitanos, marginalized and impoverished Andalusians have been subjected to hundreds of years of social inequalities, legal discrimination and economic exploitation by the government and the ruling aristocracy which has resulted in great poverty, famines and mass emigration to America in earlier centuries."[1] The tradition of flamenco has not enjoyed the same faithful written record (often court or government-sponsored) that ballet or other classical forms have. As a result, the chronology of flamenco history often lacks consistent documentation of artists' lives and performances. And, although Andalusia enjoyed wealth and power in antiquity, during the late nineteenth and early twentieth centuries, it was the poorest and least industrially developed region in Spain. However, the caution surrounding the discussion of the dance, as opposed to the song or the guitar, seems to be a result of dance's perceived proximity to bodies themselves—bodies dark and poor, criminal and sensual, bought and sold: regal, thieving, drunk and prostituted bodies.

Traditional flamenco scholarship perpetuates a gloriously modernist binary of dark, and light, Apollonian and Dionysian. The song, lifted out of

Guitarist José Luis Rodriguez, focused intently on the dancers of Bailes Ferrer, in Flamenco in the Sun 2005 at the Broward Center for the Performing Arts in Fort Lauderdale, Florida. Photograph by Liliam Dominguez, used with permission.

the body, may transcend the disgrace of the body and enter the realm of the intellect. And Apollo, one must remember, is the god of music. But flamenco dance carries with it always the taint of hunger, intoxication, poverty, and, often, sexuality. For those scholars invested in the recuperation of the dance for the intellect, the flamenco body must be transformed from a grotesque body to a classical one.[2] Even as descriptions of the dance seek to embody textually the nobility of the outcast, these accounts reaffirm the supremacy of the intellect and its capacity to distill from dangerous bodies a heroic essence.

This tendency is distinctly intelligible in descriptions of the dance from flamenco histories, both foreign and Spanish. When, in a lengthy discussion of song or guitar, the dance emerges, it is inevitably a moment of disjuncture from the "objective" or "scholarly" voice. The reader is transported, through the telling, into a realm of immediacy and longing, and the void may be filled by a host of unattainable desires—the unapproachable woman, the untouchable and violent man, an exotic "primitiveness" or "dignity" forever lost through civilization, and the apparent capacity for deep feeling that accompanies it. These qualities always exist as a mask for hidden fears, as well—the limited, temporary, but devastating castrating power of the attractive woman, the revolt of the repressed man and the transgression of societal mores that maintain order, power, and legitimacy. The most curious aspect of these ambivalent associations with the dancing body lies in the attribution of these qualities to the *essence* of the dancing body, rather than the retrospective *effect* of its representation. In these histories, the notion of the body coalesces as a host of assumptions that support a "naturalized" configuration of race, gender, class, and national identity. In each work, the body moves as an expression of some fundamental interiority: a gypsy dances passionately as a result of his or her bloodlines, a woman's dance articulates an essential femininity, a man's dance reveals the virility intrinsic to his sex, the lower classes demonstrate their coarseness through their movements, and the image of the flamenco dancer captures the innate nobility and passionate nature of the Spanish people. These associations are assumed as *a priori* truths merely expressed through the dancing. The social construction of the categories of gypsy, woman or man, Andalusian or Spanish in a specific cultural and historical context is erased.

The project of this book is to examine, to unmask, to make intelligible, the writing of dancing bodies in isolated historical accounts from flamenco history with specific attention to the ways in which truth and authority are constructed in each context. In this analysis, the categories of gypsy, man, and woman give rise to a complex matrix of meaning and power in an international dialogue. The examples represent periods of crisis in flamenco history: the end of the Golden Age, the years of tourism during Franco's regime, and the years following Franco's death up to the present. The years before the Spanish Civil War (1936) attest to the circulation of the image of the dancing gypsy as poetically embodying the innate nobility of Spaniards despite the (perceived) backward influence of the gypsies. Discussion concerning the contaminating effects of commercialism and the taint of prostitution characterize the dialogue among flamenco aficionados when they write about the decade of 1950s. Later, in Chapter 3, the debates on authenticity and the origins of flamenco concern authors from 1980 to the present. In each instance, the flamenco body fills a space of nostalgia and speaks to qualities "lost" even as they are "found" in representations of the dancing.

International Exposure

One of the first published works on flamenco dance outside Spain in the twentieth century was written by the British dance enthusiast Cyril Rice. *Dancing in Spain (Argentina and Escudero)* was published in 1931. Rice chooses two of the most internationally famous dancers of the time, Antonia Mercé ("La Argentina") and Vicente Escudero, to serve as the performers representative of dance in Spain. The work is neither a strict history nor a technical manual, though it contains elements of both. In his foreword to the book, he prefaces his account with a disclaimer:

> This book is not intended as an exhaustive technical account to the professional, but rather it is an attempt to give some idea of the richness of this unique art, and a few examples of its most typical manifestations. I believe it to deal with a subject on which there is no existing work in English. If it persuades any readers to see Spanish dancers whenever the opportunity occurs, and enables them more fully to appreciate their art, it will have answered its purpose [1].

His purpose, then, is to make an informed account of Spanish dance available to English-speaking audiences, couched in a language and organizational structure accessible to an audience unfamiliar with the history and conventions of the art form. In his first chapter, entitled "Dancing in Spain," he provides a brief history of regional dances, directing most of his attention to the dances of Andalusia. After tracing the development of various classical Spanish forms, he moves into a discussion of flamenco. Immediately, he cautions the reader against the association of these forms with an overtly sexual address:

> Though this dancing emphasized [sic], so clearly and so repeatedly, the body and the glory of the flesh, it cannot be dismissed as erotic. Provocative though these gestures may be, especially when gypsy influence preponderated, the

suggestion was only in the nature of a condiment, and the sense of dignity innate in the Spanish, their feeling for style, preserved them from vulgarity [22].

Paradoxically, Rice's descriptions of the "richness of this unique art" depend upon an elision of the dancing body in order to represent the nature of the dance and its practitioners. The "provocative" elements of the dance, particularly in performances by gypsies, should be viewed as secondary to the meaning of the dance. Indeed, any sexual connotations implied should be consumed only as "a condiment," that which teases the palate but only serves to augment the taste of the staple ingredients. The dance becomes something that can be consumed very much like a meal. According to the logic of the metaphor, the sustaining element of the performance should be the "innate dignity in the Spanish."

The concept of a biological predisposition for a kind of nobility among the Spanish appears repeatedly in historical representations of flamenco. Rice attributes this characteristic to the flamenco comportment of the torso, back and hips. He even ventures a scientific hypothesis to account for the posture of the dancers:

> Curiously enough, it is an anatomical fact, first established by Duchenne in 1866, that in Spanish women the spine is more curved than in other races, as if a slight pressure had been exerted at either extremity.... Proof of the importance attached to this part of the body is provided by the practice, common to both sexes, of wearing garments which fit like a skin from the hips to the chest [23].

This description sets up for the reader the perspective of viewing the Spanish dancer as biologically, and therefore racially, Other than he or she is. The distinction is further exaggerated in Rice's earlier contrasting examples of gypsy practice and Spanish practice, where the gypsy is still more Other on the spectrum of exoticism. The discussion focuses, despite his previous denial of the sexual connotations of the dance, the reader's attention to the erotic bodily terrain spanning from the breasts to the hips. The female flamenco dancer, with her skeletal anomaly further exaggerated by her costume, appears as a figure that invites the predatorial gaze even as her stately bearing denies the satisfaction provided by the condiment: a fleeting moment of piquancy at the tip of the tongue.

Model Exotics

Rice chooses the famous classical dancer La Argentina as the figure representative of the feminine role in Spanish dance. His choice is significant

Portrait of the elegant La Argentina in *bata de cola*, ca. 1920s (Jerome Robbins Dance Division, New York Public Library for the Performing Arts, Astor, Lenox and Tilden Foundations).

for at least two reasons: La Argentina toured widely throughout Europe and the United States during the 1920s, it is possible that her name or her reputation as "the Pavlova of Spanish dancing" (36) would be recognized; and though she is acknowledged by flamenco historians as a virtuoso dancer of flamenco and regional dances, particularly for her skill in playing castanets, she is generally recognized as a classical Spanish dancer (*bailarina*) rather than a flamenco dancer (*bailaora*). This distinction should not be overlooked, particularly in light of Rice's earlier comment about the "provocative" nature of those dances in which "the gypsy influence preponderated." Since gypsies are always associated with the flamenco forms among Andalusian regional dances, La Argentina serves as a palatable flamenco artist, exotic but dignified. Rice insists on this distinction throughout his text. "The work of the gitana is a living marvel and a thing of vivid beauty, but Argentina reaches another plane; it is a fact of vital importance that, in this process of refinement, she has sacrificed but little of the intensity which is inseparable from the dancing of her country" (38). In this single sentence, a hierarchy of class and race forms: the gypsy is located on the lowest rung of the ladder, the "refinement" of Argentina places her on "another plane," as a Spanish classical dancer she "sacrifices little of the intensity" of her native country to achieve the nobility of a Spaniard. The highest position, unseen, is occupied by the author, an Englishman, whose birth and education allow him the perspective to see the difference.

Racial difference is then further complicated by sexual difference. In one description of Argentina's performance of a dance from the "primitive, direct, realistic world of the gypsy" (42), Rice exploits the sensual and feminized characteristics of flamenco:

> [S]he is the flamenca endeavoring, by sorcery and incantation, to appease the jealous spirit of her dead lover. The strident beating of her heels echoes the anguish and foreboding in her heart; then, coming down the stage with swift, soft steps she stamps once and draws herself erect. Anxiously she fans the glow of the brazier; encourages it with the nervous snapping of her fingers, the recurrent hissing between her clenched teeth. Gradually, a more hopeful strain insinuates itself into the music. As it becomes stronger and then dominant, the load of fate is lifted from the shoulders of the gitana, and in the final phase she becomes like a child, transported by relief and joy [43].

In this brief choreographic narrative, as Rice recounts it, La Argentina is consumed by her passionate emotions. Because this section of choreography is situated within a larger narrative, a performance of Manuel de Falla's *El Amor Brujo*,[3] he assigns her gestures a discursive, almost pantomimic, quality. The metaphors he employs in this passage emphasize the close relationship between the exotic dancing woman and her body, its capacity to express deep, earthly emotions and the childlike quality intrinsically linked to the representation of playful primitiveness. Rice's emphasis on the amiable side of her performance serves to downplay the potentially threatening vulgar and sexual characteristics of her exoticism. As a palatable Exotic, she is infinitely more accessible, less threatening, as a commodity.

The image of the male partner in the exoticized dancing couple must be configured differently from that of the female dancer. In Rice's text, the descriptions of La Argentina stand in marked contrast to the accounts of Vicente Escudero. Both are international stars of the 1920s, but while Argentina represents femininity and classicism, Escudero signifies masculinity and gypsy flamenco (48). In his description of Escudero's *Farruca*, Rice conjures up hyper-masculine imagery:

> [T]he dancer appears to be possessed by a raging fury while yet retaining complete mastery over his movements. His legs might be rooted to the floor; they ripple as the heels and toes produce their continuous stabbing rhythms at incredible speed. Suddenly, with a bound, Escudero is at the other end of the stage. Jumping, he stamps firmly with the whole foot and comes to an abrupt stop with one of those sudden pauses which are so integral a feature to flamenco, and indeed, of all Andalusian dancing. First softly, then with increasing violence he beats on the ground with the ball of either foot in succession as his body trembles with the vibration; occasionally he makes an arm movement, always, however, clear and sharp-cut; more often he has one hand on his hip while the other holds fast the point of his chaquetilla. In a moment, he hurls himself to the ground, seems stretched at length, and is, all in the same instant, once again upright [53].

Escudero, like Argentina, is "possessed" by intense feeling, but unlike Argentina he maintains "mastery" over his movements. The descriptions of the choreography invoke unquestioningly masculine qualities: the "stabbing" of his footwork, its increasing "violence," and the "clear and sharp-cut" movements of the arms. He asserts, through *zapateado* (rapid footwork), with his arms drawn in close to his body, an unrelentingly erect posture. Even through the execution of a *caída*—a traditional flamenco step that involves a fall into a deep lunge—the representation of Escudero never compromises the verticality of his body. In fact, at that point he appears "stretched at length."

The *Farruca*, unlike Argentina's role in *El Amor Brujo*, has no apparent narrative, so Escudero's body does not serve as the vehicle for the expression of a story. The choice to represent the feminine body as a transparent vessel for the tides of passionate emotion and the masculine body as a differentiated instrument for technical display marks the separate, and hierarchized, spheres of activity assigned to the feminine and masculine roles. Rice's description of Escudero's dancing provides important details that make visible the labor of the dancer: he stabs his heels into the ground, bounds across the stage, jumps, stops, beats, and then hurls his body to the ground. These movements accomplish an end within themselves. Escudero displays technical proficiency through his performance of a specific vocabulary. By con-

Vicente Escudero, displaying the uncompromising verticality of the traditional masculine role. Photograph is undated but was likely taken in the 1920s. (Jerome Robbins Dance Division, New York Public Library for the Performing Arts, Astor, Lenox and Tilden Foundations).

trast, Argentina expresses her heartbeat through her footwork, she pantomimes a struggle with the brazier, then her effort disappears as she is "transported by relief and joy." While Escudero is celebrated for his virtuosity,
Argentina is admired for her emotive performance. Rice's descriptions set
up some important chains of signification within the field of connotation surrounding these representations. The excess of femininity contrasts the control and measure of the masculine role. Emotional expression is the effect of
one performance, virtuoso display results from the other. The feminine role
culminates in submission to passion, but the masculine role ends with an
assertion of mastery. These contrasting qualities serve as mutually constituting entities. The parameters of the feminine role mark the boundaries of the
masculine role.

However, the exaggerated quality of the masculine performance, the
constant reiteration of the structures of legitimacy and phallic power, reads
as a kind of excess that produces the very associations it prohibits. The conventions of representation that mark the feminine and masculine roles constitute a hierarchy in which the masculine role signifies power and the
feminine role signifies a dangerous potential for disruption of the masculine
order. The spectatorial gaze, in this case, the position of the author, occupies the most powerful and implicitly masculine role in performance.[4] The
dancing couple is feminized and dominated in this configuration. However,
the representation of excessive masculinity in descriptions of the masculine
dance simultaneously suggests and erases the possibility for an erotic engage-
ment of the male dancer by the masculine spectatorial gaze. The male dancer
moves in the space allocated to exotic objects, but he reflects the qualities of
the gaze: masterful, measured, dominating. The dangerous, passionate power
attributed to the feminine role deflects, or perhaps absorbs, the homoerotic
tension between the male dancer and the gaze.[5]

Notice that Rice chooses to present his readers with a flamenco couple,
as opposed to a single dancer or a series of dancers. Perhaps he is concerned
with an economical use of textual space: Argentina and Escudero serve ade-
quately as contemporary representatives of the masculine and the feminine,
classical and gypsy, elements of Spanish dance. The structure of these binary
categories eliminates the possibility for a more complex consideration of the
racial and class distinctions among the many regions of Spain. With this pair,
Rice collapses layers of difference on top of each other to construct the model
Hispanic dancing couple. Both La Argentina and Escudero perform regional
dances as well as flamenco forms. In a given context, either dancer can stand
in as Catalan, Basque, Andalusian or Gypsy, conflating these ethnic differences as equal and interchangeable characteristics on the site of a single dancing body. As a couple presented as dancing together under the category of

"Spanish dance" within the text, their sexual difference, not the ethnicities they represent, is reasserted constantly. The position of the author stands apart from his desire's creation. A similar relationship between the Latino male/female dancing couple and the colonizing gaze has been explored by tango scholar Marta Savigliano:

> But it actually takes three to tango: a male to master the dance and confess his sorrows; a female to seduce, resist seduction, and be seduced; and a gaze to watch these occurrences. The male/female couple performs the ritual, and the gaze constitutes the spectacle. Two performers, but three participants make a tango. However, the gaze is not aloof and static; it is rather expectant, engaged in that particular state of detachment that the creators hold toward the objects of their imagination. The gaze can substitute for the male dancer; the gaze can double itself and dance instead of the tango couple.[6]

While Argentina and Escudero do not dance as a couple in any of the accounts within the text, and neither performs the tango of Argentina, as representatives of the Hispanic dancing couple, they function as representations of the spectatorial object of desire in terms of the performativity of the text. They are subject to the same discursive conventions as any other exotic objects, which are interchangeable by nature. As the third participant in this theoretical tango that produces exotic objects, Rice's authorial role constitutes the spectacle of exoticism. The passionate space of the Exotic marks that which circumscribes the identity of the desiring subject.

The boundaries between the Exotic and the expectant gaze must be maintained at all times. In his "Conclusion," Rice situates flamenco dance within a discussion of European ballet. Flamenco dance, like ballet, deserves patronage. However, he insists upon the difference between flamenco and classical dance from other countries: "The unambitious, more personal, dancing of Andalusia has never been the product of a standardized or academic school. Their dancing cannot be confined within fixed, irrefragable rules—it is too spontaneous, too sincere, too urgent" (68). The existence of schools and a standardized vocabulary for ballet speaks to the legitimacy of the dancers' labor. Rice erases the production of the dance and dancers within a tradition by suggesting that flamenco dance springs forth from the soul of the dancer as a spontaneous expression. He then removes the dance from the economy of commercial performance as he contends that the art form must not be allowed to "fall into the hands of 'gypsies from the music hall, manufactured in series in Sevilla.'[7] They would display, not the true embodiment of a living tradition, but merely those elements which are most effective theatrically, adulterated with extraneous tricks" (74). Once again, he demonstrates the need to rescue this art form from its "native" practitioners. He fears the degradation of the form in the one setting where most European audiences would have access to flamenco performance: tourist venues such as the music hall. For Rice, flamenco must be protected from classical standardization as well as commercial contamination. Only educated aesthetes such as he can correctly preserve the simplicity and purity of the tradition.

Paradise Lost

The dangers of commercialism for flamenco are widely discussed by flamenco historians, usually non–Spaniards who treat flamenco as a scarce resource. Something essential can be protected from the demands of an uneducated audience and from the compromises of its "corrupt" practitioners. In a more contemporary (1985) discussion of flamenco, a series of essays published under the title *Flamenco: Gypsy Dance and Music from Andalusia*, only one chapter is devoted to a discussion of the dance.[8] In a moment characteristic of many flamenco scholars, the chapter entitled "History of Flamenco" by Marion Papenbrok traces only the development of the *cante*, or song. Parenthetically, she remarks that "*baile*—dancing—plays a less important role historically" (36). In the chapter called "*Baile Flamenco*," Madeleine Claus gives a possible explanation for the conspicuous absence of material concerning the dance element of flamenco in historical texts by flamencologists: "More than with singing or guitar playing, dance has suffered under Spain's steadily growing tourist industry, which bills flamenco as its main attraction" (92). She attributes the commercial popularity of flamenco dance to its accessibility to foreign audiences as a "gorgeous image of physical movement." Claus separates the dance from the other aspects of flamenco performance, then reassigns the dance within the category of contaminated objects. Physical movement, the body, and sexuality remain in the domain of visually accessible, easily consumable cultural products.

According to Claus, the song and guitar elements are less accessible, and therefore remain more pure in their development over the course of the century:

> This inaccessibility was a blessing in disguise. To avoid shocking the casual listener with this rasping, forbidding and introspective kind of singing, it was performed only as an accompaniment to dancing. The great flamenco singers sang only before small groups of aficionados or made recordings ... they were able to preserve their songs by not having to pander to the tastes of the public, which in its clamor for less challenging entertainment never suspected— and still does not—the gaudy, high-spirited stage show has nothing to do with flamenco, but is simply a prostitution of this centuries-old art form [92].

Claus assumes that "outside" influences, like the technology of recording or the unequal class relationship between aficionados and performers, made no compromising demands on the tradition of the *cante*. Like Rice, she uses words like "preserve" to refer to a tradition of purity that begs protection from "the tastes of the public," those who destroy the form through capitalist consumption. However, her construction of "true" flamenco outside of the realm of commercialism does not change its status as a commodity. Rather, pure flamenco is veiled, kept hidden from outsiders like a virginal bride. The paradigm of the marriage contract provides the structure for meaning in this context, and the bride is elevated as a commodity for exchange above the figure of the prostitute. Both figures can be sold, but the bride price is negotiated between the heads of families and serves to reassert the social structures of kinship. The sale of the prostitute cannot be recuperated within the tradition, just as she cannot be contained within the family structure.

Claus isolates a period of purity within the dance tradition prior to the commercialization of flamenco. She claims for the dance at the turn of the century the status of "true flamenco." Though she consults a handful of written sources for her reconstruction of flamenco history,[9] her main framework for the formulation of her theory of the Golden Age stems from testimony by a dancer named La Joselito:

> La Joselito was born at the beginning of this century, when the first professional flamenco artists were just reaching the peak of their careers. The quality of such performances was never again to be attained. Why? Probably because these people were the last to experience a time when Andalusians and gypsies, under the veil of oppression, sang, played and danced flamenco strictly among themselves, a time when concepts of life and death, love and work, routine tasks, fear and joy were only too well understood [89].

Claus's positioning of La Joselito as a representative of the Golden Age is significant to her own claims of authority within the text and a testament to her knowledge of "true," or "pure," flamenco. In order to accomplish her goals, she retrospectively rearranges the chronology (however unstable) of flamenco history. For example, despite Claus's claims that the Golden Age was free from the constraints of commercialism, professional performance within the *cafés cantantes* have been chronicled by flamencologist José Blás Vega as early as 1847.[10] While the turn of the century marks a period of ascendancy for commercial flamenco performance, it is not the first evidence of widespread professional activity. What's more, the actual year of La Joselito's birth is "unknown," making it difficult for the intrepid researcher to "locate" her position within the spectrum of the Golden Age. As Claus remarks later in the text, the performer has conveniently "forgotten" her age (90). Claus bases her judgment on the quality of past performances in comparison to those of the present or more recent past on the testimony of La Joselito. Her account of the mythical time of oppression and simultaneous innocence at the turn of the century simplifies the complex network of social relations that surrounded the performers of the Golden Age. Claus ignores, or dismisses, the economic and political tensions presented by agrarian reform, Civil War, and the Franco dictatorship in the region of Andalusia.

The interview with La Joselito, then, installs the performer as a living museum piece in the history of flamenco dance and places Claus at her elbow as the informed biographer and scholar of flamenco history. La Joselito's story contains several references to famous figures of the flamenco canon. When La Joselito was a child, La Macarrona smuggled the underage dancer into her first performance (106). An early cross-dressing female artist named La Tanguera physically attacked La Joselito for stealing her *farruca* (107). And, while the two were on a European tour of the ballet *El Amor Brujo*, the famed La Argentina asked La Joselito for flamenco lessons in exchange for castanet coaching (110).

The most important aspects of La Joselito's discussion of flamenco history in this analysis are the ways in which pure flamenco is constructed and how frequently La Joselito criticizes various female flamenco dancers for dancing outside the conventions of traditional flamenco. These issues point to the relationship between the perception of purity in the tradition and the clear-cut gender roles in performance. Claus attributes the degradation of flamenco performance, particularly the female role, to commercialization:

> La Joselito has the body of a woman born into the world of flamenco at the start of this century. Spurning seductiveness, she bewitches her audience not with her body, but by focusing their total attention on the art itself. Commercial productions, on the other hand, use "flamenco" to display the charms of frenzied, coquettish, plastic, imitation "Carmens." Alternatively, more ambitious productions of gypsy–Andalusian flamenco stress technique and virtuosity as ends in themselves. In either case, the ancient essence of flamenco is lost behind pomp and picturesque slickness, driving the duende into exile: Adieu Dionysus!—you've been banished by perfectionism and commercial interests [97].

Claus points to flamenco dance's problematic proximity to the body. *Flamenco puro*, in her description, relies on well-developed craft rather than youthful wiles. Her reaction against the image of Carmen addresses the stereotypical, exoticized, and sexualized image of the female flamenco dancer. But her argument still reinforces the relationship of spectator to performer as the "informed" construction of an exotic object. The tension of seduction supports this connection. La Joselito serves as a receptacle for the desires of a flamencophile. Her bewitching performance is not conventionally seductive, and her sense of craft does not cross the line into vulgar displays of virtuosity. This sense of perfect measure in performance reinforces the authority of the text and the spectatorial position it represents. La Joselito, an incarnation of noble exoticism, dances the desire of the subject. The writing of La Joselito creates her as a symbol of innocence lost, convincingly rendered to appear as a fundamental "essence" merely expressed through description.

Like Rice, Claus heralds the "essence" of flamenco that cannot be expressed through the burlesque of the *tablaos* or the standards for virtuosity established in other forms of classical dance. The problem with commercialism, for Claus, lies in its "false" representation of what is "true" flamenco. Inherent in Claus's text is an anxiety about mass production, with its loss of romantic individuality. The sheer number of dancers produced by the tourist industry would imply a lost "essence."[11] Such an essence is integral to the construction of the exotic object. The desiring subject must continually reconstitute the ephemeral essence of the passionate object at the parameters of being, as if seeing her for the first time. The construction of the exotic object portrays her as always threatened and always in need of protection.

Claus's goodbye to the *duende*, the spirit that takes over the dancer in an inspired performance, is significant to her exoticism of the true flamenco dancer. In an essay in the same collection on "The Spiritual World of Flamenco," Marion Papenbrok defines *duende* as an "irresistible power which possesses an artist only at very special moments and which leads the participants in such a 'reunion' to such a state of ecstasy that they are led to rip their clothing, seem indifferent to fatigue or hunger, and are given to unrestrained crying or even aggressive actions" (54). Claus, as a spectator of such a performance, watches the dancer lose herself to the passion of the *duende*. It is this process that proves the dancer unstable and prone to excess.

Claus's desiring narrative locates a lost Dionysian passion in the performances of La Joselito. Passion becomes not only a vital, but a scarce resource in her writing. This particular configuration of the exotic object differs from Rice's portrayal of Argentina and Escudero because the figure through which this desire is cathected,[12] La Joselito, appears to be complicit in the construction of herself as an exotic. Unlike Rice in his portrayal of Argentina and Escudero, Claus engages with La Joselito in the context of an interview. This setting allows La Joselito the limited opportunity to speak to her position in the tradition of flamenco and gives Claus the aura of authenticity that accompanies "the insider's story." La Joselito, in turn, plays with her own authority during the exchange, as indicated by the example of how she "conveniently forgot" her age.

La Joselito delivers to her audience a product ripe for consumption. Like Argentina, she appropriately embodies the figure of the palatable exotic. As an "authentic" flamenco dancer, she provides the perfect object of desire for a flamencologist in search of evidence from the Golden Age. The collaboration benefits Claus as a scholar and La Joselito as a teacher and performer of traditional flamenco. Neither one acknowledges her position within the same capitalist economy as the tourists who contribute to the deterioration of flamenco. From different positions, each produces flamenco as a commodity and asserts for herself the role of agent in the exchange.

The Taint of Tourism

The problems of commercialism and contamination play an important role in discussions of flamenco since the 1950s. The American flamencophile Donn E. Pohren lived in Spain during Franco's Years of Development (1950s–60s), a period in which the tourist industry was supported largely through the profits from commercial flamenco in the *tablaos*. A self-proclaimed purist, he wrote three major texts on flamenco: *The Art of Flamenco* (1962), *Lives and Legends of Flamenco: A Biographical History* (1964), and *A Way of Life* (1980). *Lives and Legends* serves as a point of reference for two important reasons: First, he arranges flamenco history in the form of a genealogy, and second, he divides the genealogy of performers into two separate categories, male and female. His work may seem to be a rather unconventional form of a genealogy. That is, he does not trace the development of a bloodline, but instead maps the chronology of performers, generation after generation. While "flamenco families"[13] play a key role in the perpetuation of the tradition, as a legacy flamenco passes from teacher to student, and frequently those students are parents and children. His structure emphasizes the way in which the teachers transmit, orally and physically, information to their students.

Pohren's history of flamenco is performative in two senses: it charts a lineage of performers, and it reproduces the structures that create the tradition. He cements these parameters through the adherence to established standards for cultural intelligibility. Pohren recognizes the performers as flamencos by naming them within a tradition. One of the most important standards for inclusion within this history (and he chastises some performers, alive and dead, for breaking this rule) is the maintenance of separate spheres for the masculine and feminine dances. Once again, the damage done by commercialism appears in the blurring of gender roles for performers.

Like other flamenco historians, Pohren deals with the dance in a separate section from the other components of flamenco. Within this section, he includes a brief introduction, followed by "Biographies of Dancers, Male and Female." In the introduction, he establishes the origin of flamenco dance in the ancient Hindu dances of India. Presumably, these dances entered Spain through the import of temple dancers for entertainment sometime during the Greek empire 500–250 B.C. (174). While some contemporary scholars concede this pattern of development, and have analyzed the similarities between *kathak* and flamenco dance techniques, one might have difficulty in sustaining the belief that an evolutionary pattern can be traced according to racial characteristics across several cultures and centuries. However, the plotting of such a development betrays an interesting and effective narrative strategy, which will reappear later in a discussion of Allen Josephs's *White Wall of Spain.*

Pohren points out the pitfalls of a theory asserted by Spanish musicologists, who claim that flamenco developed as an art form in Andalusia "free from outside influence" (176). He argues that the dismissal of gypsy contributions to flamenco reflects an intense Spanish national pride and a latent notion of racial purity. He asks the important question, "There are few pure gypsies left in Andalusia, and as for pure *andaluces*, just what is a pure *andaluz?*" (176). He then begins to trace the "recorded history" of flamenco dance from 1842 through the decade of the 1950s. During the *cafés cantantes* period of flamenco, which segued into the Golden Age at the turn of the century, performers of flamenco were mainly gypsies. Pohren describes the movement characteristics of early flamenco:

> The footwork of the men was relatively primitive; the women, with few exceptions, used almost no footwork at all, but concentrated largely on the more feminine arms, hands and upper torso in general. This type of dance was soon to be altered by two revolutionaries of the *baile flamenco*: Antonio el Bilbao and Carmen Amaya, both of whom came on the scene like cyclones to change the trend of the flamenco dance from non-technical to technical, from simple and direct to difficult and complex [178].

Pohren, like Claus, sets up the standards for true flamenco according to the movement conventions performed at the beginning of the twentieth century. Bilbao and Amaya, as representatives of those dancers who broke from the tradition through their performance of rapid, complex footwork, are separated by a period of about twenty years. He gives the years of birth and death of both artists in his biography, Bilbao c. 1880–1945 and Amaya c. 1913–1963. Again, like Claus, he associates the move toward technical display as a movement away from true flamenco. More significantly, he disapproves of the entrance of footwork into the female dance vocabulary. He writes disparaging accounts of

> the tendency of *bailaoras* to go beyond their more conservative, feminine footwork, also at the expense of the upper torso, arms and hands, into direct competition with the men, turning much of the *baile* flamenco into a non-aesthetic race toward high-speed, intricate, overly-extended footwork. This has gone hand-in-hand with another development: a confusion of the sexes

in the dance. How many present-day *bailaoras* dress in male clothing and emphasize almost nothing but footwork and brusqueness in their dance; and, conversely, how many male dancers look everything but masculine while dancing. The condition that men be men and women, women, or at least appear to be, is an absolute necessity in the *baile* flamenco if it is to be effective [179].

Good flamenco, according to Pohren, has specific standards of sexual difference that are maintained in the distinct movement vocabularies performed by male and female dancers. It is interesting to note that while men must be men, women need only appear to be women. However, this is not a passing reference to drag performances of the female role. Such an idea is outside the scope of Pohren's imagination, unmentionable. Instead, the two polarities of being he sets up here follow a slippery, and mutually reinforcing, logic: men must appear masculine in order to be men; those women who do not appear feminine must not be real women. Pohren cites the gender slippage in the performances of the famous American dancer José Greco as "an example of the devastating effects of commercialism." Though Greco traveled the world as a performer in the '40s and '50s, his dancing suffered from the demands of success:

> As his name grew, his dance deteriorated; each year he was less effective. In my mind his trousers symbolize the change in his dance; it seems as they became more satiny and flamboyant (i.e. skin-tight satin, champagne color and the like), Greco took on an airy, ballet style, and the characteristic virility and duende of his dance suffered badly. This deterioration was augmented by acrobatics and gimmicks, and with time Greco became converted from a moving purist into a crowd-pleasing sensationalist [201].

It is significant that the loss of potency that Pohren attributes to Greco's dancing is focused directly on the type of trousers he wears. As a spectator whose gaze constitutes the spectacle, Pohren is uncomfortably compelled to stare at the crotch of another man. The feminized Greco, whose heterosexual romantic conquests are catalogued at length in his autobiography,[14] disrupts the operation of the gaze as it constitutes the spectacle. Note that Greco's lack of virility precedes in importance his movement toward technical display, which only "augments" the "deterioration" in his dancing. The implementation of a classical movement vocabulary within his performance of flamenco does not strengthen his dancing; instead he appears as a feminized grotesque. Classicism in La Argentina's performance read as "refined," while Greco's attempts at dandyish, high-class mimicry are unsuccessful and somehow threaten the relationship of the spectator to the spectacle.

Pohren maintains his standards for sexual difference and excellence in performance through his textual reconstruction of performance conventions

The Brooklyn-born flamenco, José Greco, performing here with Nila Amparo in an example of the "acrobatic displays" that developed during the 1950s (Jerome Robbins Dance Division, New York Public Library for the Performing Arts, Astor, Lenox and Tilden Foundations).

from the Golden Age. Ironically, he traces the first female dancer to cross-dress and perform the masculine dances to the period of the Golden Age. Trinidad Huertas, "La Cuenca" (c. 1860–1920), was the first female dancer who "went into direct competition with the male." Retrospectively, he attributes the subsequent "deterioration" of the feminine dance to her: "[S]he will have to bear the brunt of the results; setting the fashion for this type of thing, which has adversely affected the feminine dance, often to a disgusting point for those of us who still prefer our females feminine" (216). La Cuenca was the inspiration for another early *flamenca* who performed the male dances, Salud Rodríguez, "La Niña del Ciego" (c. 1870–1930). In the biographical entry for Rodríguez, Pohren writes his most scathing criticism of all his attacks on cross-dressing female dancers. He connects her success in the male roles to a biological aberration from "normal" females:

> Thus Salud equipped herself with *trajes cortos*, boots, and the other masculine dancing paraphernalia, spent numberless hours practicing her footwork, and eventually achieved her goal. She became in her dance what, through some glandular confusion, she was best suited to be from birth: a man [220].

Part of the unnaturalness of Salud's performance seems to be aligned with the amount of labor required to transform her from female to male impersonator. His emphasis on the excess of her labor points to the lack of discussion surrounding the training of other female dancers. Female labor is either masked, or female talent seems to arrive naturally at the moment of birth. Technical display of *zapateado* by a female dancer is always conspicuous because the footwork is the one part of dance that is supposed to require effort. Not without significance, this area of the dance has been traditionally confined to the male role.

However, within Pohren's biography of flamenco performers, it appears that Carmen Amaya's much-publicized entrance on the flamenco scene during the late 1930s as a female dancer doing the masculine dances was not without precedent. Interestingly, Amaya emerges from this flamenco history as the single exception to his overall condemnation of female cross-dressing and dancing. He calls her "*la única* (far superior)" among other dancers and even credits her with "unwittingly caus[ing] the emancipation of the feminine dance" (230). His surprising embrace of Amaya reflects a strategic decision: recuperate her within the textual genealogy, and by extension, within the canon of flamenco history. Despite her outrageous international success as a performer of the "trouser dances," in Pohren's history, "Carmen gradually began outgrowing her masculine type of dance. As she matured she began altering her style, adding more elements of femininity, more ruffles, more flowing arms and hands, more tranquility, a more subtle fire and passion and a suppressed sensuality formerly lacking" (232). It is only through a feminized refinement of her dancing, which transforms her from a rebel to a convincing figure of Passion, that Amaya can be included within Pohren's purist history as a great *bailaora*.

Scholarly contributions to the canon of flamenco history by foreign

In this photograph believed to have been taken in the 1950s, Carmen Amaya (right) and her *cuadro* pose in a *tablao* setting. She wears the ***bata de cola***, the quintessentially feminine dress, a contrast to her famous "trouser dances" (Jerome Robbins Dance Division, New York Public Library for the Performing Arts, Astor, Lenox and Tilden Foundations).

flamenco aficionados reflect the social and political tensions that endow dancing bodies with their problematic corporealities. These writings re-present the caution surrounding the presence of the dancing body as a symbol for threatening excesses that cannot be contained by discursive and regulatory practices in specific contexts. Rice's accounts of the early twentieth century and the careers of Escudero and Argentina echo the modernist dualities of masculine vs. feminine, expression vs. technique, and gypsy vs. Spaniard. Those dualities continue to have currency in the world of *flamencos*; they serve as important polarities between which meaning is constructed. The binary categories that emerge just as flamenco enters the global stage do not "wither away," just as Spivak contends in "Can the Subaltern Speak?" Instead, they deepen and gain complexity as the context for meaning shifts.

Claus's portrait of La Joselito reasserts the tensions that accompany the flamenco body following the period of the *cafés cantantes* but prior to the Spanish Civil War, a time when the conventions for the stage spectacles are defined as separate from the popular practice of flamenco in non-theatrical settings. Paradoxically, the public enthusiasm for flamenco performance, the very attention that brings flamenco into the international spotlight, and the attending demands of commercialism intensify the anxiety surrounding the representation of flamenco in those venues. The stereotype that could be dismissed as some Frenchman's fancy becomes the only means of access for many audiences hungry for the consumption of flamenco.

At the same time, the display of "technique" through rapid, building displays of footwork, more complex figures for the arms, the addition of jumps and turns, replaces the improvisational moment in which the *duende* is invited to inhabit the performer. The intimacy of the small, educated audience, familiar with the structures of the *palos* and the *compás*, yields to the distance of the proscenium stage and the spectacle of the music hall. That distance evokes the ghost of Merimée's Carmen and the estrangement of exoticism, key fuel for the international flamenco marketplace.

Pohren's work follows the period in the history of flamenco following the huge international success of artists like Carmen Amaya and José Greco, the appearance of flamenco in Hollywood films, and the establishment of the tourist trade in Andalusia under the Franco regime. His history anchors authenticity in the gendered performance of flamenco practitioners. The artists who traveled the globe during this era, represented by empresarios like Sol Hurok, brought flamenco into a new framework for intelligibility as an exotic object.

Despite any dispute regarding the "authenticity" of their authorial voice, or the "legitimacy" of their scholarship (after all, these authors do not claim to be academic in their training or intentions, and follow a different kind of rigor in their access to a notion of the "truth"), these texts serve as a kind of canon for English-speaking flamencophiles, particularly works by Donn Pohren. They construct a field of knowledge in which the flamenco body performs and achieves meaning in particular ways. The information that is included or excluded in these texts, the shape of the narratives, the preferences, passions and prejudices voiced by the authors—all of these elements combine to produce the imaginary space of desire for an Exotic Other. One could argue that they speak more to the nature of the desiring subject than to the object of that desire, but it is too easy, and incorrect, to dismiss these texts as dated or unsophisticated. They speak eloquently to the creation and perpetuation of the flamenco stereotype and the anxieties it provokes among audiences and performers alike. More recent scholarship attempts to analyze flamenco outside the realm of the exotic imaginings of desire. However, those new histories can no more escape the "spectacle" of signification, and the problems of representation, than earlier aficionados.

3

Imagining Andalusia

Divine Inspiration: Origins Reconsidered

While the previous chapter dealt with the written work of foreign flamencophiles from the early twentieth century through the 1980s, this chapter will focus on examples of "academic" flamenco scholarship outside Spain from the 1980s through the 1990s. In Chapter 2, flamenco served as the object of exotic fascination for authors who "studied" flamenco as educated audience members, aficionados. Their accounts, lovingly compiled over decades of research and living among practitioners, echo the intimacy of their contact with the subject. The texts take on the narrative structures of the compelling story. They "read" as travel diaries, memoirs, biographies, and interviews and construct a desiring relationship between reader and subject.

More recent flamenco scholarship constructs the "authority" of the subject in different terms from the examples in the previous chapter. In those texts, despite the fastidious attention to detail involved in the compilation of previous "histories," the authors did not claim to be producing academic scholarship. Instead, they hoped to illuminate a previously obscure and misunderstood art form for other foreign flamencophiles. Authors like Allen Josephs, James Woodall, Timothy Mitchell, and Loren Chuse employ the methodologies from different disciplines like history, sociology, anthropology, and cultural studies to frame their inquiries in a way that would make them intelligible to a differently educated audience: academics. If previous histories resembled the engaging story, then these works claim the authority of the scientific model using hypothesis and proof. This is not to say that earlier histories were not well-researched or sophisticated in their analysis, nor that more recent scholarship does not seduce using the conventions of good storytelling. Rather, in terms of information that is privileged, disregarded, included or excluded, each example reveals a specific construction of desire for the Other. This Other is always feminized, if not female, and she dances. In Loren Chuse's scholarship, she also sings.

The contested body of the female flamenco dancer has been retrospec-

This 2005 publicity still for Bailes Ferrer features Niurca Marquez in a pose reminiscent of the "Callipygian Venus." Photograph by Liliam Dominguez, used with permission.

tively reinscribed with divine significance in Allen Josephs's study of Andalusian culture, *White Wall of Spain* (1983). Recall, in Pohren's work, how the femininity of the flamenco dancer must be constantly reasserted as a reaction against the overly masculine tendency toward rapid footwork and overtly masculine cross-dressing. Both of these aberrations are interpreted as an entrance into competition with male dancers for the position of "mastery" over the form and its traditional conventions. In Claus's history, the tendency toward the use of acrobatics and the vulgar display of sexuality among contemporary female dancers must be tempered by a demand for the feminine dance of old, characterized by postures of dignity and the calculated control of emotional abandon. Josephs also deals with the "problems" of femininity and sexuality as they are performed by *bailaora*, but along different tropes of representation. He uses the "originary" narratives of flamenco to trace its development from "Oriental" temple dancers and prostitutes and to reconstruct a linear history from ancient times to the present.

In a chapter called "Dancer of Gades," Josephs locates the first dancing priestess/whore in the second century B.C. The landmark for his history is a statue of the "Callipygian Venus," a Greco-Roman figure of a woman looking downward over her shoulder as she lifts her tunic up to display her buttocks for the viewer (67). The first mention of this statue in connection with a dancing slave girl from antiquity was made by the nineteenth-century hispanophile Richard Ford,[1] who connected the statue to historical accounts of a slave named Telethusa. Ford's "discovery," and the resulting revision of flamenco history, are lauded by Josephs: "If we follow that thread from antiquity to the present, we can begin to understand the complex and strangely beautiful world of ecstatic mime and ritual dance that Ford was attempting to concatenate in his own illuminatingly Romantic fashion" (67).

The exoticism of the contemporary dancer as a descendent of temple prostitutes reflects two important narrative conventions that have shaped the discourse surrounding flamenco, particularly in travel diaries written by European tourists from the nineteenth and twentieth centuries, but also in the academic analysis of these texts as a kind of discourse. One, these descriptions portray Andalusian culture as a whole as Orientalized, and two, they align flamenco dancers, the emblem of Andalusia, with prostitutes.

Andalusia, with its 800-year history of Arab rule and its actual proximity to Northern Africa, falls easily into the nineteenth-century traveler's imaginary geography of the Orient, an amalgam of "Eastern" cultures produced largely through the exotic imaginations of French and English travel writers and authors of fiction. Flamenco, with its mysterious ties to ancient Arab and Indian cultures, allows for a deeper immersion in a lost Orientalist fantasy. Merimée's Carmen populates that imaginary landscape, but she is not alone.

The figure of the dancing prostitute is necessary to the construction of the Orientalist aesthetic.

In the 25th anniversary edition of his pivotal text, *Orientalism*, Edward Said describes the mute casting of the Oriental in much the same way that Gayatri Spivak discusses the "subaltern":

> There is very little consent to be found, for example, in the fact that Flaubert's encounter with an Egyptian courtesan produced a widely influential model of the Oriental woman; she never spoke of herself, she never represented her emotions, presence or history. *He* spoke for and represented her. He was foreign, comparatively weathy, male, and these were historical facts of domination that allowed him not only to possess Kuchuk Hanem physically but to speak for her and tell his readers in what way she was "typically Oriental."[2]

Telethusa, another dancing courtesan, emerges through the descriptions of the men who served as her lovers, audience and patrons. Like Flaubert's Kuchuk Hanem, she embodies the "illuminatingly Romantic" equation of the body, sexuality and dance.

Josephs begins the chapter with an invocation of Telethusa through the statue of the CallipygianVenus. "Here was a goddess—a nearly naked, superbly sensual, dancer-courtesan goddess—worthy of having been modeled from Telethusa herself." He follows with an analysis of the history of dance: "From time immemorial dance has been considered a magic or religious activity, as numerous prehistoric cave paintings and early Egyptian and Mesopotamian works illustrate" (74). He then traces ritual dance through accounts from the Bible to the empire of Rome. According to his reading of the Roman writer Lucian, dance was always associated with temple rites for the gods Dionysus and Aphrodite. Based on this connection, Josephs makes the following assumption:

> Since these Oriental cults came eventually into great vogue in Rome, it ought to come as no surprise that the most sought after dancer-courtesans were their original Oriental practitioners. The most celebrated dancers in Rome were precisely the descendents of the Phoenicians, from Syria as the region was called by the Romans, and from Cádiz [a city in Andalusia] where the rites of Astarte (Aphrodite or Venus) had already been celebrated for a thousand years [75].

Josephs seems to find little difficulty in connecting the representations of sacred dances from cave paintings to the dancing slave girls of Cádiz (*puellae Gaditanae*) and finally, to the flamenco dancers of twentieth-century Andalusia. He turns to a Spanish historian to validate his theory, Ramón Menéndez Pidal: "The eminent historian replied that he believed that some racial characteristics—we would probably say ethnic or ethnological—could last even three milleniums, and that one example was the sense of rhythm of the Andalusian people, of the *puellae Gaditanae*" (78). He goes on to cite a Spanish flamencologist, Fernando Quiñones, for further support of his argument, "although this is to associate fantastically a yesterday and a today separated by twenty centuries, all the connecting links are there, a view shared by the musicologists and ethnologists who have studied the problem in detail" (79). Unlike the generations of flamencophiles who precede him, Josephs carefully documents the "authoritative" sources from which he derives his analysis. However, he depends on a history of scholarship that naturalizes dance as a practice and assumes an essential racial history for its practitioners, as if people lived (and danced) unaffected by social, political and economic tensions.

Despite his reliance upon travel diaries from figures like Richard Ford, George Borrow, James Michener, and Walter Starkie as primary sources in his reading of flamenco history, Josephs does not discuss the effects of the very complicated relationship between European spectators and lower-income women who perform for tourists. In fact, very few flamenco historians remark upon the association between flamenco dance performance and prostitution. However, the fearless flamencophile Donn Pohren, in *A Way of Life* (1980), sketches the flamenco landscape of Sevilla in 1956:

> And the whores, a most complete line-up of whores of all ages and dimensions, also looking to be hired, for in the flamenco juergas in those days flamencos and prostitutes usually went hand-in-hand. Sevilla had fame of being a wide-open city and attracted wealthy señoritos from all over Spain and from the farthest reaches of Europe, and such lively aficionados demanded, and got, the *complete* juerga treatment [16].

Though Pohren does not indicate whether the *bailaoras* served as prostitutes as well as dancers, his recollection of the environment in which flamenco was performed for tourists and wealthy Spaniards supports an often alluded to, but rarely discussed, alignment of the position of the dancer with that of the prostitute. Josephs locates the figure of the prostitute in another age and in a setting of religious observance, rather than one of contemporary economic exchange. But the shadow has been cast, and it clings to the figure of the flamenco dancer as a sign of backwardness and vulgarity.

Josephs traces an ancient history of exoticized, overtly sexual dances in an attempt to rescue these dances, and, by extension, Andalusian culture, from the context of the "primitive" to the realm of the "primordial." His framing of the flamenco dancer as a descendent of dancers from antiquity endows her with the authority of ancient times and transcends any negative connotations that may be associated with the dance:

> The wanton performances of the *puellae Gaditanae* have been transformed into a hieratic rite within the trimillenary forge of Andalusian folk culture,

and the courtesan has turned back into a high priestess whose choreography, primordial but stylized, now suggests less a prostitute than a goddess. Through the stylization of certain Gypsy artists, the *baile* (dance) has been returned some share of its original purpose, a recovery impossible in most of the nineteenth-century world and perhaps only possible along the timeless corridors of Andalusian culture [94].

While Josephs establishes the figure of the priestess/whore as the Rosetta Stone for flamenco dance, he insists on the erasure of the image of the prostitute. The "original purpose" of these dances situates Andalusian culture in the past, even as they continue to be performed in the present.

This hearkening backward evokes the tango embrace of Desire, Passion, and the spectatorial gaze, only in this case the tango is enacted through the relationship between the scholar and his exotic object. With respect to the different rewritings of flamenco history, the passionate object—the female dancer—constantly demands containment and legitimacy through the structures of tradition and history. Simultaneously, the representation of the female dancer is reproduced as excessive in spite of the efforts made to limit her sexuality, her femininity, and her technical displays of "mastery." This excess, produced and constrained at the same time, propels the historical narrative forward. The *bailaora*, then,

> is guilty of Otherness or, to put it differently, is accused of being an Otra in that she lacks and exceeds in "something" compared to the male. Her excessive passion and her lack of control over it beg for the male's embrace and leadership.[3]

The categories of male and female here do not reflect biological categories, but positions of subjectivity. A female dancer can occupy the male position of spectatorship and control in relationship to other female dancers in performance. Also, the embrace does not refer only to a movement enacted onstage. The scholars of history who represent the female dancer in their texts are performing a theoretical embrace of Desire. As Spivak concluded in "Can the Subaltern Speak?": "Representation has not withered away."[4] The threatening capacity of the Other is kept contained by the historical narrative.

Passionate Nature: The Academic Appeal of a Universal Humanity

Contemporary flamenco scholarship interrogates the political and social contexts that have produced the art throughout the centuries. James Woodall's *In Search of the Firedance* (1992) traces the history of flamenco song, dance, and guitar forms from their disputed geographical origins to contemporary performance settings in Spain and the rest of the world. Woodall's account draws from several different scholarly traditions in cultural history as well as flamencology. He sketches a portrait of Spain and Andalusian culture chronologically arranged from the occupation of the Muslims from 711 to the present. It is a dense and lengthy work, painstakingly researched. Woodall examines important parallels between the complex economic, political, and social history of Spain and the evolution of flamenco as an art form. In addition, he provides information about the cultural exportation of flamenco to Europe and the Americas and the effect this exchange had upon the practice of flamenco in Spain.

Like many British Hispanophiles before him, Woodall takes the position of the flamenco aficionado—an informed outsider, supposedly the ideal audience member for flamenco in its "pure" form. He focuses primarily on the development of the song forms, which, for him, represent the main body of flamenco proper. Including several examples of verse forms, he speaks to the predominance of certain styles during specific historical periods. Since the popular enthusiasm for the dance and the guitar components of flamenco virtually eclipsed attention to the song during the twentieth century, he takes great pains to preserve evidence of the song, particularly the *cante jondo* (deep song) forms, during the years of foreign as well as Spanish fascination with commercial productions of flamenco.

Woodall maintains the historical tradition that posits the gypsies as the primary innovators in flamenco. While he acknowledges, even emphasizes, the contributions of other ethnic communities to the development of flamenco, he insists that gypsies practice a more authentic flamenco than non-gypsies (89). At times he locates the "innate grace" of the gypsies in the simplistic, if not racist, correlation between their blood and their abilities. In other instances, he comments on the dominant role flamenco has played in gypsy culture, and, correspondingly, the success of gypsy artists in the history of flamenco. As a well-informed "outsider" to flamenco as cultural discourse, Woodall manifests the scholarly tendencies of the foreign purist: he stresses the necessity for the maintenance of the tradition in its most "pure" form, he derides practitioners who popularize pseudo-flamenco, and he speaks in negative terms about audience members who can't tell the difference. From this position he attempts, in effect, to save flamenco from itself by guiding its audiences along a more "correct" path of appreciation, governed by a loyalty to "pure" flamenco. Woodall describes at length the categories of song which are included in the domain of flamenco proper and points out the "poetic licence" [sic] that produces something other than "true" flamenco in song and verse. But the dance, characteristically slippery and changing, seems to evade his systematic evaluation.

Commercial flamenco dance, as it was recounted before in Pohren and Claus, became a lucrative tourist attraction during the Years of Development (1961–73) in the *tablaos* (flamenco nightclubs) of Franco's Spain. According to Woodall, the popularity of the dance in these venues contributed to the degradation of "pure" flamenco; he links the visual accessibility of the dancing body to sexual display onstage and prostitution offstage (252). It is no surprise, then, that Woodall focuses on the "firedance" only in his final chapter. Immediately, indeed in the second paragraph of the chapter, he addresses the eroticism of the dance in performance:

> The seductiveness of many of the movements in the female *baile*, the prominence of the breasts and the working of the hips, perhaps above all the stroking intimacy of the hands, is more Mediterranean play than concupiscence, an expression of effulgent physicality and body confidence, and so it is with the male *baile* too. If in the case of men, the stamping and muscularity, the rhythmic pulse, the fury and the sweat, the almost phallic straightness of line and gesture seem to amount to an all-too-obvious metaphor for sex, an important point has been missed: sexuality is there, but it is more display than action, more a danced confirmation of individuality, of identity, of—most especially if you are a gypsy—your place in the world than an imposition of prowess [327].

In this rather lengthy quote, Woodall acquiesces to all of the possible sexual connotations of the dance, but insists that they are misplaced. Instead, he proposes a "Mediterranean play" located in the performance of the flamenco body, indeed, an "effulgent physicality and body confidence." Again, the exotic body threatens to exceed its boundaries despite its childlike, unspoiled nature.

In his discussion of the *cante*, which takes up some three hundred pages preceding this analysis, Woodall recounts the political and social environment that surrounded flamenco from its disputed origins, none of the same contextualization couches his examination of the dance. Instead, he returns to a "universal" perspective. He claims the "passionate" nature of the dance has allowed it to be understood as merely erotic rather than expressive of "the pleasures and pains of human separateness, and of being alive" (327). The dance, positioned at the end of the book, contains all of the necessary elements to draw together his analysis of a specifically configured cultural phenomena and elevate it to the status of a quintessentially "human" experience.

Woodall then switches the terms of the argument from sex to death, and the "humanness" of this aesthetic problem. The Andalusians' fondness for death as a subject in art demonstrates their "active, hedonistic anthropomorphism, a cultural tendency that reveals a delight in the tactility, sensuality and realness of things. The realness of death has the shape of inescapable actuality, and must be and is faced with all the resources one's humanity can muster (327).

Playful, sensual, ennobled by their capacity to express a Romantic ideal of human struggle, Southern Spaniards fall headlong into the stereotype of the exotic, passionate Other. Woodall summons other distinctly Spanish images to support his contention that the Andalusian notion of death and struggle is uniquely suited to horrify and move the viewer: the bullfight and the paintings of Pablo Picasso. Sexuality, death, then hunger:

> ...a hunger for livelihood and sustenance, for recognition and acceptance within the constraints of a society which has never been fast to acknowledge the racial and emotional truths flamenco encompasses. In the best flamenco, material hunger belies a hunger of the soul, a search for the most galvanizing and most euphoric expression of happiness and despair [329].

For Woodall, flamenco, particularly the dance, distills from life the most basic needs common to humanity. A dizzyingly idealistic portrait, but it persuades through the manipulation of those very assumptions that have proven "damaging" to flamenco in the previous pages. The flamenco body, constrained and constituted by political upheaval, class stratification, ethnic tension, economic disadvantage, gendered hierarchies and sexualized narratives of conquest and domination, ironically serves as the metaphor to transcend the very powers that produce it. More specifically, it must be a dancing body, synonymous for "the body," conceived as the "universal humanity" shared by all despite social conventions, that represents this basic exercise of "nature."

If the dancing body has the capacity to express all bodies, then through dancing one can glimpse an essential humanity, a material presence that social constructions shape but do not originally form. From this naturalized assumption about "the body" follows a rapid series of meaningful assumptions: everyone has a body, and these bodies contain a biological sex and race. Certain sexes and races are predisposed to specific behaviors, some are capable of deep feeling, others excel in the realm of the intellect, some are fragile, others are strong, etc. etc. But the excuse for these rationalizations lies in the basic belief that human beings are all bodies, and they share some kind of notion of human dignity, despair, happiness, sexual norms, and cultural standards. It seems paradoxical that the gesture to unite all bodies and all identities as equal should set up the very structures of hierarchy and power, unless it is acknowledged that the notion of identity, of self, depends upon a recognition of difference. Difference is predicated by an underlying violence that distinguishes between the self and the other, the woman and the man, the Spaniard and the Gypsy, the author and the subject. Jacques Derrida calls this condition of writing "archeviolence."[5] It is a condition for the production of knowledge within the inescapable, regulatory function of power. Representation reproduces itself.

Woodall's work falls into, for lack of a better term, a "genealogy of modernist flamencologists." From the turn of the century until the present, flamenco history has, with few exceptions, followed the same basic narrative structure. Authors plot an origin point, periods of ascendancy and deterioration, and then conclude with a plea to preserve flamenco from the degradation caused by commercialism. All of these histories, from Rice to Woodall, mean to recuperate a much-maligned presence in history by speaking to its true, misunderstood, nature. These authors attempt, through the gathering of facts to support an educated hypothesis, to discover essential beauty or truth in the artifact. This essence is interior and can be recognized by the secondary characteristics on its exterior. The aesthetic crisis of modernism is held in a dynamic tension by binary oppositions: Dionysian and Apollonian, authentic and fake, gypsy and *payo*, colonizer and colonized, male and female, virgin and whore, barbaric and refined, joy and sadness, life and death, the gaze and its object, self and other. These oppositions depend on the categorical assignment of difference, the enduring legacy of Romanticism and global colonialism. Among the foreign flamencologists who have compiled a history of the art, few have challenged the basic ideas that define the canon.

Sober Clinicism: Demystifying the Other

In *Flamenco Deep Song* (1995), Timothy Mitchell provides a potential model for an inquiry into the conventions of traditional flamenco scholarship and their pitfalls. Like Woodall, his approach to flamenco is multidisciplinary, and he maintains the song, specifically *cante jondo*, as the center of his analysis. However, from the first few pages, Mitchell maintains his separateness from the line of flamenco scholars before him: "Before I go any further let me stress that I am not a flamenco artist nor a flamenco aficionado in the traditional sense of the term. For those readers seeking an insider's account of flamenco or the flamenco way of life, alternative reading is available in English" (4). Here, he footnotes first Donn Pohren, then another American aficionado, Paul Hecht, and the Englishman Walter Starkie. Unlike previous flamenco scholars, who rely upon their own intimacy with flamenco as a practice, or flamencos as a community, Mitchell does not speak from the same position of authority. Instead, he calls upon a position of what one might term "scholarly disinterest," a profitable distance from the inner cir-

cle that endows his account with a different sort of authority, the "objectivity" of the theoretically informed, "scientific" (social scientific) gaze. He says
of traditional flamenco scholarship:

> Although such works have their charm, they are often beholden to romantic
> or mythical notions of flamenco that can actually impede a true understand-
> ing of the music in its overall social and cultural contexts. My approach is
> scientific in the broadest sense of the term, and my overall ambition is to con-
> solidate and give impetus to the drastic reorientation of flamenco studies that
> has just begun [4].

By his account, the authorial position claimed by Mitchell is free from
the intoxicating influence of myth or romanticism, and by virtue of his sobri-
ety, he may have access to the "truth." Although other authors rely on rigorous attention to scholarly issues of citing established flamenco experts to
prove their accounts, Mitchell is the only one to actually label his methodology as "scientific in the broadest sense of the term." For Mitchell, the space
of "innocence" is located not in a nostalgic longing for a mythic past, but in
a methodological approach rooted in the "objectivity" of science.

From his position as the clear-headed scientist, Mitchell dismisses most
flamenco scholarship as "parochial." He relies on a definition of parochial-
ism by social constructionist Bruce Lincoln to clarify his point: "The construction of a socio-epistemological border and hierarchico-taxonomic
distinction between the knower, known, and worth-knowing, on the one
hand, and the unknown and unworthy of knowledge, on the other" (17). In
other words, flamencologists rely on their embedded position within the
flamenco community and their familiarity with a specific jargon or system
of meaning to persuade the reader of their version of the "truth." Not dras-
tically different, than, say the position of the author who, accomplished and
well-versed in the realm (and the sometimes impenetrable language) of the
social sciences and contemporary cultural studies, assembles an argument,
based on the "scientific model," and thereby convinces the reader of an
"objective truth." Somewhere between an idealistic hope for the "truth" and
the dizzying "myths" of flamenco folklore, Mitchell self-critically arrives at
a compromise: "I maintain that a respect for the facts is not incompatible
with compassion, that insight into psychological motivations does not have
to be entirely intuitive, and that one can evaluate the contributions of
Andalusian gitanos without falling into racism *or* romanticism" (17).

For all of his self-reflexiveness and his attentiveness to "the experts'
background or ideological affiliations" (17), Mitchell maintains that there
are facts to be known and that they may be deciphered from the "massive
edifice of pseudo-knowledge built up over the years" (18). For Mitchell, the
truth is out there, waiting, beneath the layers of evidence. He does not, how-

ever, entertain the possibility that the knowledge he desires is always produced at a specific cultural moment and that frequently racism and romanticism are foundational concepts in the articulation of truth. For him, the
frame merely surrounds the spectacle of exoticism and obscures our true
vision of flamenco. Mitchell's account is no less a product of socio-cultural
tensions than the legacy of the "parochial" flamencos who preceded him.
And, if racism or romanticism constitute meaning within flamenco history,
it is difficult to believe that the "essence" of flamenco can be distilled as separate from the mixture. Ironically, Mitchell's perspective differs very little
from that of the scholars he critiques: There is a "true" flamenco, and he is
uniquely equipped to distinguish between the authentic and the imposters.

The "socio-epistemological border and hierarchico-taxonomic distinction between the knower, known, and worth-knowing" is formed, in
Mitchell's analysis, through a detailed discussion of theorists from the Frank-
furt School and structural Marxism, particularly in the area of anthropology. In the first chapter, "Style and Ideology," he sets up an important
correlation between the values of a given culture or subculture and the conventions of the music that it produces. Once ventured, he retreats again to
the position of the objective outsider in pursuit of "a nonevaluative or at least
a less evaluative understanding of ideology (and, beyond that, a clearer picture of musical styles of flamenco)" (24). He then suggests the limits of cultural relativism and the efficacy of theories from constructivist structuralism
in anthropology, specifically those of the Thompson group. These researchers
provide, according to Mitchell, a model that "shows how one may stand
apart from the fray and observe how each way of life needs all the others as
reference points—and foils—in order to develop its own coherent style of
legitimation" (26). This "hermit's perspective" is attentive to the ideological bias of all the players in the scenario, except one: he who stands apart
from the fray.

Unimpeded by "prejudice," Mitchell stresses the radical possibilities
inherent in his methodology. "An unbiased approach to cultural bias has the
potential to revolutionize flamenco studies" (26). For, as he demonstrates in
two highly charged quotes by some of Spain's most highly regarded flamencologists, cultural bias has run rampant, and virtually unchecked, in the history of flamenco. Anselmo González Climent bemoans the education of the
gypsies as a deterrent to good flamenco and its inherent (illiterate) tragedy.
Félix Grande rages against social injustice in Spain with an emotional zeal
that is more often found among poets and protesters than in serious academics. In their confessional tone, the "parochial" authors of flamenco's past
clearly articulate their investment in and the agenda behind their claims to
truth. What remains unexamined, however, is the cultural bias that consti-

tutes Mitchell's methodology: "Superior to parochial and insider views of flamenco, it would be the closest thing yet to a nonbiased, nonideological way of dealing with a musical style whose study has been dominated by one ideological bias or another" (37).

From his "psychohistorical" or "psychosocial" perspective, Mitchell examines many of the assumptions that foreground the debates in flamenco history. Among them, he focuses on the "purity" of gypsy lineage, the "devastating effects" of commercialism, and the need for preservation of traditional forms to "save" them from "adulteration." He also discusses such taboo subjects as alcoholism, prostitution, and the cult of flamenco *machismo*.

In "Deep Song Sociology," Mitchell describes the complex regional, class and racial tensions that produced a flamenco subculture in the late 18th century.

> The defiant young men of Lower Andalusia were particularly responsive to the lumpenproletarian style engendered within their region's *gitanerías*, the low neighborhoods in which gitanos and subcultural others interacted and shared many of the same problems, vices, beliefs, values and amusements [39].

Alienated from the social and economic movements that swept Europe, and from the nexus of political power in the North, Southern Spanish men of the lower classes created an audience for a song style that emphasized rebellion against the ruling classes. Mitchell's argument is indeed fairly radical, for it asks new and different questions of flamenco's history. Instead of asking whether gypsies or Andalusians invented flamenco, and assuming that the presence of any ethnic motifs in the music indicates "ownership," he attributes the emergence of flamenco to the habits and values of a specific subculture composed of many ethnicities. Indeed, he suggests that the very concept of ethnicity is less a biological category than a social one.

Mitchell then examines, in the course of several chapters, the constellations of various social groups, besides gypsies, that contributed to the development of *cante jondo*: "moriscos, gitanos, beggars ... peddlers, pícaros, criminals, and drifters ... horse and cattle thieves, bandits, and smugglers ... an incipient industrial proletariat ... a segment of the rural proletariat ... and daily-wage laborers called *jornaleros*" (67). By effectively calling into question the exoticism that predicates the isolation of the term "gypsy" as a singular, pure race, Mitchell pulls apart the threads that have held debates among flamencos in tension. Without the mythical, uncomplicated, and fully fabricated configuration of the gypsy as Spain's unique and exclusive social outcast, he expands the debate to consider the complex phenomena of social stratification in Spanish history.

Further, Mitchell insists that the genesis of flamenco as we have come to know it was dependent upon the patronage of the upper classes. The *juergas*, the private flamenco parties now prized by flamenco purists as the only opportunity to witness true flamenco, began as events funded by upper-class señoritos for their own pleasure: "The word señorito was used to address unmarried young men of the leisure classes whose love of song, dance and debauchery, allied with a certain dosis of romanticism or musical nationalism, frequently led them to consort with pleasure professionals of the lumpenproletariet" (42).

The accusation waged by purists of the past has been that, had flamenco dance not been seized by the tourist industry as a tool to revive a sagging economy, the art would have remained pure. According to Mitchell's analysis, the more embarrassing aspects of commercial flamenco, alcoholism and prostitution, were part of the private *juerga* subculture well before flamenco became a tourist commodity. Mitchell cites several periodicals from the early nineteenth century attesting to widespread "antiflamenquismo," a mainstream fear of flamenco performances as "immoral" practices. He goes on to suggest that, if flamenco had not been circulated as a practice stereotypically aligned with Spanish national identity, it would never have been recuperated by the upper classes as a "classical" art form.

Having at least complicated, if not dismissed, the passionate arguments among flamencologists regarding the "purity" of gypsy identity and the "innocence" of flamenco prior to commercialization in the tourist industry, Mitchell suggests a future for flamenco that is "beyond ethnicity." In the final, and incredibly brief, chapter to his book, Mitchell ventures a theory that celebrates, rather than denigrates, the appeal of flamenco in the contemporary context of a global music community. He insists that people who are not flamencos may enjoy flamenco for its emotional value, and for the way in which it represents and transcends trauma:

> For many, flamenco music will be a mood, that is, a structured affective state involving a set of linked conscious and unconscious fantasies about Spain, gitanos, passion, sorrow, and so on, mixed perhaps with personal, unconscious early events that color one's perceptions of exotic music. The particular moods evoked will vary from individual to individual, but it seems logical to expect that the most successful internationalized flamenco music will produce a commodity-flamenco that corresponds to a given nation's "social representation" of Spain (or gitanos) as well as to unconscious emotional needs of a more personal variety that may converge with that representation [225].

This statement addresses some of the underyling fears surrounding the expansion of flamenco into the wider global marketplace via the internet. Historically, flamenco has been an international art form, but the unmediated access created by digital technology further distances flamenco from its native terrain. For many aficionados, the personal enjoyment of the uninitiated should be regulated by a presence that insists upon substantial knowledge of flamenco and its history. Within flamenco history, the "exoticism" of the art form and its practitioners has led to the exploitation of flamencos and gypsies, and to the perceived artistic prostitution of flamenco as a tradition. After all, one might suggest that Prosper Merimée, in the creation of the famous fictional gypsy Carmen, produced "a commodity-flamenco that corresponds to a given nation's 'social representation' of Spain (or gitanos) as well as to unconscious emotional needs of a more personal variety that may converge with that representation" (225). Despite his arguments for a "non-ideological" evaluation of flamenco history, Mitchell finally proposes an ideal spectator, an uninformed layman who appreciates flamenco for its exotic appeal, for the ways in which flamenco represents a fantastical image of Southern Spain in a global context. Mitchell's position, then, is firmly grounded in ideology, the familiar narrative of colonialism.

Throughout this discussion of histories written by non–Spanish flamencophiles, the exotic spectacle of colonialism returns again and again, like a refrain from a familiar song. The issues of ethnic identity, national pride, artistic purity and the role of commercialism in flamenco are no less controversial in the international flamenco community today than they were in Spain in 1922, when Manuel de Falla and Federico García Lorca organized the *Concurso de Cante Jondo* in Granada. Their intention was to preserve an ancient song form from the contamination of commercial influences featured in early flamenco performances of the *cafés cantantes*. The idea that flamenco as a tradition existed or exists as an unchanging, static practice is belied by the fractious multiplicity of those narratives that bear it forward. To take hold of the *cante jondo* and project a vision of what it once was back in time is to "give it a history and legitimacy that only tradition and longevity could impart."[6] First viewed through the eyes of foreign travel writers, flamencos struggle from the early twentieth century to engage, respond to and contradict representations by other authorial voices, to decolonize themselves, to transcend the muteness of the subaltern.

According to Edward Said, in his work *Culture and Imperialism*, the reinvention of tradition occurs not only among the European elite as a means of asserting colonial power, but also among post-colonized peoples like Algerians and Muslims as an attempt to "create images of what they supposed themselves to have been prior to French colonization."[7] Flamencos exercise this kind of post-colonial subjectivity. Today, in online and print journals such as *La Caña de Flamenco*, produced by the Asociación Cultural España Abierta in Madrid, or *Acórdes de Flamenco*, a commercial production from

RDM Editorial, through websites like *www.flamenco-world.com*, the same issues concern contemporary flamenco aficionados in Spain as they did a hundred years ago. These voices include artists. The transformation of flamenco from a popular folk practice to a classical art form during the twentieth century, shaped by regional, national and global events, has prompted a multitude of voices to speak to and for flamenco in an international dialogue. In the infant days of the twenty-first century, flamencos all over the world engage in heated debates about the future of the form. Anxious traditionalists fear that the current popularity of flamenco in a global market threatens to eradicate its "orthodox" roots. On the opposite side of the table, flamencos argue for innovation through the fusion of different musical forms with traditional flamenco structures. Two questions emerge in this debate, from opposite ends of the spectrum: In order to save flamenco from extinction, by whose authority must it be "rescued" from its practitioners? And, what are the cultural and economic implications of demystifying flamenco? For if groups such as Ketama, who have inherited flamenco (not only as a blood right, but as a family business spanning several generations) have no legitimate claim to the articulation of a flamenco aesthetic in the eyes of aficionados, whose culture is being preserved? Flamenco has a long history of upper-class patronage and exploitation, as well as the perhaps inescapable accommodation of and, at times, shrewdly transgressive complicity in this arrangement by flamencos, gypsy and *payo* alike. It becomes increasingly difficult to discuss the "cultural appropriation" of flamenco when some respected practitioners and scholars of the art come from outside Spain, from countries such as Japan and the United States. All of these issues converge at the site of the flamenco body, the achingly beautiful image of the female flamenco dancer, with arms raised in half-moons above her head and her skirts swirling around her hips. Her image expresses centuries of history in a single moment, and stories erupt from the rows of ruffles that adorn her dress. But flamenco histories, inasmuch as they ostensibly attempt to elucidate her presence, function as a means of concealing her absence. For, as Michel de Certeau observes, "the dear departed find a haven in the text because they can neither speak nor do harm anymore. These ghosts find access through writing on the condition that they remain forever silent."[8] The subaltern cannot speak, because ideology, history and representation only allow for the articulation of the subject. However, the multitude of voices vying for the position of the speaking subject has changed during the course of the twentieth century. The struggle to be heard above the din reveals competing agendas and conflicting perspectives. As a result, the future of flamenco appears to be open to the embrace of many histories. The inclusion of a diversity of opinions has eradicated the possibility of a single, definitive narrative. Ironically, or perhaps predictably, the characteristics of the exotic stereotype have become a viable modus operandi for the survival of flamenco. The threatening excess of flamenco resists all efforts to contain it. These attempts yield a continually unfolding dialogue that further augments the established canon and allows for a precarious balance of tradition and innovation.

(Re)discovering the Women in Cante

The multiplicity of voices present in contemporary flamenco scholarship allows for the inclusion of stories that have been previously excluded from the written history of flamenco. Loren Chuse's *The Cantaoras: Music, Gender and Identity in Flamenco Song* (2003) capitalizes on the most recent progressive scholarship on the *cante* in Spanish and English, combined with original research among contemporary female singers to flesh out the role of the *cantaoras* in the history of flamenco. Although female singers have made and continue to make important contributions to the art form, she says, "Flamenco music has traditionally been considered a male genre, with the exception of female dancers" (3). She goes on to say that "women's presence in cante flamenco had either been ignored, or considered to be quite minor and unimportant" (5). Her inquiry, based in the discipline of ethnomusicology and borrowing from scholars in anthropology and sociology, reconstructs the established timeline of the *cante's* development, with attention to the previously unwritten complexities of gender in flamenco and Spanish cultures. Chuse addresses the absence of scholarship surrounding female singers, despite their important presence in flamenco history.

Important to Chuse's analysis of the "sophisticated and subtle layering of identities and subject positions, as well as skillful and often subversive manipulations of expressive forms" (17) by female flamenco performers is the model provided by Pierre Bordieu's discussion of *habitus*, which she parenthetically defines as a "theory of embodiment." Practice Theory, and by extension, Practice Anthropology, explores, in this case, "music and performance practice as a site in which identity, gender and social hierarchy is enacted, constructed and negotiated" (18). Further, scholars of Practice Anthropology, and Chuse in particular, also employ Antonio Gramsci's concept of ideological hegemony as a means of examining "the possibility of resistance as well as accommodation, and addresses the tension that exists between shared understandings and idiosyncratic stances of individuals" (18). These models provide a conceptual framework for the production and negotiation of meaning within the multilayered culture of flamenco, suspended in a constellation of power relations that define the consideration of nation, region, class, race, and gender.

Chuse grounds her adaptation of Practice Anthropology in scholarship specific to Andalusian and flamenco cultures, through the work of Gerhard Steingress, Cristina Cruces Roldán, and William Washabaugh, among others. Steingress and Roldán represent the cutting edge of flamenco scholarship in sociology and anthropology from the University of Seville, while the U.S.–based anthropologist Washabaugh was the first foreign flamencophile to suggest "what he terms the 'ironic history' of flamenco and argues for a polysemic, complex analysis that eschews the essentialism of previous work on the history of flamenco" (26). Washabaugh's scholarship provides the framework for the consideration of the documentary style in Carlos Saura's films in Chapter 5. Chuse's analysis reflects the integration of traditional flamenco scholarship and discipline-based postmodern theories.

Thus prepared to investigate the absence of scholarship surrounding female flamenco singers, Chuse then provides the reader with a concise overview of musical structures in flamenco and a history of the development of the *cante*, inclusive of periods of ascendancy, innovation, and stagnation. This framework allows for a reconsideration of nineteenth- and twentieth-century *cantaoras*, who are presented in biographical entries, and a discussion of the "Social and Political Conditions for Cantaoras in Twentieth-Century Spain." Chuse's original interviews with living *cantaoras* span at least two generations and several regional styles. She also addresses the limited presence of female guitarists in flamenco and the cultural conditions that prevent a more expansive participation of women in *el toque*. She analyzes the theme of woman, from the mother to the lover, in flamenco *letras*. Finally, she ventures a theory of the "Social Construction of Flamenco Identity" and the cultural production of "Identity, Aesthetics, and Emotion."

Chuse's scholarship stands out among the work of other musicologists or flamencologists in its relentless focus on the construction of gender in each context under consideration, from the days of the *cafés cantantes* to contemporary Spain. Perhaps as a consequence of this focus, she discusses in depth the taboo topic of prostitution and its relationship to flamenco culture. Like other flamenco scholars in this chapter, she identifies the role that prostitution played during the era of the Golden Age of flamenco. She cites the respected flamenco historian José Blás Vega, who contends that the *cafés cantantes* and other venues for flamenco from the turn of the century frequently led to

> authentic orgies, where the euphoria created by alcohol and the presence of women not only created a highly erotic environment, but often resulted in scenes of lust and lasciviousness that were large part of the cause of the rejection that a great deal of Spanish society felt toward flamenco.[9]

She links the sexualized environment of the *cafés cantantes* to the prevailing exotic stereotype of flamenco held by nineteenth-century Europeans. Her treatment of this environment differs from the work of other scholars in that she suggests that

> female performers were well aware of the stereotypes, prevailing fantasies and expectations of their clientele, both the national and the foreign variety. They played the role, living up to their scandalous reputations, and earning good money while doing so. That this performance was accompanied by more than a little irony and conscious manipulation is clear in the often mocking performances that have been recorded: singers and dancers who parodied the bullfight, strutted around the stage in imitation of roosters or mocked Andalusian and often male, customs [62].

Chuse argues that flamenco women were complicit in their perpetuation of sexualized stereotypes of Andalusian femininity, and, apparently, masculinity. This perspective differs radically from the accounts that attempt to distance practitioners from the taint of prostitution and the highly sexualized exotic stereotypes of the art form. However, as many of her interviews with living performers reveal, the negative associations with flamenco prevailed until after the death of Franco and the social changes that followed in Spain. Chuse insists:

> The stigma of disrespectability haunted the profession for female performers. As was the case with Pastora Pavón's mother, most parents did not want their daughters to be professional singers or dancers. The association of flamenco with brothels, bars, heavy drinking and low-life in general was so pronounced in the early days that women from middle class backgrounds did not become performers. A woman's mere presence in a bar or taverna brought into question her reputation, in the gender-separated and strongly *machista* cultural terrain of Southern Spain. Good women belonged at home, especially in the late-night and early morning hours when the flamenco shows took place [86].

Chuse then delves into the changing roles for women in Spain during the Second Republic, prior to the Spanish Civil War. During this time of reform, women were granted the right to vote and divorce. According to Chuse, "For the first time in Spain, women could act as witnesses, sign contracts, administer estates. No longer were employers formally able to dismiss women merely because they had married" (93). However, these reforms were reversed after the Spanish Civil War, under Franco's regime. In an attempt to reify the roles of wife and mother and emphasizing the importance of the domestic realm for women, "married women were also to be 'freed' from the workplace and the factory. The law of July 1938 established the family subsidy (paid to the father) ostensibly so that women should no longer need to work" (100–101). However, the laws went beyond creating options for Spanish families. Compliance with the state agenda was mandatory: "From 1942 on, all labor regulations stipulated the dismissal of married women. The Family Subsidy Law of March 1946 deprived men whose wives worked of the state-paid family bonus." At the same time that the Franco regime celebrated the role of the mother in the home, and prevented women from gainful employment outside the home, many women were deprived of a male head of household by war, forced labor or prison. During the 1940s, Chuse recounts,

> The main work for poor women was prostitution. Despite the official Puritanism of the New State's ideology, this was one activity from which women were *not legally debarred* until 1956, when brothels were criminalized and prostitution became even further privatized [102].

The irony of the options available to women in Spain, literally the Madonna or the whore, echoed in the representations of flamenco at the time. The Franco regime used film as a means of disseminating propaganda to the masses, and adopted flamenco as the means by which these messages were to be deployed. Chapter 5 deals more extensively with this phenomenon, but here, Chuse identifies two extreme, divergent representations of women in folkloric promotional films:

> The positive female roles were of the suffering mother, the submissive wife, the saint or the glorious heroine, all gifted with the qualities of New Spain: Catholic, imperial and hierarchical. These depictions contrasted with the antiheroine, the frivolous woman of easy virtue, often evil or cruel, the incarnation of past liberties (105).

The genre of *Cine costumbrista* (folkloric films that specialize in Andalusian customs) reproduced these stereotypes of the Madonna and the whore using flamenco dancers, especially, to embody a falsely innocent notion of Spain prior to the Second Republic and the romantic stereotype of the anti-heroine.

Interestingly, the *cante* is more easily appropriated in the nostalgic representation of Spain in the later years of the Franco regime as part of the *nacionalflamenquismo* movement. Dance, always problematic in its association with bodily urges, appeared in television and film representations of flamenco as the symbol of excess. These representations affected the practice of flamenco, where and how it could be performed. Chuse explains:

> The regime discouraged the lowbrow cultural environments that drew women in to "shamelessness," to the bars and taverns. Flamenco bars in Andalusia were frowned upon and were nudged out of existence, while the regime encouraged the development of *peñas*, organizations for the cultivation of

flamenco. These predominantly male clubs, licensed and subjected to surveillance, focused on the serious, de-politicized appreciation of flamenco [108].

In this environment of control, the practice of flamenco was reframed, re/territorialized in a masculine sphere of dominance, while other social practices reinforced the role of respectable women in the home, subordinate to the husbands, fathers and the state. Here, flamenco music, gendered masculine, separates from flamenco dance, gendered inappropriately feminine. As the Franco regime appropriated flamenco to promote its vision of Spain, the low-class positioning of flamenco performers in marginalized settings, engage in "bodily" practices like drinking, dancing, and sex, was replaced by an aesthetically pure environment where the *cante* and the *toque* figured most prominently.

The *Rito y Geografía del Cante Flamenco* series (1971–73) marks the waning years of Franco's regime, and the first stirrings of resistance to the official representation of flamenco. According to Chuse, these programs "picked up on some of the largely unnoticed innovations in both content and style made by women artists during the Franco years." These portrayals "advanced a presentation of women deeply involved in flamenco, yet still thoroughly honorable, a depiction that contrasted with the gender imagery promoted by Franco" (108). While first Washabaugh and then Chuse claim that this series advances a critique of Franco's use of flamenco by claiming for it a respectability denied to practitioners for many years, it is clear that the "allowable" representations of flamenco still meet the criteria for appropriately gendered activity in spheres marked as legitimate. Chuse admits:

> The *Rito* programs never mention brothels or prostitutes despite the fact that these places figured prominently in the history of flamenco. Nor were juergas depicted since these were occasions for excessive drinking and womanizing. Flamenco was recentered in the family and the household, away from streets and bordellos. Like the writings of García Lorca fifty years earlier, the *Rito* films aimed to redeem flamenco, to lift it up out of the debasement into which it had fallen in the Franco years [109].

Key to this re/territorialism of flamenco within Spanish culture was the focus on the music, not the dance. While *cantaoras* were depicted as icons of motherhood and promoters of tradition, the figure of the dancer still carried the weight of flamenco's shame:

> Depicted as central figures, the *cantaoras* in the *Rito* film series are active agents, a far cry from either passive or decorative roles. Some programs mocked the traditionally conceived "flamenco woman," such as a scene in which a local *bailaora*, elderly, portly and comical dances, a lascivious, mocking rumba in a tavern outside a gypsy housing project in Sevilla. Such imagery

was considered to be a flagrant deviation from acceptable Franquist imagery, so much so that similar footage of dancer Juana la Pipa was pulled by television censors the following year [109–110].

Certainly, any agenda of resistance against the Franco regime would have to be deeply buried within the representations of the *Rito* series; however, what even the most progressive flamenco music scholars, like Chuse and Washabaugh, fail to appreciate in the "reading" of these texts is the complicity of these seemingly resistant images through their use of the dancing body. The portrayal of singers as virtuous mothers and dancers as faintly ridiculous receptacles of sexuality is absolutely in keeping with the dichotomy of the Madonna and the whore. While the *cantaoras* can be made respectable, the dancer cannot escape the associations of the body and its excesses.

To be fair, as scholars of the *cante* and *toque*, their focus on music is appropriate. However, it is interesting that the theories of embodiment that provide the foundation for scholarship by musicologists or anthropologists rarely incorporate readings of the dancing body, or consider dancing as a signifying practice, the way that lyrics or musical structures function. These theories allow for the consideration of metaphorical bodies and movements, like the body politic or cultural movements, but they do not engage the dancing body beyond its implicit, inescapable associations with sexuality. That being said, the richness of Chuse's contribution to flamenco scholarship should not be diminished in any way. First, she integrates the historical canon from Spain as well as the most progressive contemporary scholarship in the foregrounding of her work. Second, her work is the first among serious scholars in English to privilege the construction of gender in flamenco. No other foreign flamencophile examines with such detail the material conditions that create gendered bodies in flamenco history. Third, she unmasks the ideological affinities between the Franco regime and the movement toward purism in traditional flamenco scholarship. Finally, her frank discussion of the practice of prostitution within the consideration of other regulatory practices that govern and construct bodies throughout flamenco history make it possible to map a landscape in which the consideration of the dancing body may occur.

4

Fatal Filmic Flamencas

The Spectre of Carmen

She haunts. She can be invoked—a spirit—simply by calling her name. Carmen, the eternal stereotype of dangerous femininity. She always dances. The history of flamenco dance is constructed around the lascivious curves of her body, whipping and furling like the flounces of her skirt. She is the unavoidable stereotype, a figure to be evaded or embraced, but in any event the choreography must accommodate her presence. Other characters in the narrative may be organized around her, set up in opposition to her, but her presence provides the center of a landscape in which the action may occur.

Previous chapters deal with the Hispanic Exotic and the elusive character of the dancing body in flamenco histories. In this chapter, representations of the female flamenco dancer in contemporary films illuminate the problems that emerge in the analysis of historical texts. Descriptions of movement in these films examine the choreographic and filmic conventions that construct flamenco bodies. Like written accounts of flamenco performance, choreography and film rely upon a system of codes to formulate meaning within specific ideological structures. However, the visual image of the dancing body, with its iconic rather than arbitrary resemblance to material bodies, presents its own problems for analysis in the context of flamenco history. The naturalization of the production of meaning in written texts is amplified in filmic texts. If, in previous chapters, the position of the authorial voice erases the mechanics of its own writing in flamenco histories, it is still more difficult to pin down in representations on film. In order to attempt a comprehensive analysis of flamenco bodies on film, two strategies must be deployed: attention to how movements are represented onscreen and a theoretical examination of how the dancing body on film achieves signification. The discussion that follows is heavily influenced by psychoanalytic theory, the predominant theoretical model for the consideration of perception and the visual image. While Marxist theory provides a template for the consideration of class hierarchies, the psychoanalytic model excels in its capacity

Photograph of Antonio Gades, c. 1972–73, shows him performing with the angular virility that imbued the characters he danced on film (Jerome Robbins Dance Division, New York Public Library for the Performing Arts, Astor, Lenox and Tilden Foundations).

to articulate difference and sexuality. In the context of an overall analysis of the flamenco stereotype, the description of the dancing body in these films is intended to supplement previous discussions of race, class, gender, regional tensions in Spain and the image of flamenco as a symbol of Spanish national identity.

That Obscure Object of Desire *(1977)*

Spanish surrealist filmmaker Luis Buñuel, a contemporary of Salvador Dalí and Federico García Lorca, created one of the most imaginative configurations of the flamenco dancer in the final film of his career, *That Obscure Object of Desire* (1977). Buñuel uses the tensions of exoticism and the history of Orientalism to construct a relationship of perpetually unattainable desire between Mattieu, a wealthy, older Frenchman, and Conchita, a young flamenco dancer in Paris. The character of Conchita embodies the eternally duplicitous nature of fatal women, literally, in two bodies. Cool, elegant, French Carole Bouquet and warm, earthy, Spanish Angela Molina play the two sides of Conchita, a lover who promises herself to Mattieu but will not allow him to possess her sexually.

Conchita dances very little in the film; however, her role as a dancer is key to the narrative. References to the history of exoticism between France and Spain, and to the stereotype of the flamenco dancer, allow for the dramatic tension between the lovers to emerge and propel the narrative of desire. Footage of Seville runs during the opening credits, accompanied by a guitar playing a *salida por alegrías*, a traditional "entrance." This footage leads into the first scene of the film, which captures the moment following a violent interaction between the lovers. Mattieu is ready to leave Spain and return to France. His manservant is only too glad; he is "tired of eating steaks fried in oil." This first reference to the cultural backwardness of the Spanish establishes the hierarchy of sophistication developed through the film, in which the rational Mattieu is driven to distraction by the unpredictable Conchita.

The director reveals the history of the lovers through a series of flashbacks, as a story being told to French travelers departing on a train from Spain. Already, conversing in French, the protagonist imparts his history to a receptive audience. As he tells it, Mattieu meets Conchita when she appears in his Paris home as a poorly trained but beautiful chambermaid. He attempts to seduce her and she disappears. He finds her in the shabby apartment she shares with her aristocratic but poor mother, and he attempts to woo her.

In an early chapter of the film entitled "Conchita's Talents,"[1] Conchita dances for the first time, some 40 seconds of movement, foreshadowing her performance later in the film. The first sounds of the guitar *falseta* are audible as Matthieu slips from his reverie on the train to his ascent on the darkened staircase outside Conchita's apartment. The viewer sees the image that Matthieu is denied. Behind a closed door, she performs a *llamada por soleares*, a "call" within the rhythmic structure of the *palo soleares*, and then begins an *escobilla*, a section of footwork. She is working with "El Morenito," the guitarist and part of a band of flamenco "criminals" who surround Conchita and menace Matthieu throughout the film. Mattieu enters without knocking and interrupts their rehearsal as the door shuts behind him.

Conchita dismisses El Morenito. She undresses and bathes before Matthieu, then sings to him and sits in his lap. Despite their intimacy, she won't allow him to make love to her. She repeatedly promises to be his lover, then denies him because he tries to buy her like a prostitute, by giving her elaborate gifts or slipping wads of money to her conservative Catholic mother, who is only too willing to look the other way in exchange for his financial support.

In a moment of desperation to rid himself of her forever, Mattieu asks his cousin, a lawyer, to ensure that he never sees her again. The cousin uses his rank and privilege as an upper-class Frenchman to have Conchita and her mother immediately deported back to Spain. But because he is too much in love with Conchita, Mattieu pursues her in Seville. Led, as if by magic, but quite literally by a Catholic devotional procession, Mattieu walks by her new house. She spies him and invites him to come to watch her dance at a local *tablao*, El Gurugu.

At Gurugu, a group of flamencos perform on a raised platform for Japanese and other tourists. The audience is filled with attractive women, grooming themselves, prostitutes who are "working" the room. The singer croons about "money, money, money" as four women in bright costumes dance *sevillanas* complete with shawls, flowers, and castanets, stock repertory for *tablao* shows. As Matthieu enters the bar, Conchita performs a *rumba* as the *cantaor* sings a *letra* about a man on a staircase in the darkness. She abruptly leaves the stage to join him at a table. Reunited, they reaffirm their love for one another as Matthieu asks her to stop dancing and come to live with him. She agrees.

As the promise is made, a woman reminds Conchita of the time. "They make us take half-hour naps," she explains. "If not, we daydream onstage." Matthieu promises to wait for her. The mood changes and the singer begins a somber *soleares*. A blond woman, reminiscent of Marlene Dietrich's Blue Angel (Beware, remember Rath!) joins Matthieu, claiming to be a friend of Conchita's. She laughs at his innocence and tells him to go up the stairs to see where Conchita is "resting." Ascending a darkened staircase for the second time, he fumbles and then pulls aside curtains that separate a private room to see Conchita onstage, naked except for her accessories: a pair of stockings, a flower, jewelry, and her shoes. As she performs some *marcaje por alegrias* (marking steps in the *palo* of *alegrias*), the camera pans across the room. Downstairs, the audience was dominated by women. The upstairs room is filled with Japanese and American men. As an American shouts a toast to her "beautiful body," another man announces her as "the typical Spanish dancer, Conchita!" Matthieu breaks in and empties the room. He accuses her of lying, and she retorts, "We dance nude for tourists. Even kids know that! Don't tell me you didn't know!"

Buñuel relies upon the character of Carmen and the passionate associations with flamenco to endow the character of Conchita with her qualities as a fatal woman. Duplicitous and opportunistic, she uses her dancing body to manipulate a world controlled by men. Mérimée's besotted Frenchman is reborn in Matthieu. The more she repudiates him, the deeper is his desire to possess her. The film relies upon the Orientalist tendencies of the French in Southern Spain, the history of exoticism of the Spanish dancer, and the stereotypical associations with flamenco to achieve meaning. After all, Conchita would be a very different character if she were a bank teller. Unlike some representations of flamenco, which use the symbolic references to flamenco, like a fan or a flower in the hair, but not the musical and choreographic conventions of the form, Buñuel works more deeply within the stereotype, anchoring it in recognizable rhythmic patterns, or embedding commentary on the action in the lyrics.

In *That Obscure Object of Desire*, Buñuel exploits the image of the flamenco woman and her capacity to signify unattainable desire. However, in his Surrealistic film style, he simultaneously reminds the viewer that the image is not what it represents. Although he uses "real" flamenco references, they serve as metaphor, not reality, a difficult distinction. In another scene in Seville, gypsy women holding a baby approach Mattieu, begging to tell his fortune. He smiles, tickles the "baby," who is actually a pig, behind the ears as he hands them some coins. It is this combination of the authentic and the imaginary that makes his representations so compelling and "real."

The use of specific choreographic conventions by flamenco artists on film simultaneously taps into the wellspring of associations with the dancing body and destabilizes the chains of associations that traditionally accompany the image of the Spanish dancer. The limited use of flamenco as a vocabulary in *That Obscure Object of Desire* creates a landscape in which action may occur. In the film narratives created by director Carlos Saura and choreographer Antonio Gades, the two explore the structures and conventions of flamenco as a language and eventually create more distance between the object and its representation by calling attention to the ways in which the choreography creates meaning. The two produced three collaborative film projects during the decade of the 1980s: *Bodas de Sangre* (Blood Wedding) (1981); *Carmen* (1983); and *El Amor Brujo* (Love, the Magician) (1986). In each work, the figure of the female flamenco dancer moves from the center of the narrative. Her actions seem to determine the fate of the community—men die and women mourn as the result of her excessive passions. Her body serves as the site of racial conflict, class struggle, sexual tensions, and national identities. She metaphorically represents the embattled history of flamenco. In each instance she is invoked, conjured up like the spirit of the *duende*, and the continuing practice of flamenco dance is reestablished in relationship to its past.

Marked: The character of La Novia in Blood Wedding *(1981)*

In the first film of the three-part series, *Blood Wedding*, director Carlos Saura and choreographer Antonio Gades reinterpret Federico García Lorca's play of 1933 as a flamenco ballet. The ballet, staged as a dress rehearsal, serves as a *mise-en-scène* within the diegesis of the film, and differs from Lorca's play in several significant ways. In the play, the dialogue between the characters insinuates a complex history of bloodlines and violence that precedes the wedding of two families from different social classes. The wealthy bridegroom (El Novio) is engaged to marry a young woman of a lower class (La Novia). He is the only surviving male member of his immediate family: his father and his brother were murdered by members of the Félix family. The bridegroom's mother clings to her remaining son and vows to have vengeance upon the Félix clan. On the other side of the tracks, the bride (La Novia) prepares to make a loveless but lucrative marriage with the wealthy bridegroom (El Novio). Three years before she had a passionate but doomed relationship with Leonardo, from the Félix family. Their relationship was interrupted by Leonardo's marriage to a cousin of the bride, to whom he had been betrothed since childhood. Leonardo's wife (La Mujer) suspects, through the gossip of the community women, that her husband has been meeting secretly with her cousin, the bride.

In the absence of spoken dialogue, Gades and Saura use choreographic and filmic conventions to construct complex characters. The gendered vocabulary for flamenco first establishes the categories of sexual difference and then expresses the tension between Leonardo and his wife. As the scene opens, the camera focuses on the choreographer who watches from a place "offstage." Gades turns his head to signal for the singer to begin. She is Marisol, a highly respected flamenco *cantaora* (singer). She sings without accompaniment Lorca's verses of a *nana*, a lullaby that chronicles the death of a child. The Wife of Leonardo is seated on the floor, looking into and rocking an empty cradle. She raises her head and her gaze to the camera. She rises and frames her face with one curved arm. She departs on the diagonal, away from the camera. The camera tracks back, the mirrors are again visible, as well as the other company members, seated and watching. The Wife lunges, and pulls her dress against her thighs. She reaches out with her arms crossed and then executes a series of turns to land facing the mirrors and the other company members. She looks beyond them for her absent husband. She returns to the cradle, performing the sequence in reverse. The camera cuts to the singer, who continues her song. She sings for the mute Wife. The sound of footsteps is audible, then the camera cuts to the feet of Leonardo as his strides approach his wife.

The camera cuts to the Wife, framing her torso and head as her eyes trace the vertical line of his body. The trajectory of her gaze propels her to standing. She wraps her hands around his face, brings her face close to his, eyes pleading. The camera cuts to a shot of her upturned face from a position above her husband's shoulder. Her eyes loom large, accentuated by heavy, Orientalized makeup. He throws her hands away from him; she clings again; he moves away from her. She turns away from him, traces her hips and breasts with her hands and their tapered, spiraling fingers. Her arms frame her face, then reach out to him as she follows, arms extended toward him. With each gesture he moves away, his arms slashing out in the space between them. Each time she manages to wrap her arms around him from behind, he throws her off, stamping a sharp, insistent rhythm on the floor. They circle each other, dueling, spinning to face one another. She falls to the floor, he pirouettes along the diagonal to view the empty cradle. The camera cuts abruptly to her as she collapses in a heap on the floor, and again the company is visible in its frame. She slaps the floor with her palm, matching his denial with her demand. She grasps her skirts and comes to standing. She runs along the diagonal to hold the cradle in her arms. Her eyes move up his body once again, accusing, then she turns away.

In this movement sequence, the choreography for the Wife pushes the vocabulary for the female dancer to the point of excess. The wife performs signature feminine movements: she frames her face and torso with arms curved in semi-circles, her fingers and wrists articulate serpentine shapes, and her upper back and torso arch. She grasps her skirt in her hands so that it emphasizes her hips and reveals her legs. She places her hands on her waist and thrusts her breasts forward. These movements all fall into the realm of the traditional vocabulary for the female flamenco dancer, but the Wife exaggerates these gestures: her arms drag across the surface of her body, rather than travel in the space immediately surrounding it. The play of her own hands across her body suggests an auto-eroticism, a display of excessive feminine desire, in an attempt to capture the attention of her errant husband. But he continually repudiates her, her performance goes too far. The masquerade of femininity she assembles does not attract, it repulses. She is dangerous. Mary Ann Doane reads the masquerade of femininity as one tactic of the *femme fatale*. She cites Montreley's discussion of the threat implied in such a performance:

> It is this evil which scandalizes whenever woman plays out her sex in order to evade the word and the law. Each time she subverts a law or a word which relies on the predominantly masculine structure of the look.[1]

The Wife uses her excessively feminine danced vocabulary to hide a masculine agency, the attempt to acquire a phallus of her own: a baby, or the phallus her husband repeatedly protects from her insistent advances.

The character of Leonardo is the only role that bears a name in the play and the ballet. Marked by the name of the Father, a proper name, he can be recognized as a figure of authority. It is not a surprising coincidence that Antonio Gades chooses to perform the principal role. As the choreographer, he is the most powerful member of the company. In the ballet, he dances with uncompromising virility, characterized by understatement and the display of technical control. His arms slice away from his body in angular shapes, his hands move from flat (knife-like) shapes into fists, and his body always remains relentlessly vertical. He is the only character, at this point, who performs footwork. He "speaks" in a discursive space that excludes the other characters, who must rely on gesture and pantomime. He has the phallus; he is a man—not through his anatomy, but instead by means of his status. The qualities of masculinity, and therefore dominance and authority, are displayed in the solo which follows the duet between Leonardo and the Wife.

Standing, facing the diagonal, Leonardo's arms travel out away from his body, his hands move from flat to fisted, and his torso remains absolutely vertical. The camera shifts positions. It has framed his face and body from the diagonal and now switches to a frontal position, echoing the structure of the proscenium arch. His legs extend in a lunge—he appears to grow still longer—he never compromises the rigidity of his bodily posture. He moves backward along the diagonal. The camera follows him, his whole body is visible in its frame. He executes a slow turn on half-pointe, his arms travel up to form a brief, elongated frame above his head. He repeats this sequence and executes another slow turn. The moment his arms reach the shape of framing, he rises with a leg extended behind, breaking the frame. He completes yet another slow turn. He sinks onto one leg and extends the other in a long straight line. His arms travel out and away from his body.

Leonardo's slow and measured movements contrast the fiery flamenco solos usually associated with male dancers. Gades substitutes slow and flowing movements for a building display of *zapateado*. Gades demonstrates control through the precision he uses when he shifts his weight in the same way he might claim mastery over a rhythmic phrase through rapid footwork. In this film, the choreographic conventions of masculinity, as signs, are juxtaposed on top of bodies to signify authority. Gades mimetically enacts, through his choreography, the function of the phallus. The presence and absence of authority depend on the use of gendered choreographic codes. This process first creates gender as an effect of representation, then obliterates that moment of signification.[2] The choreography appears to emerge as an expression of a biologically masculine body: "He is a man, therefore he dances in a masculine style," rather than "Because he dances in a masculine style, he can be identified as a man."

The duet is immediately followed by a solo for La Novia. The camera cuts to a close-up shot; La Novia's hands cover her face. The music intensifies.

She wears an expression of panic as she focuses on her hands, then explodes into an angular stance, lunging forward toward the space once occupied by Leonardo. Her arms stretch out straight from her sides and push against the space in front of her. She moves along the diagonal, feet biting the floor in clipped, short footwork. The reverberations from her *zapateado* move up her body, carry her along, as her hands move up along the erotic terrain where his hands once were. She stops, arms stretched overhead, again completely vertical. From offstage, two male singers begin their song for the bride, "Awaken, bride, awaken on the day of your wedding..."

The two men move toward her; they frame her body in the camera's eye. She begins a traditional flamenco solo, not looking at the men closing in on her. She moves between their bodies, her gaze pulls inward. The men foreground her as they slowly exit the space; she moves in and out of sight, behind and between their bodies. She backs up on the diagonal, chased. Her footwork is more insistent now; the camera focuses on her feet. The camera pans back to reveal a woman, a dresser, beside the piano "offstage." The bride takes a bouquet of white flowers from the dresser's hands and throws it to the floor. The woman picks up the flowers without expression and puts them back in the hands of the reluctant bride. Immobile, she makes no move as the woman puts a white dress over her head and crowns her with a circle of lace.

In this scene, La Novia performs a feminine role that contrasts with the dance of the Wife. While the Wife described abundant curves on and around her body, the bride flattens the curves of her arms to a position that is defiantly vertical and, I would argue, phallic. Leonardo demonstrated similar angles of limbs and an uncompromising verticality in his solo, earlier in the ballet. The performance of the Bride resists a configuration of desirable femininity. The Bride represents a woman dangerous not in her ability to manipulate the constructs of femininity, like the Wife, but in her indifference to those codes of femininity. Sarah Kofman describes the dangerous elusiveness of such a woman in her reading of Freud: "She loves only herself, she is sufficient unto herself, and leaves the man who loves her unsatisfied; she always maintains 'an enigmatic reserve,' gives herself without surrendering...."[3] The Bride, then, is a character who is potentially criminal, a *femme fatale* who may be crafty enough to emerge from the narrative unpunished.

In her extended solo, the Bride performs the most abstract (as opposed to pantomimic) movement in the work. Her movement transgresses the borders of the realm of the discursive; its meaning cannot be easily translated into language. When framed by the bodies of the two singers, she moves around them. She resists her exchange in marriage as she continually escapes the framing of her body between the two men. The choreography transforms her body into a fluid which leaks and swells against the structure of the Law of the Father and the apparatus of the camera. Though she moves somewhere near (in, out, around, and through) the discursive components of language, her body "speaks" in a different way. In order to understand the dynamics of this "language," perhaps one must, in the context of choreography, "read" in a different way. Luce Irigaray discusses a similar leakage in "The Dynamics of Fluids." When "the woman-thing speaks," in order to understand we must remember

> that it is continuous, compressible, dilatable, viscous, conductible, diffusable.... That it is unending, potent and impotent owing to its resistance to the countable ... that it allows itself to be easily traversed by flow by virtue of its conductivity to currents coming from other fluids or exerting pressure through the walls of a solid ... and that it is already diffuse "in itself," which disconcerts any attempt at static identification....[4]

La Novia's dancing flows and resists the "meaning of the proper," blurs the confines of discursive structures like language and pantomime to signify a position that is alternately resistive to and accommodating of the phallogocentric order that produces subjects.[5] Because she has demonstrated her capacity for slippage, it is uncertain where her crown will "fix" her in place.

As one might suspect, Leonardo and La Novia run away together on the day of the wedding. The Groom sets out with a group of riders, seeking his revenge. In the final scene of the film, the Groom and Leonardo perform a fatal, erotic duet across the body of La Novia. The duet begins as the search party finds the illicit lovers. The two men lock gazes, remove coats and withdraw knives. The bride steps into the background, framed by their two bodies. The company, offscreen, breathes a collective gasp. The two men connect in a circle of tension formed by torsos, arms and legs. As they pass each other, their bodies overlap. The camera circles the two men, joins their two bodies in its frame, and positions the bride in the background, between them. They move in slow motion, their heavy breathing the only sound that breaks the tension of the silence. Slowly, painfully, Leonardo slashes toward the groom with his knife. He misses, and the groom lunges toward Leonardo. As they struggle, the bride slowly performs a series of gestures between and behind the outline of their bodies. She clutches at her head, she hides her eyes, and she reaches out toward the couple. The camera focuses on their feet, advancing and retreating, interrupted by a pair of white heels. The camera continues to circle. The breathing of the two men is heavier; their faces shine with sweat. Their bodies clasp, joined. The bride continues to watch, then hides her face behind her hands. The circle traced by the camera tightens. The company begins a low, contrapuntal clapping. Leonardo stabs/penetrates the groom in the side. The tempo of the clapping increases, punctuated by shouts and grunts from the "audience." The groom throws back his head as he stabs/penetrates Leonardo. The groom sinks to the ground; Leonardo falls slowly after him. The clapping increases in volume and speed. The camera traces the limbs of the two men as they make contact with the floor: thigh, waist, wrist, elbow, back, face. The groom is dead. The camera cuts to the face of Leonardo, lying motionless on the floor. The clapping and shouting stops abruptly. Again, the company sings, "Awaken, bride, on the day of your wedding...." The bride walks between the bodies of the fallen men, her face cast downward. She walks toward the mirrors; her hands trace her breasts. As her hands moves toward her hips, they leave behind a trail of blood. She looks to her own face in the mirror. The bodies of the two murdered men lay in the background, elegantly folded in death, matching poses like bookends. The credits run over the marked body of La Novia.

The duel between Leonardo and El Novio plays on two powerful undercurrents of desire. The fight is, on the one hand, a recognition of the connection between the two men in their rivalry for La Novia. Leonardo, as the one named, represents the position of the Father in an Oedipal drama. The bride serves as an acceptable stand-in as Mother to El Novio. Newly equipped with his phallus/knife, the groom must slay the Father. La Novia cannot look upon the scene of the two men coupled in struggle. It is an inverted primal scene, or a primal scene of inversion, from which she is completely excluded as the object of desire. This primal/primary drama taps into the always burgeoning desire between the men as the competitors for the bride-as-phallus. Each man must kill the other to prevent his own castration. This struggle has all of the dynamics of passionate lovemaking. The two men's bodies are joined. They writhe, sweat, and breathe heavily. The rhythmic accompaniment provided by the company builds to a crescendo as the two men penetrate each other and reach the climax of the duet. The threat of violence that runs beneath the surface in the play calls attention to the homosocial/homoerotic underpinnings of the marriage contract. In this skewed Oedipal drama, the death of the Father is accomplished, but no Son survives to assume the position of having the phallus.

Instead, the audience is left with the lingering image of La Novia in her stained bodice. What kind of *femme fatale* is this? What kind of subject emerges from this struggle of desire and power? As a woman, she is always already castrated. The doubled stain of blood echoes the traumatic image of the open wound. However, as a fetish, the mark does not disavow, but calls attention to, her exclusion from the Law of the Father. She wears this mark as an ironic fetish. She is not "the bearer of the open wound, she exist only in relation to her castration and cannot transcend it," as Laura Mulvey articulates the problem of female positioning and filmic representation. According to her reading of psychoanalytic theory, a woman's position in the symbolic order is one of "bearer of meaning, not maker of meaning."[6] The character of La Novia escapes the binary positions available to her in the symbolic order. She gains entrance into the symbolic at the moment she recognizes herself as castrated in the mirror, but the self-consciousness of her double marking suggests that she occupies strange space. This position is not static; it exists on the margins and can only be accessed by movement. Though, at times, she accommodates the structures of the Law of the Father, she is capable of resisting those structures by the "mechanics" of her fluid being. She is not absent, but her presence is complicated by the rules of intelligibility, just as her movement cannot be "read" as pantomime. Luce Irigaray asks, then answers, "Woman does not exist? In the eyes of discursivity." And those women who speak, take up temporary and unstable positions on the margins, where they clamor for attention? "Interpreting them where they exhibit only their muteness means subjecting them to a language that exiles them at ever-increasing distance from what perhaps they would have said to you, were already whispering to you."[7] The bride's relationship to meaning balances on a series of appropriations and displacements of the structures of intelligibility already in place.

Perhaps the most important subversion of the roles assigned to La Novia is her performance of the *femme fatale*. Not only does she appropriate masculine qualities and movement vocabulary rather than an excess of femininity, like the Wife, but she survives the ending of the film. Unruly women usually die to allow closure in a narrative. In a discussion of the great heroines of the opera, Catherine Clement laments,

> Dead women, dead so often. There are those who die disemboweled, like Lulu at the knife of Jack the Ripper, in a cruddy attic of smoggy London; there are those who die for having embodied too well the false identity of a marionette-woman or for having simply affirmed that they are not where the men are looking for them....[8]

La Novia dances away from, flees, escapes the place where the men are looking for her, yet, unlike her predecessor Carmen, she remains alive. Perhaps the red stain is meant to be read as a scarlet letter of some kind; after all, she is an adulteress. But here the bloody bodice reads as an ironic fetish, a mark of the wound that a proper fetish would have to mask. This fetish can only function coupled with irony, as it is discussed by Donna Haraway. This irony is "about the tension of holding things together because both or all are necessary and true.... It is also a rhetorical strategy and a political method..."[9] The use of an ironic fetish in this reading of *Bodas de Sangre* calls attention to the mechanics of choreographic and filmic representation that produce an intelligible female dancing subject, a fatal woman who survives the resolution of a narrative.

An attempt at such a reading has important implications for the feminist analysis of the image of the female flamenco dancer on film. The performance of the bride, and the ballet as a whole, provide a text ripe for the kind of analysis envisioned by film theorist Teresa de Lauretis. In her words,

> ...feminist work in film should not be anti-narrative or anti-oedipal but quite the opposite. It should be oedipal narrative and oedipal with a vengeance, working, as it were, with and against narrative in order to represent not just a female desire which Hollywood, in the best tradition of Western literature and iconography, has classically represented as the doomed power of the fetish (a fetish empowered for the benefit of men and doomed to disempower women); but working, instead, to represent the duplicity of the oedipal scenario itself and the specific contradiction of the female subject in it.[10]

A reading of the bride's contradictory embrace of and resistance to the constraints of her role in Lorca's narrative and the flamenco ballet on film opens up a window of opportunity through which one might glimpse the characters in Gades and Saura's most famous work, *Carmen*.

Carmen *Revisited (1983)*

Gades and Saura, through a deliberately constructed, extremely self-conscious authorial perspective, modernize the stereotype of Carmen in ways that reveal the power of the stereotype, her capacity to signify a multitude of transgressive characteristics, while also acknowledging the limits of traditional choreographic and filmic narrative strategies to contain her presence. Like other collaborative works by Saura and Gades, *Carmen* operates on a number of narrative levels. The film is somewhat autobiographical. Gades plays the role of a choreographer for a flamenco company in rehearsal for a contemporary production of *Carmen*. He retains his own name, as do several other cast members like dancer Cristina Hoyos and guitarist Paco de Lucía, throughout the film's development.

Two stories are enacted within the film and eventually blur to the point at which they are indistinguishable from each other. Gades plays Don José in the flamenco production, and he has an affair with Carmen, the dancer/ actor, during the rehearsal process. As Susan McClary succinctly points out, "He soon falls desperately in love with her, Pygmalion-style, and the two narrative strands (their relationship, Merimée's story) become confused—both to Antonio and to the spectator, who is often given mixed cues as to whether the action concerns Carmen or the affair between Antonio and his protégée."[11] Gades's role as the narrator and the choreographer who directs the movements of the company echoes the authorial voice of Merimée in the original. The viewer hears Gades recite parts of the text as a voice-over, just as the narrator delivers the story to the reader. In Merimée's version, the character of the French narrator assumed authority and mastery over Carmen by gaining access to Romani, her language, as well as narrative control over her unruly presence by orchestrating her story-death. Similarly, Antonio Gades, as the narrator/choreographer, attempts to establish control over the character of Carmen in the film by designing her choreography and, as Antonio/Don José, kills her with a knife, in a series of penetrating stabs, as Bizet's score plays.

Gades and Saura play with several overarching narrative strategies within Merimée's story, Bizet's opera, and the film they create together. First, they provide the presence of a narrator in the film as there was in the original, an element left out of Bizet's opera and several productions based on the opera. Second, they emulate the seductive teasing of Carmen's sexuality through the inclusion of partially developed dance scenes from the rehearsals for the performance. Just as Merimée's Carmen (and Buñuel's Conchita) revealed parts of her body through the folds of her dress, and promised, but never delivered, sexual satisfaction through lovemaking, the film entices the viewer with fragmented dance sequences that begin to develop as independent narrative elements, but then end abruptly and segue into the action of the film. The viewer never has a sense of fully suturing into the filmic or the choreographic narratives. Even at the end, the viewer walks away unfulfilled, because the narrative is unresolved. After Gades stabs Carmen, the camera pans out over the rehearsal space. The other company members appear unaware that a murder has taken place. The viewer is presented with contradictory imagery—what just happened? Did Antonio kill Carmen, or did Don José murder her as in the original?

The film Carmen repeatedly invokes both Merimée story and Bizet's opera, but then skews the meanings attendant to the "originals." In an early scene from the film, the camera looks upon a rehearsal in progress. Dancers practice footwork as the musicians go over the guitar and lyrics for the production. Antonio Gades is listening to a reel-to-reel tape of Bizet's music, and the opera threatens to drown out the sound of the musicians. As Antonio listens, he thumps out the *compás* for *bulerías* over the measures of Bizet's *seguidilla*. The musicians immediately take his cue and adapt the melody to a *bulerías* structure. Bizet's orchestration is too slow for dancing, they contend. The layering and contrast of Bizet's *Carmen* to the flamenco *Carmen* is accomplished through a series of intercutting camera shots from the musicians to Gades. Paradoxically, as the choreographer attempts to cite the "original" in his production, the musicians struggle to reinsert the "authentic" (flamenco) into the "original" (opera).

The tension between the legacy of the stereotype and "real" flamenco characterizes the film as a whole. In the next few scenes from the film, Antonio the choreographer must somehow make the character of Carmen "work" within a flamenco context. At the same time, he tries to work within the narrative framework of the opera *Carmen*, which has little to do with flamenco. In fact, references to gypsy dancing in the "originals" only appear as indications of Carmen's exoticism. As an artist steeped in the tradition of flamenco, he must recognize the persuasiveness of the stereotype while at the same time he must produce a work in the flamenco idiom. The transformation takes place in the pedagogical and sexual relationship between Antonio and Carmen. The oppositional tensions of the stereotype and the real, as well as the categories of "respectable" and "criminal" women, are embodied in the performances of Carmen and Cristina/Micaela.

After the musicians have adapted Bizet's melody, Antonio calls over the ballet mistress, Cristina Hoyos, and instructs her to follow his lead in an improvised series of movements. She adeptly matches him, step for step; however, she will not play the leading role. Cristina serves as the respectable foil for Carmen's character, as Micaela was created in Bizet's opera. However, unlike Micaela, who was virginal and chosen by Don José's mother as an appropriate bride, Cristina Hoyos is the most accomplished female dancer of the company.

Gades searches for the "authentic" Carmen among the professional flamenco dancers in company auditions. Gades uses the portrait of Carmen from Merimée to evaluate the suitability of the different candidates. Through a voiceover, he muses about her "wild and strange beauty," the "voluptuous but surly" character of her expression and the racialized, animalistic qualities of her eyes: "Gypsy eyes, wolf eyes ... as the Spanish saying goes." His search for Carmen brings him to a class of María Magdalena's dance students at the Amor de Dios studios. The teacher is a well-known *bailaora*, who shares with her students a humorous and deliberate knowledge of the stereotypical image of the flamenco dancer. As she corrects the dancers, she advises, "The breasts are like bull's horns, warm yet soft."

Carmen is not among the determined, hard-working students present at the beginning of the class. Instead, she arrives late. As she joins the rest of the class, Antonio recognizes his Carmen:

> I looked up and I saw her. It was Friday ... I'll never forget it. At first, she didn't please me. I went back to my work. But, as is customary with women and cats who don't come if you call, but come if you don't call, she stopped in front of me and spoke to me.

The portrait of the exotic provided by the French Romantics has become a self-conscious, but equally seductive, stereotype. Carmen's animalistic and transgressive characteristics have been internalized by the artists in the film and by Gades as the choreographer. Just as the Romantics had to search to find the perfect image of the gypsy to satisfy their Orientalist imaginings, Gades must scrutinize several dancers in different contexts to find his Carmen. The metaphor of animal qualities and movements reappears frequently in the discussion of the character of Carmen and the attributes of flamenco dancing. Carmen has "the eyes of the wolf," she advances and retreats like a cat; María Magdalena suggests the female dancer's breasts must be like "the horns of a bull," and Cristina Hoyos insists, later in the film, that the dancers' hands should move "like doves." Again, the characteristics of animals are integral to the portrayal of the gypsy/flamenco dancer and more specifically, the female flamenco dancer.

The "*Tabacalera* (Tobacco Factory)" scene demonstrates the integration of Carmen the dancer and Carmen the stereotype. In Merimée's text and Bizet's opera, the scene in the tobacco factory occurs at the beginning of the story, after the introduction of the principal characters. Don José arrests Carmen after she has slashed the face of another factory worker. In the film, the scene in the factory and the seduction of Don José by Carmen in the jail cell are collapsed into a single choreographic event. Also, Cristina/Micaela plays the role of the woman who insults Carmen in the factory and rallies a group of women in opposition to her.

The camera pans across the faces of the *cantaoras* seated at long wooden tables. These women are all within or past their 40s, with lined faces and heavy figures. They sing in broken, "flamenco" voices about the dangers of "brambles that have thorns." Cristina rises from her seat, and walks with swaying hips to the center of the room. She grabs the folds of her skirt and turns to address individual women in the room. She stamps in keeping with the rhythm of the *compás*. She approaches Carmen. "In this factory," she sings, "there are more bitches than good girls." Cristina leans over Carmen's shoulder, abruptly turns and offers flamenco's ultimate insult: she kicks up the back edge of her skirt, then shakes her hips at Carmen without looking at her. The women cheer, and Carmen returns, "Don't you annoy Carmen!" Cristina sits and ignores Carmen; Carmen rises slowly from her chair. She flips her skirt open to reveal a red spandex-clad thigh, pulls the fabric up around her hips and swings her hips as she sings, "Don't you annoy Carmen! Carmen has a knife for those who annoy her!" Carmen sinks into a wide stance and gyrates her hips in a circle. The two women face each other, retreat with swaggering steps, and the company repeats the refrain, "Don't go near the brambles/ The brambles have thorns...."

Cristina challenges Carmen by rushing at her with stomping feet; Carmen answers back in kind. Carmen advances toward Cristina, her arms raised. Cristina retreats, mirroring the shape of Carmen's arms. Cristina then chases Carmen; the two women turn away from each other and frame their heads and shoulders with their arms. They approach each other, deeply seated on bent legs, torsos cast forward, and arms defensively guarding the space around them. They rise up and begin a circle of dueling footwork. As the *zapateado* builds, the other women leave their seats and organize in two groups behind Carmen and Cristina. A few women remain in their seats to maintain the *compás* as the groups face off in lines behind their leaders. They retreat and then attack in twos, one side against the other, all maintaining the rhythm in unison. They pass each other, accentuating the downbeats with wide-legged stances, and assemble once again at opposite sides of the room. Advancing and retreating, gathering and dispersing, the dancers add more turns into their footwork patterns. They organize in a circle at the center of the room, moving counter-clockwise around the pivotal couple, Cristina and Carmen. The two women lock gazes; the groups retreat for the final attack. A stampede of footwork, and then Cristina backs Carmen up against a table where a knife has conveniently been placed. Carmen hides the knife in the folds of her skirt as they continue to drive toward one another with turns and footwork. Carmen whirls, then slices at Cristina's throat with her knife. Silence. The women slowly support Cristina and lay her down on the floor.

The two groups stare at one another, and the sound of a march introduces the men, the restorers of law and order. Don José leads them in a military march. He looks at Carmen, who returns his gaze. She tosses away the knife, and two men grab her by the elbows to escort her away. She stops, looks at Don José, frees her arms, and plants her fists on her hips. Don José circles Carmen and scrutinizes her. He grabs her elbow, and she circles him with undulating steps. She boldly appraises him, circles him, rubs against him, and takes off her shawl. She presses her breasts against his chest. He attempts to put her back in line, as the escorted prisoner. The two approach the mirror, she circles him, watches them together in the mirror and then simply exits. His eyes follow her, then his head snaps back to attention. He breaks character to address the company.

In this rather lengthy scene, several elements of the plot coalesce. Carmen the dancer becomes Carmen the character through her training with Cristina. The character of Carmen acquires authenticity through the proximity of several "true" flamencos, trim professional dancers and aging priestesses of song. The choreography incorporates the signature hip movements for Carmen and the other women, marking them as gypsy, poor, sensual, and violent. The woman's sphere, the factory, signifies the potentially explosive and dangerous lawlessness of Carmen's character. She is also aligned with the lower classes who work in the factory. The military men appear to reestablish legitimate authority, the power of the state, and the interests of the dominant classes. Carmen pantomimes killing Cristina, and the antagonism is displaced from the two women to the couple, Carmen and Don José. Immediately, the tension becomes sexualized, and Carmen usurps Don José's position of authority through the display of her body. She maintains this powerful position until the end of the film.

The reversal of the positions of power from Don José to Carmen and Antonio to Carmen plays off the categories of masculinity and femininity. While masculinity has been aligned with the authority of the choreographer, or the power of Don José in his military regiment, femininity has been embodied in Carmen's elusive deflection of advice and affection. Most importantly, Antonio/Don José has been the bearer of the look, he who evaluates, scrutinizes, judges, and harangues. Carmen has been the object of the gaze, she who is evaluated, scrutinized, judged and harangued. However, once the seduction of Don José by Carmen has been danced out within the film, Antonio loses his authority, and Carmen gains hers.

As the character of Antonio/Don José dissembles, the choreography presents conflicting images of unstable masculinity. As Carmen gains more autonomy in the filmic and danced narratives, Antonio's character becomes more vulnerable, feminized as the threatened *macho* who clings to a woman who has the agency to negotiate her own exchange between two men. The primary relationship, however, is between the two men, a toreador and Antonio/Don José. They posture, compete, and threaten to erupt into violence over the possession of Carmen. Positioned between them, she is a commodity, a fetish for a relationship between two men who occupy positions of power as men. However, she disrupts this dynamic by leaving the frame their bodies provide for her. She chooses neither one of them. Her punishment is death.

The scene opens on the toreador admiring himself before the mirror. Decked out in gilt braid and sequins, his trousers tightly cling to his legs, the cummerbund cinches his waist, and the short jacket with epaulettes crowns the muscular column of his torso and legs. An elderly man adjusts his wig, while another tests the drape of the toreador's cape. The image of this spectacle of masculinity and desirability dissolves as the curtains part to reveal the walls of the studio, and company members enter the frame of the camera.

The musicians start up, and the dancers pair off. The scene has the air of a fiesta, a celebration of the toreador's victory. Carmen and Antonio dance together, she smiling, and he staring intently at her. With a fanfare, the toreador enters, surrounded by his entourage of men. He plays to the crowd, waving and nodding at individuals. His eyes take in Carmen as she stands at Antonio's side. His gaze moves up and down her body, then he takes her hand to invite her into his embrace. She leaves Antonio to dance with the toreador, and the rest of the crowd resume their activity. Antonio is still and staring at the couple. He moves toward them, grabs Carmen's arm, and pulls her away from the toreador. The bullfighter responds to this insult with understated outrage. He backs up, taking measured steps and playing *pitos*. His cronies surround him, placing themselves in the path between the two men, protecting the toreador.

The musicians strike up a *sevillanas*, and the couples resume their dancing while the camera frames Carmen and Antonio. Over the shoulders of the dancers, we see them argue. Carmen gestures in frustration as Antonio attempts to pull her into his arms. Disgusted, Carmen departs to join the circle of people around the toreador. Again, Antonio inserts himself and grabs Carmen's arm. The toreador spins to face Antonio, and his comrades draw their knives. The men of Antonio's company rush to surround their leader. The toreador signals his men to put the knives away. He begins a masculine solo of voluptuous control while his friends play *palmas*, sing, and shout *jaleo*. His wrists circle as he raises his arms to frame his torso and head. His slippered feet slide and soundlessly punctuate the accents of the *compás* as he moves with infinitesimal steps along diagonals and in semicircles, never turning his back on his opponent. With each step, his hips sway slightly. His arms and their fisted hands cross and uncross, shielding and then baring his chest as he moves toward Antonio, then backs up again. He pirouettes and halts with an attenuated flow of momentum, then repeats his advance forward and retreat back. He turns again, and brings his arms forcefully down to his sides as his chest puffs up.

The challenge issued, Gades responds with a masculine solo of a different character. The heels of his boots crash down as he slices his arms across his chest. His steps carry him forward, carriage uplifted. His heels accent the *compás*, a solo voice among those of his friends who have rallied around him playing *palmas*, singing, and shouting *jaleo*. He uses isolated movements of his shoulders and torso to punctuate the phrases as he stands on tall legs. His turns are abrupt, and he follows them with building phrases of *zapateado*. He snaps his arms into positions at the level of his chest, almost as if he were holding the reins of a horse. As his solo reaches a climax, Carmen interrupts him with her exit.

The solos of the two men illustrate opposing embodiments of masculinity. The toreador appears almost effeminate in his scarlet and gold costume.

His slippered feet do not assert the characteristic masculine voice of *zapateado*. He frames his head and torso with his arms, moves his hands in sinuous circles, and slightly sways his hips with each step. The oblique diagonal passes of his choreography are more suited to female solo roles than the traditional male role. And yet, there is no mistaking the virility of this performance. The turns, softened at the end, and the frequent puffing of his chest seductively and dangerously remind the viewer that this is a man capable of violence even though his manner may seem subdued. He teases the emasculated Antonio Gades/Don José with the confidence of a man who has nothing to lose.

Underlying the sexual competition between the two men, a class and race competition also occurs. The toreador represents a man of the lower classes. He shares with Carmen the status of an outlaw, however celebrated he may be in performance. He presents a contrast to Antonio Gades/Don José, who represents authority as a choreographer or representative of the state. The "feminine" aspects of his performance underscore his status as subordinate, but dangerous in comparison to Antonio Gades/Don José, whose "masculine" display reasserts his position as a representative of the dominant class.

The contest over who will possess Carmen already implies a loss for Gades, the thwarted lover. The taunting quality of the toreador's performance emphasizes the almost desperate display of masculinity in Gades's solo. He slices his arms and legs through the air, brings his heels down with emphatic *golpes*, breaks the line of his torso with staccato shoulder isolations, and abruptly spins and halts as he executes his turns. His arms rarely travel above the level of his sternum, while the toreador framed his head and upper body with curved arms. Gades moves forward and back and turns in place, but he never presents the oblique line of his body through diagonal pathways, as the toreador does. And finally, though his hips sometimes displace to the side as he thrusts his legs beneath him, Gades does not employ the toreador's lilting sway of the hips.

The two male positions within this duel/duet bring into focus the struggle for power between two men that is fought over the body of a woman. They compete for each other as they vie for Carmen's attentions. Their virility, their manliness is at stake here. Ironically, it is the toreador, with his dangerously effeminate display of sensuality, who is the most masculine. Despite his thunderous footwork, Gades/Don José lacks the fundamental element of male prowess, the woman. His "lack" feminizes him in a relationship of power in which masculinity is aligned with supremacy. The toreador maintains his masculinity through the communal recognition of his erotic power and through his temporary possession of the prize, Carmen.

The contested category of masculinity in this scene is further informed by the relationship of the performers to the (meta)spectator, the camera's eye. If the exoticized Hispanic dancing couple (even if they are two men, especially if they are two men) is always positioned as subordinate to the gaze that constitutes the spectacle, and that gaze is, by virtue of its political, economic or narrative mastery, gendered masculine; then, these two men betray a threat to their masculinity through their conspicuous display of masculine characteristics. In the arena of international politics and the unstable configurations of national identity that have shaped flamenco history, the positioning of these performances must be read in the context of the stereotypical image of Hispanic and Latin *machismo*.

Since the popular perception of exotic Latin stereotypes renders them interchangeable—remember the confusion of Carmen Miranda, the "Brazilian Bombshell," and the "Human Vesuvius," gypsy Carmen Amaya—the dynamics of their signification can be compared as similar instances of misrecognition. Tango scholar Marta Savigliano writes:

> Machismo, in particular, is an outcome of international struggles over manliness. "Macho" is the Spanish word for "male," but it has been adopted by other languages/cultures to refer to a "wrong" kind of maleness—an unmanly maleness. Manliness here is contrasted with maleness. Macho men are not so much unmale as they are unmanly. Machismo is a synonym for the barbaric, uncivilized "virility" attributed to latinos.[12]

When a man dances a solo that expresses the qualities of excessive masculinity and incipient violence, the history of how Latino men have been stereotypically configured with respect to the foreign gaze comes into play. Gades and Saura offer two incarnations of flamenco machismo: one effeminate but virile, the other masculine but feminized. As a flamenco couple, the two are feminized by the gaze of the spectator. This spectator is positioned as he who looks, a corridor of mirror reflections: the French Romantics, upper-class señoritos, Hollywood filmmakers, fascist dictators, and international film viewers. The relationship of the dancers to the camera's eye emulates their relationship to international structures of power, and reveals the ease with which the dynamics of seeing inherit the legacy of colonialism. As Savigliano concludes, "Bourgeois manliness and modern imperialism [are] one and the same ideology, one and the same practice. Colonialism, in its different stages—born of the competition with other races, classes and nations of men—feminized and turned unmanly the peripheral world."[13]

But what of Carmen? Wouldn't it be interesting if the story ended at the fiesta, resolved by Carmen's exit from a conflict that no longer concerns her? Two men remain standing, and dance to their deaths, or at least until exhaustion sets in, and their friends tire of the posturings and disperse? The final image would be the silhouette of Carmen, striding off into the sunset, her hips slightly swaying as she bites into a blood orange. But her violent end is necessary to restore a masculine order and to reaffirm her place as the object of exchange between men. Her transgressiveness titillates only when her threat is contained through her murder in the final scene.

After Carmen interrupts Gades's solo, he starts after her, grabs her arm and spins her to face him. A series of clutches follows, with Carmen wrenching herself from his grasp as he repeatedly begs her to stay. Gades wraps his arms around Carmen and tries to kiss her. She thrusts him away, saying, "I've had enough! I don't love you any more! It's finished!" He backs her against the wall, her body hidden from the camera in a recess as he clutches her once more, draws a knife from his pocket, and stabs her three times. The music soars as she collapses, visible again, in a heap at his feet. The camera pans across the studio, where people sit at tables and talk, seemingly oblivious to the murder that has taken place.

The choreography for this final scene metaphorically embodies the narrative dynamic that insists upon Carmen's punishment for her exotic criminality. Gades repeatedly attempts to contain Carmen's body with his own. She resists each time, and finally Gades brings her into submission by penetrating her with his knife. His sadistic mastery of her unruly body parallels the narrative containment of her presence. On yet another level, the spectator observes the spectacle of feminized men in conflict over who shall possess Carmen's body. Contemporary feminist theory in film studies has articulated the parallels between the mechanics of desire and object-formation. In her pivotal articles on visual pleasure and film, Laura Mulvey uses psychoanalytic theory to describe certain foundational concepts for spectatorship and identification with respect to the celluloid world of Hollywood cinema: "Woman as Image, Man as Bearer of the Look."[14] The image of woman on film, with all of her potentially castrating but pleasurable possibilities, determines the active/passive roles of looking for the spectator and the rules of narrative coherence in traditional film structure. The woman is displayed as the erotic object of desire; in pursuit of her the hero passes through the storyline, yet she constantly threatens to disrupt the seamless flow of the narrative. The spectator may identify with the ego-ideal of the hero, an "active," masculine, heterosexualized positioning. When the spectator identifies with the male hero, he may, by extension, "possess" the erotic object of the camera's gaze, the female love interest. Female scopophilic pleasure relies on a guilt-ridden cross-gendered identification with the sadistic, controlling masculine gaze or the passive, masochistic acceptance of the position of the object of the gaze.

When considering this argument in the context of *Carmen*, one must resist the temptation to directly apply these theories across the boundaries of Hollywood cinema and contemporary European, and more specifically Spanish, film. However, certain points resonate and deserve further discussion within the context of Mulvey's arguments. In her writing, the figure of the woman on film presents such a pernicious threat, even as she satisfies the erotic desire in looking, that she must be sadistically undone by the male protagonist. Her image must be fetishized in order to disavow the threat of castration it implies.[15] As a character, Carmen is both erotic and dangerous, threatening through her capacity to signify the castration of the male protagonist even as she provokes his desire and, by extension, the desire of the spectator. However, Mulvey's theory does not take into account the tensions of gender, race, class, national identity, and the legacy of colonial expansion as it is performed in Gades and Saura's film.

The use of Merimée's story, the choreographer's deliberate play with stereotypes of gypsy identity and flamenco authenticity, and the positioning of Spanish film in a transnational context following the dissolution of Franco's regime demand that the spectator negotiate several layers of meaning as s/he reads the film. The narrative of *Carmen* reiterates the relationship of the colonizing gaze and its desiring reflection of the exotic Other. The power imbalance inherent in that relationship is displaced across a host of categories, and that displacement produces ambivalences and double meanings. The protagonist is simultaneously the narrator (the ghostly voice of Merimée), the emasculated tragic hero of the film (Don José) and the macho embodiment of the jealous Latin lover (a flamenco dancer). The *toreador*, in both his comic and dramatic incarnations, plays on the humorous, sensual, and violent associations with Spanish maleness. And finally, Carmen, beloved Carmen, expresses both transgression and the inevitable reassertion of the codes of masculine authority.

Love, the Magician *(1986)*

The third work in the "flamenco trilogy," *El Amor Brujo* animates the 1925 ballet composed by Manuel de Falla. Although he is best known as a classical music composer, de Falla organized, along with poet Federico García Lorca, the 1922 Festival de Cante Jondo in Granada. Flamenco and gypsy themes appear in works throughout his career. In the final collaboration between director Saura and choreographer Gades, the filmic and choreographic conventions that mark their earlier works fall away in favor of a more traditional film narrative. For example, although the opening of the film features a slow pan through the set of a gypsy village, revealing the "production" behind the production, once the story begins, the disruptions that characterize earlier films are absent. *El Amor Brujo* differs in structure from *Bodas de Sangre* and *Carmen* in the absence of both the confessional narrator's voiceover and the plot device of the *mise-en-scène*, the rehearsal within the performance. Instead, the viewer is drawn into the story, allowed to "suture" into the highly stylized celluloid "reality."

Although almost every scene features flamenco song and dance, few scenes involve sustained dancing, and when they do, they tend to utilize the vernacular elements of flamenco. Moments of spoken dialogue, dramatic action, song and dance flow seamlessly throughout most of the narrative. The music weaves almost imperceptibly from the original score to the various flamenco *palos*. Wedding dances, laundry dances, wandering *bulerías*, and drunken *soleares* provide the landscape in which the action may occur. In this way, the third film in the "flamenco trilogy" traces the art form back to its informal social context among gypsies. Significantly, the scenes that incorporate theatrical dancing occur when the artificially constructed "reality" gives way to the spirit world, during key moments in de Falla's balletic score. The choreography injects flamenco silhouettes, framing arm movements, fluttering hands, and muffled rhythms into those more classical music structures. Although the influence of gypsy music colors de Falla's score, Gades and Saura "flamenquize" the original music with the integration of authentic flamenco *palos* and the juxtaposition of flamenco bodies on top of the score.

Like *Bodas de Sangre* and *Carmen*, *El Amor Brujo* deals with the theme of ill-fated lovers. In a gypsy village, their fathers promise that Candela will marry José when the children reach maturity. Poor Carmelo loves Candela since childhood, but he must respect the vow taken by the elders. José and Candela marry, but he is unfaithful to her and falls in love with Lucía. One night, while out with Lucía, José is stabbed to death in a knife fight. Carmelo had fought at his side, but has the bad luck to be on the scene when the police arrive, and he is sent to jail. Candela is haunted by José's ghost. Every night, she meets him at the spot where he was killed, and they dance.

Lucía is dancing with José when the knife fight occurs. They are part of one of the groups of young people who wander through the village, dancing and singing. She is the only woman to accompany this group of men. Another man tries to dance with her, but José won't allow it. Here, the dancing marks sexual possession. The infiltrator reminds José that he is already married and has no claim on Lucía. Insults are exchanged, and the fateful brawl begins.

Lucía, the fatal dancing woman, provokes violence and disrupts the social order. José dies defending her honor, Candela lives a haunted existence, and Carmelo serves a prison term because of her. Like the character of Carmen (in fact, the same actor who played Carmen plays Lucía, Laura del Sol) the narrative is propelled by her unruly behavior. In the end, she must be brought into submission by a communal rite that consigns her to the world of ghosts with her lover, José.

The developmental arc of the "flamenco trilogy" first establishes the categories of sexual difference in flamenco and then explores the stereotype of the female dancer. By calling attention to the construction of Carmen the character in her array of clichés, the director and choreographer reveal the artificiality of the stereotype. They call attention to the tension between the "authentic" flamenco content of the films and the stories that have come to represent flamenco—Federico García Lorca's play, Prosper Mérimée's novella, and de Falla's ballet. This choreographic and filmic effort marks a re-appropriation of Carmen the stereotype by the exotic Other. In terms of a post-colonial discourse, the character of Carmen provides an opportunity to directly address the means by which the colonial stereotype has been imposed upon flamenco. The space of the dialogue, the very possibility of that dialogue, opens up new spaces for the analysis of flamenco's social history.

Despite, or perhaps because of, the performing and performative critique of flamenco as a cultural icon in Saura and Gades's work, the response to these works within the flamenco community, particularly among non–Spanish purists, has been one of ambivalence and caution. Although these works use fragments of traditional flamenco vocabulary and deal with familiar gypsy or Spanish themes, they also introduce new dance styles, frame them with unusual camera angles, and couch the elements of flamenco in the larger context of the epic film narrative. Claus Schreiner captures the frustration of many purists when confronted with the popularity of the "flamenco trilogy": "But what is to be made of Saura's *Carmen* or *Blood Wedding*? No matter how well Antonio Gades and his troupe dance in these films, or how well-crafted, they have little to do with true flamenco."[16] In this context, "true flamenco" is defined by the non–Spanish practitioners and scholars of the form, not necessarily by Spanish flamencos. The argument avoids direct confrontation of issues of race, artistic origin, or cultural ownership.

Instead, the criticism of these works takes place in the realm of adherence to the standards of a discipline. Since traditional flamenco dance does not follow the structure of a story, relies upon the unrehearsed spontaneity of improvisation, and follows very strict codes in terms of innovation and adulteration of the dance vocabulary, Saura and Gades's works are often regarded as splendid theatrical spectacle, but not "true flamenco." However, their collaborations serve as an important example of the investigation of the role of the dancer as a figure of performance. In contrast to historical narratives produced by non–Spanish flamencophiles, they theorize a flamenco subject capable of self-representation. The stereotype of the flamenco dancer fragments and recombines to speak for the complicity of the flamenco subject in the process of flamenco's historical subjugation. These films paved the way for future flamenco projects undertaken by Carlos Saura, which enter the dialogue of purists in the recounting of flamenco's history, the definition of tradition, and reconfigure the role of practitioners in determining flamenco's future.

5

Realism Reinvented

Following the collaboration with Antonio Gades, Carlos Saura went on to produce two more films, very different in their approach, based on flamenco/Andalusian music and dance forms: *Sevillanas* (1992) and *Flamenco* (1995).[1] Unlike his collaborative work with Gades, the two newer works do not use a play, an opera, or a ballet to serve as the basic plot structure for the film. Instead, *Sevillanas* and *Flamenco* present, in a documentary-like structure, examples of contemporary singers, dancers, and musicians in performance. In these films, practitioners from different regions—children, adolescents, adults and octogenarians, men and women—perform as performers, a "willed submission to a cluster of artistic and social mythologies," as Marvin D'Lugo suggests, but not as fictional characters, in a sequence of music and dance numbers. The ordering of these performances does not conform to a conventional narrative format; that is, there is no story of "fictional characters who are bound inextricably to fatalistic scenarios."[2] Instead, professional and amateur flamencos are shown gathered in a studio space to solemnly and skillfully display extraordinary examples of music and dance. Despite the serious, performance-oriented tone of these works, the camera occasionally captures a singer asking the director if she can do it again, or a dancer heaving a sigh once his performance is finished. The absence of characters or an overarching dramatic plot and the inclusion of "accidental" moments of informality place these films closer to the category of the documentary than the epic narrative structure of the "flamenco trilogy."

However, these films also depart from the documentary format in important ways. The performances are staged for the camera in a studio. The lighting and the angles of the camera suggest a well-rehearsed production, calculated to artfully frame each individual performance. Dancers change facing to approach the camera, and the camera pans out from the group, circles them, or frames them from the ceiling of the studio. None of the performances approximate a "real-life" event in a home, a *juerga*, or a *tablao*.

Even the inclusion of "spontaneous" moments reads as calculated break from the moment of "rehearsed" performance.

While these films do not neatly fit into the categories of either epic film drama or documentary, they contain elements of both. Saura's collaborations with Gades have played a role in the production and distribution of flamenco's popular image in an international context. *Sevillanas* and *Flamenco* introduce new concerns—such as the use of the documentary format by artists living under the Franco regime as a form of resistance—and resurrect old tensions—like the issues of purity and contamination in flamenco performance. Saura's treatment of these tensions suggests new directions in representations of flamenco on film. Saura's newer works point toward a critique of Franco's *nacionalflamenquismo* as they embrace diverse perspectives on contemporary flamenco performance.

The Documentary and Nacionalflamenquismo

Between 1971 and 1973, a flamenco documentary series, *Rito y Geografía del Cante Flamenco* was produced by Spanish National Television and aired, in 100 half-hour segments, on Channel Two. William Washabaugh, the American flamencologist, discusses the political context of this documentary series in his book *Flamenco: Passion, Politics and Popular Culture* (1996).[3] He points to at least three issues underpinning the importance of the program in its particular historical moment. First, the *Rito* series was produced by an "anti-establishment" group of "authors," Mario Gómez, Pedro Turbica, and José María Velázquez. The creators shared the tasks of directing, writing, filming and editing the segments, a socialist distribution of labor, which could be interpreted as a deliberately *anti-franquista* decision at the onset of the project. Second, these "liberal" collaborators aired their series on Channel Two of Spanish National Television, the only alternative to mainstream television programming available to Spanish viewers, and a limited number of them at that, for many of the provinces of Spain did not receive it. The development of Channel Two coincided with an increasingly "liberal" radio presence in Seville, "Radio Vida." Channel Two and "Radio Vida" shared some of the same contributors and together broadcast "anti-propagandist" programs devoted to flamenco.

The third important aspect of the *Rito* project has to do with the political undertones of flamenco performances featured in the documentary series. In the 1960s, Franco's government appropriated flamenco performance as a means of projecting an image of a unified Spain to foreign tourists and to Spaniards themselves. Given the status of flamenco under Franco, a documentary series on flamenco would not necessarily present a critique of the government; if anything, it would reinforce the *nacionalflamenquismo* rhetoric and policies already in place. The "official" version of flamenco deemphasized regional tensions and captured all of the accessible tourist images of Spain in light-hearted, entertainment-oriented stage shows for the *tablaos*. According to Washabaugh, "flamenco events were orchestrated in such a way as to give tourists the experience of sampling different facets of Spain's one diamond, different instantiations of the one body of Spain, all united in the same mystical way that the body of the Church is united" (162). However, the *Rito* project, in Washabaugh's analysis, "rescripted" flamenco. That is, "reframed [flamenco], inconspicuously fitted [it]out with a new agenda" (161).

This "rescripting" was accomplished by introducing fragmentation and ambiguity in the documentary representations of flamenco. While government-sanctioned flamenco performance was deliberately uniform and streamlined in the *tablaos* to promote the image of a multifaceted diamond, the *Rito* programs, presented in half-hour segments, used filmic conventions and directorial strategies to further undermine a single, coherent perspective on flamenco. Washabaugh's analysis of these programs points to several tactics employed in the "realist documentary" format to convey flamenco's multilayered complexity, an implicit critique of *nacionalflamenquismo*, and, ironically, a new kind of flamenco essentialism.

In Washabaugh's description of the first fifteen seconds of the title sequence, fragmented images of disembodied hands "clapping, knocking, tapping and strumming" (151) are juxtaposed on top of a *bulería falseta* performed by Pedro Peña. This series of images segues into an eight-second shot of a guitarist adjusting his guitar. The strikingly long shot of the guitar adjustment is followed by thirty seconds of credits, including "the network logo emerging from within line drawings of nineteenth-century flamenco figures" (150). According to Washabaugh:

> In the course of these sequences, viewers confront the juxtapositions of chaos and orderliness, uncenteredness and centeredness, noise and music, confusion and understanding. Each contrast is associated with a temporal phase, the past and the present, respectively. This medley of images and sounds provides viewers with the single strong impression that flamenco is a mysteriously attractive delight, though one not easily penetrated [151].

The ordering of the images, the alternation of fragmentation and long camera shots, and the insertion of nineteenth-century flamenco figures suggest a multilayered complexity that resolves in a coherent linear progression very much like a historical timeline. Washabaugh concludes, "The flamenco tradition, it seems, operates on a single line that moves from deep past to present and future, and that line varies only in intensity as it moves. Flamenco forces here seem to be analogous to geological forces. The past presses its heritage onto the present" (157). As in other historical representations of flamenco, the events of the past are isolated and then given significance through sequence so that they support the "reality" of the moment of "writing." The *Rito* series "writes" through its filmic representations, and this "writing" presents to the viewer a specific configuration of a desirable "reality," in which "authentic" flamenco is revealed in counterdistinction to the artificial spectacle of "tourist" flamenco.

The historical journey implied in the opening credits becomes a geographical one, very much like a tourist's trajectory through the different regions of Spain. The episodes in the *Rito* series take the viewer to different regions of Spain and show the diverse regional styles in commercial and private performance. According to Washabaugh:

> Almost every program in the series contains panoramic cinematography, a commonplace in travelogs. From roof tops, viewers scan Cádiz, Jeréz de la Frontera, Lebrija, and Utrera. From trains, viewers see the landscape rushing by as they travel from Despeñaperros to La Unión and from Córdoba to Sevilla.... All these different panoramic scenes with their distinctive panoramic techniques confirm the centrality of the trope of travel in the "Rito" films [167].

Here is where the ambiguity of "rescripting" subtly imparts its *antifranquista* message. On the surface, a historically accurate, travel-oriented approach to the landscape of Spain supports the state-sponsored appropriation of flamenco as a commodity intended for sale to tourists. However, the separateness of each episode emphasizes the distinction between the regions and their styles, a message that contradicts the calculated uniformity of *nacionalflamenquismo*. The heightened attention to the taxonomy and development of individual forms further underscores this fragmentation and emphasizes the diverse styles of flamenco present in a seemingly "singular" tradition. Washabaugh provides an example of this compartmentalization and attention to detail in the two episodes that show *pregones*, a song style used among vendors in one context and then "outside" its "original" context as a performance piece (169). The *Rito* series appears to be a representation of "official" flamenco on one level, but in its episodic, regional, and developmental approach to flamenco, it produces a counter-hegemonic representation of the art form's divergent paths and traditions.

The "authors" of the *Rito* series also provide, in a less subtle way, a critique of the tourist-oriented flamenco performance seen in the *tablaos*. The travelog provided by the programs features both commercial and private flamenco performances in what Washabaugh refers to as spatial terms, a "front region," and a "back region" (166). In his analysis, the "front region" is portrayed as the "artificial" spectacle of commercial flamenco, and the "back region" is depicted as the "authentic" experience of private flamenco. The programs travel "behind the scenes" of commercial flamenco performances in the *tablaos* to reveal the ways in which the spectacle is constructed for the audience. Washabaugh provides an example of one instance:

> Velázquez asks La Paquera, Manuel Soto "Sordera," La Perrata and numerous other artists whether they sing differently for public audiences and for private gatherings, a question [that] predisposes viewers to adopt a cynical frame of mind regarding public performances, even before they hear the artists' responses. Even more direct and provocative is the question addressed to José Pansequito: "It is sometimes said that singing in a tablao destroys a singer's quality ... what do you think?" [168].

By deliberately questioning the "authenticity" of public performances, the *Rito* series implies that the version of flamenco presented before commercial audiences is "artificial." Then, by providing examples of private flamenco performance, the programs suggest that the "real" flamenco exists in spaces previously unavailable to public view.

Finally, the "cinematographic tour" in the *Rito* series represents "authentic" flamenco by employing "tactics" from "realist" cinematography. The reification of the "reality" represented in these episodes is accomplished through the inclusion of everyday activities (at times deliberately staged for the camera), the revelation of "intimate" details of flamenco life, and carefully choreographed performances that contradict the images presented in commercial productions. Perhaps the most persuasive of these techniques used to depict the "authenticity" of the everyday is what Washabaugh calls "the revelation of secrets, the disclosure of things normally hidden from view, the unveiling of what is usually veiled" (171–2). These details include performances by flamenco artists who normally shy away from audiences, examples of flamenco forms usually reserved for gypsies alone, and attention to the idiosyncratic personalities of flamenco performers. By revealing to the audience those aspects of the lives of flamenco performers, the creators of the *Rito* series claim for their representation of flamenco an "authenticity" that stands in marked contrast to the state-sponsored performances of flamenco in the *tablaos*.

Washabaugh recognizes the political resistance in the strategies deployed in the *Rito* series, but he also points out the danger of misrecognizing the "realist" representations of flamenco as "reality":

> In the last quarter of the Franco era, *andalucista* opponents of Franco sought to advance their cause by undercutting Franco's uses of flamenco. They portrayed his *nacionalflamenquismo* as artificial spectacle, a tourist site to be visited while sampling Spain's delights. Real, authentic flamenco, they implied,

stands behind and beneath, in the "back region," visible only to those who are willing to set aside the artifice and propaganda of the front. Ironically, the "back region" is no less fictive—literally constructed—than the "front region." Ironically, too, filmic realism, an alleged medium of truth and enemy of fiction, is the style on which this fiction is founded [174].

For Washabaugh, what has emerged from the critique of one kind of essentialism, the portrait of Spain as a multifaceted flamenco diamond, is yet another: a purist's perspective on flamenco that only recognizes the "authenticity" of the everyday. The calculated, "realistic" choreography of the everyday is repressed at the moment of representation, very much like the effacement of the "moment of writing" in flamenco histories of the same era. Washabaugh's analysis of "realist" film techniques, and the agendas they serve, provide a solid foundation for the discussion of Saura's recent "realist" films. For *Sevillanas* and *Flamenco*, like the *Rito* series, employ filmic strategies borrowed from the documentary format and "realist" cinematography to represent contemporary flamenco performance. However, they also depart from these techniques in important ways, suggesting, alongside their historical positioning twenty-some years later than the *Rito* series, that their intention also differs.

Sevillanas *(1992) and* Flamenco *(1995)*

It is important, in a discussion of flamenco on film, to provide some background on *sevillanas* as a music and dance form. *Sevillana,* as a term, literally refers to a woman from Seville, but *sevillanas* is a traditional Andalusian folk form that was popularized through flamenco performance at the Ferias in Seville, in the *tablaos*, and as a social dance in nightclubs. Usually *sevillanas* is performed by couples in four *coplas*, and each section is preceded by a musical, usually guitar or vocal, introduction. The choreography for *sevillanas* has a basic structure that can be embellished according to the performer's wishes, but the many variations of the dance follow the standard pattern. Each section begins with at least one *paseo*, the distinctive *sevillanas* step that travels forward and back and is accompanied by *brazeo*. The *copla* ends with a *vuelta* (turn) and a *final* (pose). It can also be performed as a solo for a dancer with castanets, in a trio or a large group, and as a guitar or with different instrumentation. Most flamencologists do not treat *sevillanas* as a flamenco form, but recognize that it is often performed as a part of the *tablao* repertory. Due to its association with commercial flamenco, *sevillanas* is often negatively regarded as a "tourist's dance" by purists, but it has become so popular among flamencos and Spaniards as a social dance that it continues to be performed, enjoyed and even respected as a folk tradition. Saura's film *Sevillanas* displays a wide variety of styles and regional variations on the basic structure of *sevillanas*, from the percussive tradition of Lebrija to the balletic *escuela bolera* style, as a flamenco solo and as a duet for two guitars. At no point in the film does Saura explicitly state that *sevillanas* is a flamenco form; in fact, he is careful to label two performances as *sevillanas flamencas* and *sevillanas gitanas*, indicating that these are folk forms executed in a flamenco or gypsy style. However, some of the performers in the film are flamenco legends like Camarón de la Isla and Paco de Lucía, implying perhaps that while *sevillanas* is not a flamenco form, it has earned a place in the repertory of many respected flamenco performers.

Opening Credits *(Sevillanas)*

Sevillanas begins with a shot of a landscape. A crowd of people appear in silhouette beneath a tree at sunset. The members of the crowd pass one another, raising their hands in greeting, tipping hats, and moving their arms in patterns of *brazeo*. The title of the film is juxtaposed over this sequence. As the names of several flamenco luminaries fade in and out, the camera pans out slowly, revealing the silhouette image of the crowd as an illusion created by backlighting the dancers, who stand behind a muslin screen. The faint murmur of a crowd, talking and singing, is audible. The camera continues to pan out, and the wooden floor of the studio becomes visible in its frame. The borders of the screen also become visible, framed in by the walls and the ceiling of the room. When the name of the director finally appears, the last in the sequence of names, the camera has pulled back from the screen far enough to encompass a row of wooden chairs placed at a table.

Then, the camera switches perspective to show the participants, dressed in full *sevillanas* costumes, entering the space. The shots alternate in duration and frequency to suggest the gaze of a spectator who is also joining the group. In a series of momentary and then lingering "glances," the camera focuses on children running to the table, or on the mirrors of the studio at one side of the room. The audio track of the crowd's noise fades up as the people enter, older men and women settling at the tables, adult women adjusting the positioning of a flower or a comb in their hair, and a little girl riding in a stroller, the flounces of her skirt erupting around her. A boy and a girl practice the first steps of *sevillanas* as the crowd continues to move about in various activities of preparation. The camera focuses on the upper body of a guitarist strumming chords, then switches to a shot of teenage girls practicing *brazeo* at the mirrors as their instructors count out the *compás*. The camera slowly focuses on a tight shot of one girl's face as she takes in the path of her arms in the reflection of the mirror.

Like the opening credits for *Rito y Geografía del Cante Flamenco*, the first seconds of *Sevillanas* suggest a journey. However, rather than referring to a historical timeline, the sequence suggests a spatial journey, a shift in proximity and perspective in an enclosed area. The single image of a group gathered on the horizon in a social setting is revealed as a scene constructed for the camera. The names of professional flamenco legends like Paco de Lucía, Manolo Sanlúcar, Camarón, Merché Esmeralda, Lola Flores, and Tomatito, juxtaposed on top of the images, emphasize the setting of a staged performance. The viewer has the perspective of someone invited into a privileged space behind the scenes of a flamenco production. The shots of the participants who prepare for the performance mimic the gaze of the invited guest who peers over the shoulders of dancers and moves into close proximity to the performers, as a friend might be encouraged to sit at the family table.

While the creators of the *Rito* series used "realist" film tactics to chart a "behind the scenes" journey that portrayed the "front region" of flamenco in the *tablaos* as an artificial construction and the "back region" of private flamenco performance as "authentic" examples of flamenco life, Saura uses this opening scene to suggest the opposite. The informal, "authentic" gathering of the crowd at sunset dissembles into a carefully choreographed performance. The camera reveals the artificiality of the scene with a sympathetic, almost tender, attention to detail. The "realist" film tactic of showing the "accidental" moments of preparation for the performance implies that, while the scene has been deliberately staged and does not "spontaneously" arise from the gathering, no effort has been made to "fool" the audience. In the wake of the "purist" movement among flamencos who chose to represent "authentic" flamenco as a seamless fiction of the everyday in contexts like the *Rito* series, the opening scene of *Sevillanas* emphasizes the construction of that fiction.

Opening Credits (Flamenco)

The first image in the opening sequence of *Flamenco* is a shot of the cathedral windows and vaulted ceilings of the Plaza de Armas, a converted train station in Seville. A guitar solo, "Boceta" by Isidro Muñoz, begins, and the camera pans down to eye level. As the credits roll, the camera pans around the room, taking in the mirrors and partitions that break up the space. The reflections in the mirrors give the viewer a fragmented perspective on the interior of the space. For example, windows behind the camera appear in front of it. Many of the mirrors are tilted at different angles, further underscoring the kaleidoscope effect created by the play of light, the colors of the stained-glass windows, and the constellation of many planes reflected back at the camera.

The guitar solo accents and elongates musical phrases, and the camera matches its pacing. Scaffolding and lighting are visible in the space behind the tilted mirrors. The camera switches angles and begins to pan across the room, following the labyrinth of partitions assembled in the depth of the space. Another angle, and the camera pans from a close shot on the mirrors to the windows of the vaulted ceiling high above. The camera switches to a shot of the polished wooden floor. Lights come up, and the shadows of many legs traveling across the floor are visible. The camera opens on a wide shot of partitions assembled before stained glass windows, and chairs arranged in a large semi-circle. It zooms in on the chairs and pans along the semicircle, taking in each chair as a sequence. Cut to a sidelong shot of a few chairs placed in front of the mirrors, multiplying their numbers and again giving a multilayered perspective on the arrangement of the space. The camera switches to a wide shot of the interior of the space from the ceiling, with the cathedral windows visible on the horizon and the partitions forming an immense angular sculpture in the room. Cut to a shot of the backlit partitions, and a crowd of people visible in silhouette as they pass through the corridor formed by the muslin walls and enter a room in the maze. As the people walk behind the partition, a voice-over provides a brief history of flamenco as an introduction:

> Flamenco appeared in Andalusia, Southern Spain, in the mid–nineteenth century as a consequence of the intersection of *pueblos*, religions and cultures that gave way to a new kind of music: Greek songs, Arab poetry, Gregorian chants, Castilian ballads, Jewish laments, the rhythmic forms influenced by African cultures in diaspora (*el son de la negritud*) and the accent of the gypsy *pueblos* that came from far-off India to settle here—these elements combined and gave form to the art we now call flamenco, expressed in the song, the guitar and the dance.

Like *Sevillanas*, the opening sequences of *Flamenco* call attention to the space where the spectacle is staged. However, the use of fragmentation to suggest multiple layers of meaning is much more pronounced. The many shots of light reflecting off the surfaces of tilted mirrors reveal several perspectives from which the interior of the space can be seen. The partitions, mirrors, and scaffolding break up the vastness of the Plaza de Armas, a construction that contains the activity in a freestanding labyrinthine sculpture. Like the opening sequence of the *Rito* series, the camera's path in *Flamenco* suggests a spatial journey from chaos to organization. As the camera reaches the heart of the maze, people enter and the voice-over begins. The historical introduction to flamenco similarly guides the viewer from the chaotic origins of flamenco to the order of the contemporary moment.

The opening sequences of *Flamenco* share several representational strategies with the credits for the *Rito* series. A guitar solo accompanies and provides pacing for both examples, and both sequences move from "helter skelter imagery" (150) to a fairly coherent historical timeline that resolves itself in the present. The *Rito* series used line drawings and images from the 19th century to construct this timeline, while *Flamenco* employs a voice-over. Like *Sevillanas*, *Flamenco* suggests a spatial journey confined inside an architectural structure. The attention to the supporting structures of the building, and to the props used to construct specific visual effects, functions as a means of revealing the space, literally "behind the scenes." But, as in *Sevillanas*, this space is self-consciously displayed as a deliberately staged fiction.

The Performances (Sevillanas)

A sequence of eleven performances composes the body of *Sevillanas*. Each is marked by an on-screen label that denotes the region or style of the performance. The first performance, DE LEBRIJA, displays the style of *sevillanas* popularized in the town of Lebrija, famous for its flamenco families and "La Caracolá," the flamenco festival held there each year. The camera focuses on the faces of an older generation of men and women as they sing the opening bars of the *sevillanas de Lebrija*. Seated and standing in the arrangement of a family photo, the performers accompany themselves with guitar, *palmas*, tambourines, and household objects like *morteros*, metal mortars and pestles held sideways and played like bells. One man provides a bass-like percussive accompaniment by slapping the mouth of a clay jar with a canvas shoe.

As the second *copla* begins, a gray-haired man approaches one of the women in the group and the two dance as a couple. Her face registers surprise as she forgets and then quickly remembers a step. Their dance is not slick or technically difficult, but the small movements of their feet mark the *figuras* of the dance as their upper bodies pulse with the strong accents of this particular style. Their arms are arranged in the framing shapes that encircle the head and travel to the sides of their bodies in curves.

After the second *copla*, two elderly members of the group, a man and a woman, rise and take the place of the first couple. The third *copla* features traveling steps that spring up and down, and the dancing couple executes them with a combination of spriteliness and frailty. At times, the gentleman gestures to his elderly partner, indicating that she should move to a particular space, or travel in a specific direction. As they dance, the camera includes in its frame the other members of the group as they sit, accompany, and watch.

As the group sings the introduction to the fourth *copla*, the first couple joins the second in a quartet. The camera pans back to accommodate the dancers and the rest of the group, then zooms in on the lined faces of the dancers as they spin and pass one another. In the final moment of the song, one of the dancers falls out of her pose and corrects herself. The four dancers remain posed in a few seconds of silence, foregrounding the group.

This performance of *sevillanas de Lebrija* dramatically contrasts the stereotypical routines of the *tablaos*. The most striking element is the age of the performers. These are not healthy young bodies coaxed into attractive shapes by years of professional dance training. Their limbs do not extend into the exaggerated postures associated with Spanish dance: sternum thrust forward and backs arching above flat, lifted abdomens. As they perform for the camera, they forget steps, go the wrong direction, and stumble. They are not wearing "costumes," although they are decked out in suits and dresses. These performers have been transplanted from a social setting to a staged performance. The inclusion of their falterings, combined with their age, lends the sequence a sense of "authenticity" as it was established in the *Rito* series. If the stage dancers of the *tablaos* are an example of the artificial spectacle of tourist-oriented flamenco, then the aged *lebrijanos* represent "real" Spanish dance.

The second performance of the film, *sevillanas boleras*, displays the youthful bodies associated with professional, but not necessarily commercial, flamenco in a classroom setting. The term *boleras* refers to the tradition of *escuela bolera*, the classical Spanish dance forms that borrow from the vocabulary of ballet and regional Spanish folk dances. Young men and women dressed in ballet slippers, leotards and tights enter a room equipped with *barres*. They perform ballet stretches, play castanets, and execute *pirouettes* as the instructor moves from student to student, holding a leg extended *á la seconde*, adjusting a torso, and increasing the height of an *arabesque*. A group of musicians gathered in the corner tunes stringed instruments. The teacher calls the class to attention, and they begin a *brazeo* exercise from fifth position while playing castanets. She chooses six dancers, who line up as couples. The other students seat themselves on the edges of the space. After the introduction, the dancers perform the *sevillanas* choreography embellished with *battements, sissones,* and *battu* in exact unison. They end with a *final bien parada*, a pose that halts on the final note. Two of the dancers remain to perform the second and third *coplas* as the rest of the students accompany them on castanets.

It is difficult to imagine two more different examples of *sevillanas* than the first two performances of the film. The townspeople of Lebrija demonstrate the kind of performance usually found in popular settings, while the *bolera* students illustrate the rigorous training methods that produce professional dancers. Saura's directoral choices encompass the spectrum of several generations, regions, and class positions, suggesting that *sevillanas* as a folk and classical form has permeated the fabric of Spanish society at many levels. Like the *Rito* series, *Sevillanas* contradicts the *nacionalflamenquismo* message that flamenco and Andalusian dance stem from a single tradition. However, *Sevillanas* appears to self-consciously borrow from the "realist" cinematography of the *Rito* series to suggest the "artificiality" of the positions in the "front region" and "back region," tourist spectacle and private purism. The audience sees the missteps of the *lebrijanos*, and the preparation of the *bolera* students. In each case, though, the "documentary perspective" is tempered by the careful staging of the sequence, the choice of camera angles, and the obviously rehearsed choreography. The effect is a double critique: the *anti-franquista* message of heteronomy and difference remains, and a caution against the convenient categories of tourist and purist emerges. These same issues develop in the body of the film *Flamenco*.

The Performances (Flamenco)

Like *Sevillanas*, *Flamenco* begins with a *juerga* setting. La Paquera de Jeréz performs a *bulerías* that features four singers and four dancers in a larger ensemble. None of the performance sequences in *Flamenco* bear titles, as they do in *Sevillanas*. Unless the viewer recognizes the rhythmic structure of the forms, s/he must look to the ending credits to know the names of the forms and the names of the artists. As in all the performances in this film, the sequence begins and ends in darkness. The lights come up on a female singer who belts out the first notes of the *canción* as if it hurts her; she clutches at her sternum and throat, forcing the hoarse sounds to come out. The crowd responds with *jaleo* and *palmas*. The guitarists and other singers join in, and a male dancer rises from his seat to dance to her song. He performs an understated male solo, a flirtation of small gestures and marking with the feet. After the first solo, a male singer picks up the *letra* from his position in the crowd. An older woman emerges from the crowd to perform a solo to the group accompaniment. She wears a large *mantón*, or shawl, and, like the male dancer before her, she uses her fingers and arms to gesture toward the more full-blown shapes that characterize the flamenco silhouette and marks the rhythms with her feet.

A third male singer begins his solo. His voice has more of a nasal resonance than the other singers,' and each *melisma* seems to buzz around in his head before it issues forth from his mouth. A teenaged girl rises and performs a solo full of edges and exuberance. She wears a mini-skirt and flat shoes. Her dance, appropriate to her youthful age, is more dramatic and rhythmically daring than the previous solos. When she sits down, a fourth singer begins his solo. Another older male dancer rises to perform a solo in tandem. He employs periods of quiet, outbursts of *zapateado*, and sudden halts in his dance. When he finishes, he gathers the other three dancers in the space before the crowd, and the quartet performs a final sequence of choreography in unison as the group sings, plays *palmas*, and provides guitar accompaniment. The four dancers exit in *tablao* fashion, that is, in a line, with their arms raised in framing shapes. The song ends, and the lights fade.

The *bulerías* by the Paquera de Jeréz illustrates the *juerga* style of flamenco. Every participant is a performer, and the elements of song, guitar and dance play equally important roles. Older dancers move with as much witticism as athleticism, and the younger dancers use the opportunity to show off new steps. Clearly, though, in the final section of the dance, the movements have been choreographed. Again, the illusion of spontaneity is introduced and then disrupted. With his characteristic sense of simplicity and drama, Saura plays with the spectacle of the everyday and immediately follows with a classical performance of a *guajira* by Merché Esmeralda and her Grupo del Baile.

The *guajira* is a Cuban-influenced flamenco form, an example of the "son de la negritude," or the *cantes de ida y vuelta*, the "songs of coming and going" in the flamenco tradition. Spain's conflicted history of colonialism in Latin America is visible in the elements of this dance. The *letra* reminisces about a love left behind in Cuba, and the women wear long white dresses with trains, a nineteenth-century concession to Spanish female fashion, dresses that can still be seen in performances of *danzón* in Cuba. Merché Esmeralda performs a solo with a fan, full of the classical *brazeo* and balletic lines of the legs. Occasionally, demure phrases of *zapateado* comment on the lyrical rhythms of the *guajira*. A large group of women eventually joins Esmeralda and combines the elements of classical *brazeo* and *zapateado*— deep lunges in second position characteristic of modern dance, high leg extensions from ballet, and play with shawls and fans.

It is a sumptuous, gorgeous display bathed in a golden light. By including this established flamenco star in a film titled *Flamenco*, Saura implicitly claims that this Cuban-influenced, classically-informed dance is as flamenco as the *bulerías* performed by Paquera de Jeréz. Like the many regional forms featured in the *Rito* series, this spectrum of flamenco performance denies the *nacionalflamenquismo* message of uniformity. But perhaps even more scandalous is the inclusion of a *farruca* by international star Joaquín Cortés, a former member of the National Ballet of Spain and a "genuine" gypsy. Cortés's bloodlines make it difficult for purists, who believe in the primacy of the *gitano* contribution to flamenco, to dismiss him. Cortés, with his lean, ballet dancer's body, often displayed in shirtless, sweaty glory, grates against the purist's image of the understated masculinity of the *bailaor*. He further complicates matters by performing, in Saura's *Flamenco*, the *farruca*, the quintessential masculine dance.

In the darkness, the silhouette of Cortés can be seen departing from the corner where a trio of musicians sit playing stringed instruments. He takes off his jacket to appear in his signature bare torso and black satin pants as the trio plays an atonal, halting, barely recognizable *farruca*. The lights come up, and Cortés pauses, a shining muscular column. He alternates between the tightly controlled *zapateado* of the male flamenco dancer and expansive balletic shapes that cross the floor in seamless chains of turns. He stops to posture, often, as is his signature, but then he draws the tension of his body into his center and executes rapid, clear footwork. Occasionally, he isolates his movements in his hands, articulating the spiraling shapes associated with the female role. But then he dives back, torso lifted high above his legs, into a rhythmic phrase, and the elements of the *farruca* become clear again. He finishes his solo with a series of quick, controlled turns that whiplash and then halt. After the moment of stillness and the descent of darkness, he heaves a deep sigh, tosses his long hair, and walks, or maybe stalks, from the camera's frame in a loping gait.

In the 1990s, Joaquín Cortés was hailed as the new male sex symbol of flamenco. His agents marketed him as the new Michael Jackson, and Anna Kisselgoff described him as "A Provocateur at Large in the World of Flamenco," "dancing hand to crotch in one of his strongest heel-stamping solos."[4] He was conversationally referred to as "El Divino," as he danced, bare-chested, a female solo in *bata de cola*. Like Carmen Amaya before him, he took the U.S. and the rest of the world by storm, dazzling in his virtuosity and titillating in his gender play. But like Amaya, Cortés is a gypsy. His link to an "authentic" flamenco environment confounds the purists who would reject him on the basis of his "adulteration" of traditional flamenco. Saura's inclusion of Cortés in *Flamenco* suggests that the artist continues the tradition of flamenco, at least in the eyes of the director.

In the historical debates concerning flamenco and "authenticity," gypsies reign sovereign as the primary practitioners of flamenco. Although certain historians have attempted to downplay their role as the originators of flamenco, it is impossible to deny their part in the development of what we now call flamenco. Contemporary gypsy flamenco musicians like the members of Ketama and Tomasito, and gypsy dancers like Joaquín Cortés, combine various styles to produce popular, hybrid forms, much to the consternation of those enthusiasts who would prefer that the categories remain separate and fixed. These artists beg the question, again, "What exactly is a pure gypsy, or true flamenco?" A gypsy, at the time of Cervantes, or Mérimée, had a different ethnicity, a different community and way of life from that at the turn of the century or today. However, the category of "gypsy" retains some of its exotic, mythical significance in contemporary contexts. In flamenco dance, the "gypsy" style exists independently of gypsy bodies, or rather, constructs gypsy bodies through the layering of coded visual and audible signifiers. Gypsy and non-gypsy practitioners assume these characteristics as performers. Conversely, performers who claim gypsy heritage, no longer (if they ever were) isolated from other Spanish or global communities, adopt the musical and dance styles of other cultures in their artistic interpretations of established "gypsy" forms. In this fractal expansion of categories that overlap and blur, the "gypsy" style emerges as a set of culturally coded characteristics that simultaneously construct gypsiness as a category and are constructed by the category of "gypsy." Fusion forms developed by gypsy practitioners disrupt the illusion of coherence in the category of gypsiness, because the younger generation of gypsies performs distinctly "un-gypsy" qualities. The instability of these categories, and their "constructedness," is intelligible in the films *Sevillanas* and *Flamenco*.

Sevillanas *Flamencas,* Sevillanas *Gitanas*

In the sequence titled *sevillanas flamencas,* Manolo Sanlúcar strides, guitar in hand, toward Merché Esmeralda, who adjusts her red, ruffled dress and smoothes her hair in one of the mirrored panels that encircle half of the space. At a wooden table on the other edge of the room, another guitarist, a percussionist, and three *palmeros* sit. The musicians play the introduction to the *sevillanas,* and Esmeralda begins the first *copla.* She exaggerates the *brazeo,* flamenco style, with tight circles around the head and torso and flowery spirals of the fingers. Her *paseos* do not travel back and forth, but underneath her, causing her spine to undulate. The mirrors in the background multiply the number of musicians, making it appear as if she is performing before a larger group. Sanlúcar, seated in a chair at a distance from the rest of the musicians, inhabits the reflection in the mirror behind Esmeralda, as if he were partnering her.

Esmeralda changes the basic choreography of each *copla* so that she turns around herself, chasing her skirt, rather than a partner. She adds *zapateado* at certain places, and lunging walks that send her skirt billowing up toward her face. The set choreography for *sevillanas* describes figures on the floor, but in this version those patterns disappear. The spirals and circles wind themselves around her body instead, through her use of her arms, turns, and skirt play. *Sevillanas* involves the framing of the head and torso with the arms, creating a sort of "picture-frame" effect so the dancer may peer out at the partner. In this solo, though, the focus alternates from an external to an internal focus, so the dancer appears to look out through her arms at times and hide behind them at others. The choreographic embellishments on the set patterns of the *sevillanas* in this dance reveal those characteristics that have come to define the "flamenco style." Traditional flamenco dances are often performed by one dancer alone, especially in *juerga* sessions where musicians and dancers alternate solos. These solos take up little space, a concession, perhaps, to the small stages in the *cafés cantantes* and the *tablaos*. The insertion of developed *zapateado* against the rhythm of the music (*contratiempo*) also characterizes flamenco. And, although *sevillanas* may be performed in a large, ruffled skirt, usually the skirt's involvement in the dancing consists only of tracing the pathways of the legs after the fact. Esmeralda frequently grabs the hem of her skirts and twists them around her body, another flamenco trait. Perhaps the most subtle element of the differences between *sevillanas* and flamenco is the dancer's focus. Since a *sevillanas* dancer usually performs with a partner, the focus is projected outward to the other dancer. Esmeralda continually draws her focus inward, almost as if she were unaware of the presence of the spectator, intent upon her dialogue with the sound of the music. These elements become more pronounced in the performance of *sevillanas gitanas*.

The camera focuses on the profile of Camarón de la Isla, one of the most famous gypsy singers of contemporary flamenco. He died shortly after the filming of *Sevillanas*. The visual image of Camarón's face in profile, foregrounded by the title GITANAS, immediately signals to the viewer that what follows is to be a performance in the "gypsy style." His face, but most of all his voice, has become synonymous with the performance of gypsy identity in contemporary flamenco. James Woodall describes the reputation of Camarón among flamencos:

> The consensus is that Camarón displayed at his best everything, across a broad range of *jondo* and the lighter styles, that one could hope for from gypsy singing: immense force, pitch as perfect as can be expected by an idiom that sets little store by it, an *appoggiatura* that is almost painful in its intensity, and at the centre of all this a fearsome humanity instinct with expressive awareness of the burdens of his race.[5]

Woodall's characterization of gypsy singing includes the structural musical elements of the performance, like the broken, forceful *raspao* (raspy) voice and its attack or embellishments, but also endows these methods of projecting the voice with a sort of "racial memory," the pain that results from centuries of poverty and persecution. The question is not whether Camarón's singing results from "the burdens of his race," but whether these elements of the song style are aligned with these experiences and represent, for both the spectator and the performer, gypsy identity. Soulful and coarse, lacking the prettified elements of commercial or classical flamenco, Camarón's voice further articulates this portrait of gypsy life through the four separate *letras* set to the *sevillanas copla* structure: "Mi barrio," "Dame la mano," "Toma que toma," and "Pa que me llamas prima." These verses describe scenarios and details that are archetypal in gypsy *letras:* nostalgic portraits of a gypsy neighborhood, flamenco, *zapateado*, and familial loyalty.

Intercut with close shots of Camarón singing to the accompaniment of two guitarists, Manuela Carrasco performs a flamenco solo in the "gypsy style." Unlike Merché Esmeralda, whose long slender arms curve in almost spidery threads away from her classically proportioned body, this dancer is round and fleshy. The camera first focuses on her as she performs phrases of furious footwork that resolve in abrupt turns. The momentum of her turns cause the flounces of the skirt to swirl around her body; she grabs its hem and pulls it in the opposite direction of her travel. She kicks her knees up high to cause a cascade of ruffles. The fringes of her *mantón* fly into her face and catch in her hair. She sinks into a bent-knee stance as she performs marking steps during the *retirando* phrases of Camarón's singing; then she lashes into turns and abruptly halts. She occasionally performs the basic choreography of the *sevillanas*, but, like Esmeralda, she pulls the traveling steps beneath her, turns weighted steps into *zapateado*, and uses her arms to conceal and reveal, rather than frame, her body.

Like the *sevillanas flamencas*, this version of *sevillanas gitanas* replaces the set choreography for the *sevillanas* with elements of flamenco vocabulary. Both performances feature a solo dancer and reconfigure the space so that the dancer advances and retreats, resolving each phrase with a turn and manipulations of the skirt. Interestingly, Saura positions the guitarist Manolo Sanlúcar in the reflections of the mirrors so he appears to partner Merché Esmeralda at a distance, while Camarón and the "gypsy" dancer perform always apart, and the camera splits its attention between the two of them. The effect of this spatial blocking further enhances the solitude of the dancer or the singer and negates the partnering of the traditional *sevillanas*. While Merché Esmeralda undulates her torso and performs elegant, classical shapes with her arms, Manuela Carrasco exaggerates the abruptness of her turns, halts unexpectedly, and performs more rhythmically complex *zapateado*. The "gypsy style" features more manipulations of the skirt and an intense internal focus on the dancer's part, so that when she breaks from her absorption to gaze at the camera, she looks almost hostile, as if her reverie were interrupted by the camera's attention.

The performance of the "gypsy style" exaggerates the "unrefined" elements of flamenco song and dance. These characteristics contribute to the "untutored" aura of gypsy performance, read as more "authentic" than the classically influenced commercial or professional performances of flamenco. The intimacy of the dancer's internal focus, and the camera's apparent intrusion on that privacy, echo the spatial division of commercial and private flamenco performance established in the *Rito* series. However, there is only the *performance* of privacy and presentationality, because all of these sequences have been staged as a spectacle for the camera. There is no "front region" or "back region," but only the spectacle and the apparatuses that support the spectacle. In a symmetrical commentary on the role of the popular incarnations of flamenco, *fiesta* and *juerga* sessions where non-professional performers celebrate in song and dance, Saura ends both *Sevillanas* and *Flamenco* with large, informal group performances.

Endings: Sevillanas

The final sequence of the film, CORRALERAS, begins with a shot of Rocío Jurado standing on a raised platform in a crowd of children dressed in full Feria costumes. The girls wear short-sleeved dressed with large ruffles at the shoulders, flowers in their hair, and many layers of flounce in the skirts. The boys wear dark suits with white shirts, and a few have red scarves at their necks. The red-haired singer addresses the children: "¿Dónde estamos?" "¡En Sevilla!" "¿Adónde vamos?" "¡A Sevilla!" "¿De qué cantamos?" "¡De Sevilla!" The group cheers, and the *palmas* for the first *copla* begins. The musicians join in and the children assemble in couples. Like Camarón, Jurado sings a different *sevillanas letra* for each copla.[6] The camera pans back to reveal the adults positioned at the edges of the crowd and the familiar backlit screen. The image of the adult dancers in silhouette echoes the first image of the film, in which the crowd appeared to be dancing outdoors at sunset beneath a tree. The camera zooms back in to focus on the faces of the children as they perform their choreography with great solemnity. Their wide eyes meet the camera's gaze without flinching. The camera switches to shots of the raised figure of Jurado, who articulates her hands in flowery shapes as she sings. It switches back again to focus on the dancers' feet as they perform the unison choreography. The pattern of the camera's changes matches the rate at which it "glanced" about the room in the opening sequences. Finally, the camera pans back from the crowd and moves up to the reflective surface of the ceiling, where the scaffolding of the building and the inverted image of the dancers is visible. The credits roll on this final image, and the screen fades to black.

This final sequence approximates a performance of *sevillanas* at the Feria de Sevilla, where large groups assemble to celebrate in the streets of the city. And yet, the screen in the background reminds the viewer that the performance takes place in an enclosed building. Consistently, Saura's directoral choices point to the illusion of untouched informality and the construction of the spectacle available to the camera's gaze. D'Lugo's theories of Saura's work emphasize the role of performance, and in Jurado's exchange with the children, the performers seem to actively and self-consciously embody the "figure of the Spaniard as performer of a cultural ethos to which his own identity appears irrevocably bound."[7] Part of this performativity involves invoking cultural symbols and practices associated with Spanish or regional identities, but Saura seems to add another element to the representation of performance, the role of seeing. Documentary representations of flamenco use the camera to access sights previously withheld from the outsider's gaze. Although Saura's work borrows certain techniques from Spanish documentaries of the 1970s, it does not allow for a clear distinction between "outsiders" and "insiders," "tourists" and "purists," "gypsies" and "Spaniards." His exposure of flamenco reveals not the secret practices of closed circles, but the mechanics of representation, the construction of spectacle, and how the camera guides the process of seeing.

This disruption of the categories of the "front region" and the "back region," as Washabaugh defines them, has implications for the perception of flamenco in the new millennium. If, as Washabaugh asserts and Saura demonstrates, the categories of commercial and gypsy flamenco are equally constructed as convenient fictions, other categories, like "race" and "authenticity," begin to unravel. This betrayal of the desiring subject by the exotic object of desire marks the final performance in *Flamenco*.

Endings: Flamenco

The gypsy group Ketama, with guest artist Manzanita, begin the final sequence of the film, a *rumba*. Like *guajira*, *rumba* is a Cuban-influenced form that may have originated as early as the sixteenth-century colonizing exploits in the Caribbean.[8] And, like *sevillanas*, *rumba* has earned the contempt of many purists due to its light-hearted (as opposed to *jondo*) feeling and its popularity in the *tablaos* since the 1950s. However, among young flamencos and Spaniards in general, the *rumba* is very popular as a social dance. Indeed, the Gipsy Kings (Spanish gypsies living in France) have earned millions of dollars and adoring audiences all over the world with their recordings of *rumbas*. The young performers begin with *palmas* and sing "Verde que te quiero verde." No halting *retirando*, no *raspao* voices, no stories of persecution; this is a pop song. As if summoned, young men and women pour in through the space between the partitions and begin to dance. In couples and alone, dressed in street clothes, they mark rhythmic phrases with their feet, extend their arms above their heads and around their torsos. The women pull their hair up and flirt over shoulders. Besides borrowing a Caribbean rhythmic structure, *rumba* is a flamenco dance that allows for the swaying of the hips in the Afro-Caribbean tradition. The inclusion of *rumba* at the end of *Flamenco* suggests the future forms of flamenco in a global context. As an art form, flamenco has never existed in a cultural vacuum. Saura's choices acknowledge the past influences of cultures outside of Spain in the development of flamenco and gesture toward a future that embraces hybridization and experimentation in the context of flamenco as a tradition.

The global success of Saura's vision as a director, in collaboration with Antonio Gades and on his own, has perhaps both inspired and intimidated other directors in their attempts to represent flamenco on film. Although the array of instructional videos that have proliferated since the invention of an internet marketplace staggers the imagination, comparatively few new films about flamenco have been produced in the past ten years. The legacy of the *Rito* series and the success of Saura's quasi-documentary style have yielded more documentaries about flamenco in the global marketplace than feature films. Enthusiasm surrounding the subject achieved critical mass in 2005, when the Sala Cardamomo in Madrid produced the first flamenco film showcase. Organizers curated three months' worth of programming along three different themes: Carlos Saura films, documentary films, and Gypsy films. The festival opened with a tribute to Antonio Gades and closed with a screening of Michael Meert's *Herencia Flamenca*, a documentary that tells the story of the Habichuela clan (the gypsy family that has produced several generations of significant flamenco artists like Pepe Habichuela and Ketama) and their transformation from poverty to international stardom.

Flamenco Women *(1997)*

An unexpected documentary appeared during the years following Saura's *Flamenco* and *Sevillanas*, from feature film director and musician Mike Figgis, called *Flamenco Women*. Figgis is best known for *Leaving Las Vegas* (1995), a film that earned him two Academy Award nominations for Best Director and Best Adapted Screenplay. *Flamenco Women* (1997) follows an ensemble of female dancers in Madrid for six days, from the rehearsal process through a performance, shifting from black and white to color footage. The documentary did not receive a great deal of public attention, although the amateur reviews listed on sites like amazon.com reflect the easy rancor of the flamenco community when it comes to representations of flamenco. In this work, Figgis captures two of the most successful international stars of flamenco, Eva La Yerbabuena and Sara Baras, at a stage in their careers before they were established as world-class talents.

The film opens with some slow-motion footage of La Yerbabuena rehearsing over the sound of her thunderous footwork and then segues into a brief introduction from the director. Responding to a prompt off-camera, Figgis explains his intent for the film:

> This is a film about flamenco. Flamenco is a celebration of life. The celebration acknowledges death not only as a possibility, but as an inevitability ... and it acknowledges the mother and ... it is very feminine. I wanted to make a film which somehow captured the essence of flamenco, so I went to Madrid and I put together a company very, very quickly and in six days shot continually as we started from scratch and made a performance that on the sixth day became a public performance, so there's a lot of tension. It was an experiment and I had no idea whether or not the performance was good or whether they had enough time, but it was an attempt to create the kind of energy I thought was appropriate to a flamenco performance.

The images of death and femininity that frame Figgis's introduction recall the flamenco stereotype, but they only appear in his introduction. The documentary runs as a series of raw takes from the Amor de Dios studios in Madrid (just as Gades sought out his Carmen), through a punishing rehearsal process, culminating in a public performance that features some unorthodox costumes from "Vacas Flamencas" and a handful of celebrities in the audience.

Most of the footage reflects the rehearsal process, which involves the relentless repetition of footwork and transitions, disagreements between musicians and dancers, costume malfunctions, and gallons of perspiration from the performers. If Figgis wanted to conjure the "essence" of flamenco in this film, then it would have to be backbreaking work. Figgis captures the labor of the female performers and their struggle to communicate with musicians and other dancers steeped in the same traditions. In an interview about the process, Yerbabuena remarked, "Flamenco is highly competitive in a rather negative way. Dancers are reluctant to share the fruits of their experience. Teachers might refuse to teach their students the secret of particular steps. At its worst, flamenco is seen as a race in which you knock everyone else out of the way."[9]

In one section, Sara Baras repeats her *escobilla* for an *alegrías* several times with the musicians, each time revealing her intentions for the musicality of the footwork phrasing. To the naked eye, or untrained ear, it might seem as if she is just repeating the pattern, but with each repetition, she excavates the structure of the musical role played by the dancer in dialogue with the guitar and cajón. Both Yerbabuena and Baras are groundbreaking artists in terms of their composition of dances. Hailed as "Nuevo flamenco" in the 1990s, both artists practice in a way that has become the standard for female performers coming of age in the 21st century. They implement "el arte," or *brazeo*, the use of the arms to sculpt the space surrounding the body, in marking phrases during the *letras*, but footwork plays a much more significant role in their work than in the work of women in previous generations. Although Carmen Amaya popularized footwork for women in the 1950s, few artists could approach her level of expertise, and women still relegated footwork to the *escobilla* section of most *palos* through the 1980s. In this film, Figgis captures the way that Yerbabuena and Baras weave footwork into sections previously dominated by the work of the arms and hands, *mantón*, and skirt. Make no mistake, they perform the more traditional feminine roles, but they compose their solos much in the way that jazz musicians do, with the developing patterns that refer back to the skeleton structure of the *compás*. Most of that development occurs through footwork, and not only in the musical sections previously reserved for *zapateado*, like the *escobilla* or *grupo de pie*. Instead, footwork pervades each section, even the phrases of the *letra*, which were once done in silence to allow the singer's voice to be heard.

Although the film perhaps only intended to document an experiment or sought to "capture an essence" that is more about the poetry and imagery of flamenco, Figgis memorialized a moment in flamenco history. With Yerbabuena and Baras, flamenco women began to articulate a technical proficiency equal to the male role, with a compositional sophistication that matches the masculine world of musicianship. These women are not just "translating" the musical ideas of guitarists or singers. They disrupt the relationship between the steps and their traditional arrangements. The space they create while still falling within the realm of "appropriate" behavior—as flamencos, as women in flamenco—allows the next generation, the subject of Chapter 7, to take still more risks in performance. However, before the experiments of Chapter 7 can be make legible, it is necessary to return, once again, to the construction of the exotic stereotype to prepare the scene for its unraveling.

6

Reinterpreting the Exotic

This chapter proposes a new introduction to key concepts as well as potential directions for new inquiries into the history of flamenco. The emergence of the flamenco stereotype reveals not only the processes to which flamenco and its practitioners have been subjected over time, but the failure of those strategies to contain the dancing body. Second, the construction of the dancing body across several discursive systems, or more pointedly, the ways in which the flamenco body has exceeded all attempts to represent it, shows the possibilities for resistance to homogenization, fossilization, and extinction already present in the tradition. Third, a potentially subversive space for reasserting voices previously rendered subaltern in the process of representation lies in the moment of improvisation. Improvisation allows for the negotiation of recognizable codes among a community of informed participants, performers and audience members alike. Finally, it is the gleeful citation of shared "texts" that assures the survival of flamenco through a renegotiation of the politics of representation.

The debates in the canon of flamenco scholarship demonstrate the ways in which historical narratives simultaneously shape and are shaped by ideology. This mutually constituting relationship gives rise to a particular kind of subject, steeped in desire. The object of fascination, the flamenco exotic, transforms in response to the desiring gaze. However, as the films of Saura and Gades reveal, this process is multi-directional. Despite its genesis as a product of colonial relations, the flamenco stereotype should not be unilaterally dismissed as simply the excess of power relations destined to disempower flamenco artists.

Innumerable practitioners and aficionados participate in the reproduction of the stereotype as a means of articulating a new subject position, the authorial voice. Once established, the flamenco subject can "talk back" to its viewer and engage in the dialogue that shapes its own construction. Inhabiting the stereotype allows the flamenco subject access to the spectacle of exoticism and skews the relationship between the colonial gaze and its object.

This disruption allows a flood of competing voices to enter the matrix of power relations, which, in turn, affects the construction of meaning. The positioning of participants in the spectacle fragments, refracts, and changes continuously. Like the kaleidoscope of light in the opening sequence of Saura's *Flamenco,* multiple perspectives shift in relationship to each other, and the overall pattern transforms from moment to moment. In fact, every incarnation of the flamenco stereotype reflects a crisis of divergent viewpoints. Debates and contradictions mark a struggle for the assertion of one voice among many. The revisitation of one particular Carmen in flamenco history shows how the stereotype can be manipulated to introduce complicity and resistance in the process of representation.

Calculated Unruliness

When Carmen Amaya emerged on the international scene in 1941, the stereotype of the gypsy dancer was imbued with new meaning in the context of American politics. Her significance as an Orientalist exotic from Spain was further informed by the political relationship between the United States and Latin America. President Franklin Delano Roosevelt had, in 1928, released a statement concerning the nature of the relationship he envisioned between the United States and Latin America, a step away from the aggressively militaristic, "interventionist" policies of previous administrations:

> It is possible in the days to come ... one of our sister nations must fall upon evil days; disorder and bad government may require a helping hand be given her citizens as a matter of temporary necessity to bring back order and civility. In that event it is not the right or the duty of the United States to intervene alone.[1]

Potentially unruly and feminized Latin countries would not be forcefully met, but instead fostered toward more appropriate behavior by a "big brother" figure. This approach to international relations was dubbed "The Good Neighbor Policy." No longer would the United States take the position of imperial interloper in the developing self-governance of Latin American countries. In his inaugural address of 1933, President Roosevelt articulated the responsibilities of the Good Neighbor:

> I would dedicate this Nation to the policy of the good neighbor—the neighbor who resolutely respects himself, and, because he does so, respects the rights of others—the neighbor who respects his obligations and respects the sanctity of agreements in and with a world of neighbors.[2]

This statement eventually had important implications for the alignment of Allied Forces against the Axis Powers during World War II. By 1943,

In this undated portrait of Carmen Amaya, she appears in *traje corto*, the male dancing costume (Jerome Robbins Dance Division, New York Public Library for the Performing Arts, Astor, Lenox and Tilden Foundations).

Argentina was alone among the members of the Pan-American Union in its continuing relations with Axis governments.

In this atmosphere of filial alignment among American nations, the colonial stereotype of Mérimée's Carmen transformed into the differently configured exotic Latina. This metamorphosis in representation was facilitated by the producers of Hollywood cinema. According to the film scholar Carlos Cortés, social disruption in Europe, culminating in World War II, deprived Hollywood of a major film market, increased the economic significance of Latin American audiences, and made Hollywood more sensitive to Latin American reactions. Once the United States entered the war, Latin America's strategic importance prompted the U.S. government to be an even better neighbor.[3]

The United States' new attentiveness to Latin American audiences and performers resulted in policy changes for Hollywood film:

> The U.S. Office of the Coordinator of Inter-American Affairs, under Director Nelson Rockefeller, stressed the need for U.S. motion pictures to help solidify the Americas in common struggle against the Axis powers. The Hays Office, Hollywood's official self-censor, appointed a Latin American expert to help Hollywood avoid filmic blunders which might offend Latin Americans.[4]

However, these good intentions were calculated to fix the Latina stereotype in such a way that she still embodied the exotic Other. According to Carlos Cortés: "Two characteristics stood out in most front-line depictions of Latino in the 1930s and early 1940s—frivolity and sensuality."[5] Cortés chooses actresses Carmen Miranda and Dolores del Rio as examples of the polar opposite, frivolous and sensuous, extremes on the limited Hispanic-actress spectrum. Miranda, star of the 1940 film *Down Argentine Way*, represented the laughable Latina, through her elaborate headdresses, abstracted pseudo-samba, and singing in gibberish. According to Cynthia Enloe, she was "confined to light roles, treated by the studios as a comic or character actor, never a romantic lead."[6] By contrast, Dolores del Rio portrayed the "morally pure" component of the Hispanic stereotype. She exhibited "a special kind of sensuality, consistently restrained and ladylike (as that term was used in those days)...."[7]

In the spirit of "cooperation," American audiences greeted first the "Brazilian Bombshell" Carmen Miranda in 1939 and then the "Human Vesuvius" Carmen Amaya in 1941 as splendid examples of passionate and entertaining Latin talent and temperament. They were more than willing to see past the differences in national and cultural origins of Carmen Miranda and Carmen Amaya and to lump together the disparate dance traditions of the samba and flamenco in order to see only the transforming stereotype of

Mérimée's *Carmen,* set in what they hoped to be the appealing backdrop of U.S and Latin American relations. While dangerous and unruly, the feminized stereotype of Latin America could be seduced, encouraged in her subordinate position to the decidedly masculine authority of the U.S. The scenario was highly appealing. In an article from the *Boston Traveler,* Tom O'Sullivan links the success of Cuban-born Desi Arnaz, the Brazilian Carmen Miranda, and the Spanish Gypsy Carmen Amaya to the "Good Neighbor Policy" between the U.S. and Latin America: "There may be some doubt as to, eventually, how effective our 'good neighbor' policy turns out below the border, but there can be no doubt about the success of the South American Way in this country." [8] A reporter from the *Boston Herald* recognized Carmen Miranda, Desi Arnaz, Xavier Cugat, Don Arres, and Carmen Amaya as "unofficial couriers of Pan-American good will" after Amaya danced before President Roosevelt in the White House. [9]

Although the American press portrayed Amaya as one of a host of Latina/o exotics, she also retained some of the qualities of Mérimée's Carmen. As a "full-blooded gypsy" who toured and performed with her extensive family, she evoked the image of the cigarette girl who wandered the Andalusian countryside with her band of criminals. She was described as "serpentine, sleek and quick as a whiplash, furiously animal, exotic and exciting"[10] at Carnegie Hall in 1942. Promotional flyers produced by Sol Hurok called her "A Female Blowtorch," "The World's Greatest Flamenco Dancer," and "A Package of Primitive Passions." In one particularly telling anecdote, a photographer asked her to pose for a "sexy shot." She threatened to slit his throat.[11] In 1942, Virginia Mishnun described Carmen Amaya as "the real thing; she is pure gipsy, with tempestuous black hair, a red gash of a mouth, and a scrawny body that has the resilience and speed of an alley cat."[12] Her performance is "dance[d] straight and hot from the bowels; as it is felt in the blood, not only of Carmen, but of the ancient gipsy race to which she belongs."[13] Like Mérimée's Carmen before her, by nature of her bloodlines, Amaya promised to perform the characteristics of the Orientalist imagination.

However, an important element of Amaya's performance distinguished her from other female flamenco artists like La Argentina or La Argentinita, who enjoyed commercial success in Europe, South America and the United States during the early twentieth century: Amaya performed the masculine dances in *traje corto,* the traditional male costume. She was not the first example of female cross-dressing in the history of flamenco, and she did not perform the masculine roles to the exclusion of the feminine roles, but Carmen Amaya gained international recognition through her unique, highly competent mastery of the masculine roles.

In the short film *Carmen Amaya in Her Original Gypsy Dances* (c. 1940), she is dressed in *traje corto*—a short jacket and high-waisted trousers—but she wears the feminine dancing shoes with high heels and ankle straps. In the first movements of the solo, she elongates her spine, raises her arms above her head, and sinks into an elastic, bent-knee stance. She has an unusually wide, powerful torso, visible through the shiny fabric. With the coiled energy of a spring, she slowly sends one leg out and digs the ball of her foot into the floor. A twist of a hip, then she retracts it and sends out the other leg. Carmen builds a rapid sequence of footwork. Her fingers grasp the lower edges of her jacket, and she settles still deeper into her stance. From that open and powerful position, the weight of her upper body is drawn up and away from her legs, leaving them free to slice in and out and down, and delivering solid, clear sounds through the contact of her heels with the floor. She executes a rapid turn and halts without any excess of momentum. She attacks the floor again, turns, and changes direction. Faster now, she travels and punctuates her steps with occasional moments of stillness. An improvisational artist (it is rumored that she never choreographed her performances), she plays with the *compás*, moving in counter-time or on top of the strident rhythm. Her solo culminates in a display of rapid-fire footwork, as she grimaces and clutches the edges of her jacket. In the final moment, she brings one arm above her head in a hard-edged flourish.

Through her highly publicized gypsy identity, Amaya registered in the American cultural landscape as a contemporary incarnation of Mérimée's Carmen. At the same time, she was positioned among a spectrum of exotic Latina/o entertainers, calculated to entertain American audiences by means of their comic abilities, superb musicianship, or "innate" sensuality. However, she managed to evade these pigeonholes even as she seemed to occupy them, because her masculine dances did not fit within the prescribed choreography for the Orientalist or the Latina exotic. In keeping with the nature of the colonial stereotype, her body threatened to move beyond the boundaries of what could be expected and threatened to assert a decidedly masculine agency over her presence in historical discourses.

The excess of Amaya's performance as an international symbol of Otherness is performatively demonstrated in the fragmented narrative of her life and art: all attempts to contain her "original" presence are frustrated by contradictory evidence. The accounts of Carmen Amaya's life in newspapers, magazines, and even more "scholarly" flamenco histories vary widely in their presentation of the "facts" of her life. No one has pinned down the exact date when she was born, and she herself contributed to the mystery surrounding her life in interviews. According to one frustrated, but enraptured, journalist:

In 1941 she admits she is twenty, in 1943 she has managed to become twenty-one, but by 1944 she is twenty again.... She is allegedly so primitive she neither reads nor writes, though it is reported elsewhere that she signs all family contracts and conducts business without professional advice. It is said that a theatre has been named for her in Buenos Aires, while another article insists she bought the theater and modestly named it after herself.[14]

By the time Carmen Amaya was brought to the U.S. in 1941 by entertainment impresario Sol Hurok, she had already attracted international attention as the "Queen of Flamenco Dance" in Portugal and Spain, holding court in the cities of Buenos Aires and Mexico City. The story, often repeated in periodicals of the time, goes like this: She was born into a family of dancers, singers, and guitarists in Granada, performed at the Barcelona Exposition at the age of seven, and at eight she starred in a Paris revue with Rachel Meller. When the Civil War broke out in Spain, the Amaya family fled to Argentina, where Carmen was "discovered" by Sol Hurok.

Dance scholar Meira Goldberg has conducted extensive research on the early tours of Carmen Amaya in South America. She suggests that Amaya represented a "Heart of Darkness in the New World" through her "gypsy" style: "She embodied the Spanish Gypsy aesthetic, so fascinating to Western audiences, in a new and distinctive way. Her dance still retained aesthetic values foreign to contemporary Western theatrical dance and which may indeed be characterized—in part—as 'Gypsy.'"[15] Amaya fleshed out the gypsy stereotype with a new sinuous athleticism and vigor. The "coarseness" of her style, her appropriation of the masculine dancing role, the violence of her footwork and transitions, fit the stereotype of the "lawless gypsy."

The anecdotes surrounding her performances in Buenos Aires, testimonials to the "innate gypsiness" of her dance, were used as publicity items in preparation for her debut at the Beachcomber, a nightclub in New York. A feature article in *Time* magazine unfurls the yarn that ensnared spectators across the United States:

> In a Buenos Aires theatre last summer, white-haired Maestro Arturo Toscanini embraced a black-haired, sloe-eyed dancer and cried: "Never in my life have I seen such fire and rhythm!" Platinum-haloed Maestro Leopold Stokowski, who knows fire and rhythm, got dancer Carmen Amaya to give a special performance for him and his All-American Youth Orchestra, willingly paid a fine for keeping the theatre open after midnight.[16]

The success of her New York debut at the Beachcomber was so overwhelming that, according to the *New York Daily News*, "Though she weighs only eighty-five pounds and has no claim to beauty, 500 full-page spreads of her have appeared in the nation's foremost picture magazines since her debut last February."[17] And, despite the fact that Carmen Amaya's signature dance was a *farruca,* performed in male costume, by May of 1941 she had inspired fashion designer Arnold Constable to create affordable "soap and water" dresses in "Romany red and white stripes," with names like "Allegrias" (sic) and "Inspiración."[18]

Amaya toured cities across the United States during the next few years, performing in extended engagements in Los Angeles and New York. She left the United States in 1944 and returned only twice, in 1955 and 1962. She died of kidney failure in her home in Bagur, Spain, in 1963. On the event of her passing, *Dance Magazine* published a poem by Vicente Romero, titled "To Carmen Amaya." The last stanza speaks to the mourning of the flamenco community when she died:

> The candles grow dimmer, flicker less now
> While an Andalusian sun grows brighter—
> The wind is like the restless rhythm of the sea,
> Undulating through ancient olive groves...
> Somewhere in Barcelona, the oceans forever pass
> Through a weeping fountain, perpetual homage,
> To Carmen, Carmen Amaya, Queen of the Gypsies...[19]

Amaya was not merely a box-office sensation; she was a respected *bailaora* and *cantaora* among flamencos. She served as a conduit for the intense pride of gypsies in their lineage and artistic traditions. Her commercial success at the onset of the Spanish Civil War and during Franco's fascist dictatorship reads as a kind of "local girl makes good" story, persuasive in the hopes she represented at a time when Spain, and particularly Andalusia, suffered political upheaval and economic hardship.

Carmen Amaya's legend demonstrates the ways in which the "gypsy" aesthetic was formulated to configure Amaya as an exotic object of fascination in the context of the United States' courtship of Latin America from 1941–43. She was an "authentic" exotic, and the desire to know more about her history was tempered by the need to preserve her mystical aura. And if the uneven attempts by the American press to portray Carmen Amaya as a barbaric but pleasurable exotic mark a cultural anxiety about the relationship of the United States to Latin America—a colonial enterprise to bring the Other into submission by rendering her as seductively inviting domination—then the continual repression of Amaya's cross-dressing performance, a negation of the necessarily feminine and passive qualities of the exotic object, poses particular paradoxes for the scholar of historical narrative.

The cross-dressed performances of Carmen Amaya in Spain have also been the subject of examination by dance scholar Meira Goldberg. In her article "Carmen Amaya Wore Pants: Flamenco as a Forum for Cross-Gendered Identification Within Spanish Gypsy Culture," Goldberg analyzes the disruption of traditional gender roles that occurs within flamenco performance and the exaggeration of those qualities within Amaya's *traje corto* dances. Not only did she adopt the man's costume and the characteristic verticality, rapid footwork, and brusque turns associated with the masculine dancing role, she also appropriated the privilege of masculine behaviors such as cigarette smoking, traveling without a chaperone, participation in the male-dominated *cante jondo* sessions, and the role of the wage-earner for her family.[20] Goldberg is careful, however, to point out that while Amaya impersonated the male performer onstage, "her offstage conduct generally met Gitana standards. Amaya did not handle money and she toured with 16 members of her family."[21] She suggests that the categories of male and female, within a gypsy context, have different valences than in *payo*, or non–Gypsy, cultures. According to Goldberg, despite the prohibitions on female behavior among Gypsies, it is possible to be a powerful wage-earner *and* a woman. With this statement, she is able to make sense of Amaya's eventual return to the feminine costume and dance:

> As a mature woman, Amaya eventually put away her *traje corto,* and stopped performing the men's dances. She replaced them with the female expression of silence: a stillness in which the upper body arch could be brought into focus by slow, sustained motion in the arms, and the face could reflect Amaya's inner life with greater subtlety.[22]

Goldberg is not alone in the historical recuperation of Carmen Amaya's dalliance into cross-gendered performance and the temporary assertion of masculine authority. Donn Pohren pointed out the potentially damaging legacy of Amaya's trouser dances:

> Soon every Pepita and Paquita were clutching *traje corto* jackets and grimacing fiercely in what degenerated into an all-out competition with the *bailaor,* a competition of masculine dancing as meaningless as it was, and is, ludicrous.... When watching Carmen's imitators one gets that embarrassed feeling, that urge to turn away, for the result is almost inevitably misplaced movements, unfelt turbulence, a complete lack of originality—in a word, utter chaos.[23]

Another famous Spanish dancer, La Meri, mysteriously remarks, "I also have it on good authority that when she passed thirty years—by then back in Spain—Amaya gave up all her male flamenco dances which are traditionally done in male attire and wore *batas* that were proper for a grown woman."[24] Upon reading representations of Carmen Amaya produced within the flamenco community, it becomes apparent that her persona was not only threatening to the stereotypes perpetuated by French Romantics and Hollywood filmmakers. For flamenco historians, Amaya's legend had to be protected from possible misreadings of the transgressive elements of her performance.

The attempts to recuperate Carmen Amaya for posterity coincide with major economic, political and social changes within Spain during the 1950s. Carmen Amaya's return to Spain, and to the codes of appropriate femininity, ironically occurred at a point in time when the art of flamenco underwent a period of crisis, brought on by Franco's decision to rejuvenate Spain's sagging economy through the tourist industry. The United States government also played a role in this drama. Flamenco scholar James Woodall narrates the unfolding of the plot, assigning Spain a feminine, passive character who plays to the masculine American hero: "Her solution, a natural one considering the might of the United States on all fronts, was to accept American loans: the price—American bases on Spanish soil."[25] As in other countries where the United States established a military presence, the creation of military bases in Spain was accompanied by a tourist industry that capitalized on prostitution.[26] The *tablaos* (flamenco nightclubs) provided the setting for dance performance and prostitution. The character of the dancing suited its seductive address, emphasizing "[U]p-front sexiness on the part of the *bailaora*, in particular, with lots of leg, thrust-out breasts, exaggerated hip movements, rather than the remoter magisterial seductiveness of true *baile* ... indeed, in some tablaos it wasn't long before the girls of the cuadro were offered to the clients as part of the evening's price."[27] By 1957, "the four military bases allotted to the United States of America under the Hispano-American defence [sic] agreements of 1953 had already contributed the tidy sum of $300 million to Spain's treasury—not to mention the $500 million invested in the building of these bases and of the Saragossa-Rota pipeline."[28] Prostitution and commercial flamenco performance transformed a folk art into a fiscal institution. The exchange of the flamenco dancer between the United States government and the Franco regime solidified their financial partnership.

The tensions at work at this historical juncture are multiple, and, unlike Merimée's story, they do not follow a predictable narrative structure. It would be dangerously simplistic to suggest that Franco engineered a resurgence in flamenco performance through the *tablaos,* for he expressed contempt for Andalusian culture as a whole. Flamenco scholar James Woodall distills Franco's perspective on the South into a single sentence that reads more as a proclamation: "Let it rot...."[29] However, Franco's regime was largely responsible for the survival of commercial flamenco during this period:

> What in broad terms happened with the birth of the *tablaos* was that Franco and his ministers of tourism lighted on a fail-safe tool for bringing in cash; as far as they were concerned, flamenco must stay firmly at the heart of an essential, revenue-creating tourist infrastructure. In a strange distortion that turned its anti-establishment history on its head, flamenco—and especially the imagery pertaining to it—became an instrument of government propaganda.[30]

Again, the image of the sexualized gypsy dancer occupies the center of the landscape. In this context, the sensuality of the Orientalist stereotype was marketed by government officials, while performers negotiated the demands of her choreography. Carmen Amaya profited from her appeal as a Latina exotic and perhaps even inspired tourists to travel to Spain to see flamenco in its "native" land. Practitioners and historians juggle the pieces of this puzzle, trying to make a fit that downplays the humiliation of the tourist's desires, Franco's exploitation of impoverished flamencos, and the sense of betrayal by those flamencos who acquiesced to the demands of the paying public. In an effort to restore a sense of dignity to these historical accounts, the stereotype of Carmen has been denied, silenced and dismissed. As a colonial stereotype, she serves as a receptacle for the pleasure and anxiety of the colonizing gaze, as well as a source of pride and embarrassment for the object of that gaze, the flamenco performer. She has been murdered thousands of times onstage, but she refuses to die or to be ignored.

The dialogue about the stereotypes of Carmen demands that scholars, tourists, and performers recognize her not as a villain, victim, or heroine, but perhaps as a teacher. Post-colonial scholar Homi K. Bhabha, in his classic essay "The Other Question: Difference, Discrimination and the Discourse of Colonialism" (1985), provides a model for the investigation of this possibility. At the beginning of this work, he sets up a foundation for the discussion that "questions dogmatic and moralistic positions on the meaning of oppression and discrimination." He writes:

> My reading of colonial discourse suggests that the point of intervention should shift from the identification of images as positive or negative to an understanding of the processes of subjectification made possible (and plausible) through stereotypical discourse [149].

To use Bhabha's project as a model for an investigation of the power dynamics enacted through representations of Carmen is to agree, at the onset, that she is neither unproblematic in her innocence nor pathological in her contamination. He continues,

> It is the object of my talk today to suggest that the construction of the colonial subject in discourse, and the exercise of colonial power through discourse demands an articulation of forms of difference—racial and sexual. Such an articulation becomes crucial if it is held that the body is always simultaneously inscribed in both the economy of pleasure and desire and the economy of discourse, domination, and power [150].

Defining the parameters for the examination of the stereotype is important, especially in the context of the stereotype of the gypsy dancer. At each historical moment that she appears, her dancing body evokes an ambivalent

negotiation of visual or textual pleasure and the effects of cultural subjugation. For Bhabha,

> It is the force of ambivalence that gives the colonial stereotype its currency:
> ensures its repeatability in changing historical and discursive conjunctures;
> informs its strategies of individuation and marginalization; produces that
> effect of probabilistic truth and predictability which, for the stereotype must
> always be in *excess* of what can be empirically proven or logically construed
> [149].

The excess of Mérimée's Carmen and the contradictory legend of Carmen Amaya frame this discussion of ambivalence. They are persuasive, even
seductive, because these stereotypes encourage the viewer or reader to believe
in the essential racial characteristics of the gypsy, yet they continually provoke anxiety through their unpredictable penchant for resistance to the codes
that define them. It is not as if Carmen the stereotype has any agency or possibility for transgression beyond her scripted criminality; after all, she is a
fictional character, a presence and not a being.

Instead, the investigation must refer to the moments when the stereotype is cited through performance. In the case of Carmen Amaya, the stereotype of Mérimée's Carmen flickers in her *farruca,* imbues it with meaning,
but then the artist Amaya reconfigures the boundaries of the stereotype in
the danced moment. With every citation of the stereotype, through film,
written texts, photos, opera, or dance, the stereotype is reproduced as still
recognizable, a sign of racial and sexual difference, but the specific categories
of difference are never fixed. Like the complex matrices of power that produce the stereotype—French Romantics searching for the East in Andalusia,
American audiences looking for the "neighborly" Latina, Franco's ministers
of tourism seeking a lucrative tourist industry, contemporary flamencos nos-
talgically reinventing a space of innocence—the stereotype itself reveals the
changing positions of the actors in the spectacle. Just as it is unproductive
to condemn or celebrate the stereotype of Carmen, it is limited and potentially dangerous to universally celebrate the gypsies as passive victims of the
process of stereotyping or to assume that every non-gypsy viewer of flamenco
maliciously exploits flamenco and flamencos. Instead, again following
Bhabha's example, engage with the stereotype of Carmen *not* as a symbol of
otherness, but as "a differential *sign,* implicated in specific historical and discursive conditions, requiring construction in different practices or reading"
(151). By inserting the performer's negotiation of the representational codes
that exist in the practice of improvisation in the larger context of the discursive practices that define flamenco, the signifying power of the dancing body
emerges. This presence is alluded to in accounts of flamenco performance,
but never fully captured by narrative. The moment of live performance, per-

petually lost, provides the opportunity for an analysis of the category of difference in a transnational, postcolonial context.

Strategic Presence

Film and history form a multilayered network of representations that chronicle, in the haphazard ways of maps, a field of meaning structured by the cultural tensions that continually reproduce the stereotype of the Hispanic exotic. Even as they chart the terrain and delineate important landmarks, representations only trace the after-effect of the lived moment. The nuances of the experience and their resulting complexities achieved only through movement in real time evaporate. The "presence," that moment of exquisite articulation, is forever lost. One might ask, following Gayatri Spivak's mandate to the feminist scholar, is this a romantic, or worse, pious idealism concerning material bodies and "reality"? Idealism as a word immediately connotes ideology. What ideology governs this statement? At the foundational level, the moment when difference is established and mute subjects are cast, what information is privileged in this account? And, by implication, what information is suppressed or ignored? Timothy Mitchell attempted to create, in his history, an "unbiased perspective." However, feminist scholars like Teresa de Lauretis insist that the feminist account must be biased "with a vengeance." How does this perspective apply to analysis of flamenco bodies and on dancing bodies in particular? The discussion of dance in flamenco histories reveals the ways in which "the body" becomes a hypothetical space for the collision of warring perceptions concerning gender, sexuality, race and nationality. Film, in its uncanny resemblance to "real life," further complicates any easy equations offered between texts and bodies, texts as bodies and bodies as text. The seductive appeal of the moving body on a movie screen convinces the viewer that the relationship between the images and their meaning is transparent, rather than mediated by a series of culturally informed signifiers.

Live flamenco dance evokes a still more powerful sense of loss, of longing for seamlessness between the symbol and its referent, especially in the moment of performance. Inasmuch as this analysis attempts to propose the relationship between representations and dancing bodies as intelligible and complex, it is difficult to ignore the blissful immediacy of the dancing body in performance. In the development of these arguments concerning representation, ideology, and bodies, the "authority" of the account frequently occupies the very same position that previous scholars have assumed and embraces the very notions that serve as the subject of the critique. This analysis of flamenco relies upon the stereotypical images of the form circulated in

Damaris Ferrer of Bailes Ferrer teaches young students the proper way to hold their arms while playing castanets (2004). Photograph by Liliam Dominguez, used with permission.

European and American cultures over the past century and a half. The prejudices voiced by American flamencophiles strongly influence the choices made. Even though this historical account challenges the assumptions of previous scholars, it shares the same agenda: the preservation and perpetuation of flamenco as a tradition. Performances of flamenco that seem to cater to the most convenient and degrading stereotypes of Andalusian culture are no less difficult to bear in this analysis than in the work of previous scholars. No less confining is the rhetoric that immobilizes the dancing body in a nostalgic construction of the past.

However, in contemporary flamenco performance and film, as well as recent historical scholarship, multiple viewpoints engage in a vibrant and productive exchange. Flamenco artists all over the world are shattering the immobilizing images of the art form and complicating the paralyzing debates that threaten to stunt a rich tradition. The dancing body in performance insists upon recognition as a participant in the dialogue, but the codes of intelligibility in choreography and improvisation are only accessible through the operation of the trace in the process of representation, the mechanics of "writing" in history and film.

What becomes clear in these juxtapositions of bodies and activities is the space of interpretation, the moment of writing. Innumerable details of the dancing are lost; there is only the chase to capture something immediately absent following the moment of its appearance. And yet, the constant generation of movement, commercial and critical, in response to the initial dancing phrase continues the dialogue of dancing and writing bodies. The boundaries of the event are porous: when does the dancing end and the writing begin? Rather than pose these written texts as failed attempts to capture the danced moment, why not view them as a continued dialogue within the structure of an improvisation? In the exciting canon of flamenco history, authors refer to improvisation, but do not explore how it figures into the representation of meaning in performance.

Practiced Spontaneity

To write about the process of improvisation is to negotiate several different representational frameworks in a single instance. First, one must consider the relationship between the danced moment and the written account. How does the writing of an event speak to the "original" moment? Then, how does an improvisation make sense, succeed or fail, to the performer or spectator? Improvisation is a learned practice. Dancers and musicians gather in classrooms, rehearsal studios and other spaces to develop the concentration and skills that can be employed in a performance of improvisation. The learning itself is mediated by a series of frames: dancers watch teachers or fellow performers, synthesize that information and produce an approximation of the shapes, qualities, and rhythms of the dance. Then, other participants respond with movements and spoken word, or song. The event, the process of learning that is a rehearsal for the performance itself, involves an often halting, but sometimes fluid series of negotiations. Training in flamenco serves as the model for evaluating the transfer of information in choreographed and improvised performances of flamenco. The classroom setting provides a consistent pattern for the systemic reproduction of key values in the vocabulary and syntax of flamenco among practitioners. Pedagogical methods differ from one context to another. For example, classes in flamenco technique offered in the United States differ from those in Spain. Private classes differ from university courses, and *cursillos* (intensive, short courses) offered in festivals or by visiting guest artists follow yet another format. Individual teachers develop specific methods to teach unique audiences. Each context produces a different effect. The following is an account of a studio class offered in the United States.

The Dancing Lesson (Anaheim, California, 1995)[31]

Classes with Antonia Rojas begin when she moves to the front of the studio, draws her torso up with a breath and sinks into her stance. The students fall silent. They stop fiddling with the flounces of a skirt or the elastic band on a shoe, and follow her example. Antonia turns her head to the accompanist and murmurs the name of a form: *soleares.* The musician strums his guitar and plays the signature opening for the form. She claps, with *palmas sordas* (muffled hand claps), a rhythmic phrase, then begins a slow, repeating pattern of *brazeo.* The students watch her, and their own reflections in the mirror, as they follow her movements. The patterns, at first, are simple: two arms move symmetrically from the level of the hips, fingers spiral in flowering shapes, out to the side and then extend up to form a circular frame around the face. Gradually, the patterns become more complicated, with independent pathways for each arm, sudden attacks and slow decrescendos. She introduces changes in facing for the torso and head. Antonia watches her students in the mirrors and gently encourages individuals to deepen their stances, arch their backs, keep their heads in line with the horizon, curve their arms, and lift their elbows.

After several minutes of uninterrupted movement, Antonia chooses one of the advanced students to take her place at the head of the class and improvise as they follow. Usually one of the youngest takes Antonia's place. The girl grabs her skirt in fisted hands and leads the group in improvised patterns of *brazeo.* During this time, Antonia walks around the room and gives corrections to the other students. She places her hands on a dancer's waist, presses in and tells her to lift up through her torso. With her fingers, she instructs the dancer to roll down through her scapulae and press up through her sternum. The student's head falls back, so Antonia tells her to lengthen her neck and fix her eyes on a point on the horizon. The dancer discovers the integration of movement necessary to maintain the flamenco posture. Antonia smiles, congratulates the student, and moves on to another dancer. After some time, she relieves the dancer at the front of the room, whose brow and upper lip are marked with beads of determined sweat. Antonia leads the class in another exercise, adding footwork. She continues the practice of bringing students to the front of the room to improvise so that she can give comments to the rest of the class. By the end of the hour, they are clapping out a breathtakingly rapid *compás* for *bulerías.* Each dancer takes a solo as the other dancers support him or her with *palmas* and *jaleo.*

In this account of a flamenco dance class where improvisation figures prominently as a technique, the teacher trains students to recognize and reproduce specific images in time. Her movements serve as a template for copying and interpretation. The students constantly refer to the "original" image of the instructor, or the advanced student, in order to adhere to the flamenco style. Unlike dancers who grow up in a flamenco environment, these students must "unlearn" their daily practice in order to imitate the body orientation of flamenco, its rhythms, shapes, weight shift and transitions.

The classes Antonia Rojas teaches differ in important ways from other flamenco classes in the United States and Spain. Her focus on improvisation is unique; in many classes the instructor demonstrates and teaches "set" choreography for every form. These more standardized classes can be very valuable; they allow the beginning dancer to rehearse, again and again, the basic structures for each form. However, the mark of an experienced dancer is her ability to improvise within those structures. The dancers in Antonia's class focus on the role of improvisation within the boundaries of tradition. It is this focus on improvisation that speaks powerfully, through movement, to the debate concerning purity and authenticity waged by flamencologists. While flamenco purists write of the loss of "true" flamenco, in this community, dancers demonstrate a commitment to the preservation of a tradition in diaspora and the complex negotiation of ethnic identities in the context of the United States, where dancers are neither Spaniard nor gypsy, but long to identify as part of flamenco culture.

For a skillful flamenco dancer, improvisation provides the opportunity to display both mastery and abandon in performance. Even in the most spontaneous gathering of dancers who play *palmas* for one another as they trade solos, the codes for improvisation are strictly prescribed. And yet, dancers find innumerable ways to play in and around, to interrupt and recombine elements of traditional flamenco vocabulary. The solo is a community event. The group provides a rhythmic foundation for the dancer's choreography; the participants shout out words of encouragement, then they tease and dare the dancer to take risks in performance. The dancer can signal to speed up, slow down, dance in silence or change rhythms, but all of these decisions depend on clear communication within the group through coded steps, gestures, or phrase-lengths. The decision-making process may be spontaneous, contextually defined by the situation and the members of the group, but a successful improvisation makes sense through the invocation and subtle disruption of traditional choreographic codes. Dancers spend years working on their solos in individual *palos*, keeping certain steps or phrases while substituting new information gleaned from each improvisational performance.

The long-term development of a signature flamenco solo serves as a metaphor for an analysis of flamenco's convoluted history. At any given moment, the foundation that had seemed stable only moments before can begin to decompose. None of the categories are fixed, and the trajectory of the dance must change in response to the individual context. But the choices available always stem from recognizable structures within the tradition, and only "work" when the decisions are recognizable by the community of participants. The practice of flamenco dance provides the strategies for its own analysis. However, the role of improvisation, particularly the danced improvisation, is rarely the focus of representations in history or film. In fact, improvisation takes on a dangerous quality, capable of preserving or eradicating the "essence" of flamenco.

The Problem of Improvisation/Giving Up the Ghost

In the written histories of flamenco dance, the practice of improvisation simultaneously promises to renew and threatens to undo the structures of the tradition. Improvisation allows the opportunity for the arrival of the *duende,* the spirit of inspiration that overcomes the dancer and endows his/her movements with a sense of "authenticity" lacking in fully choreographed productions. The ideal setting for this kind of performance is the flamenco *juerga,* an informal gathering of musicians and dancers. According to Doris Niles, "The climax will be the emergence of *el duende.* Any dancer *en serio* knows that there is nothing to compare with dancing for a select few, as this becomes your personal dance in which your emotions touch those close to you in this intimate and secluded exhibition of fine art."[32]

The correlation between "authentic" flamenco and the visitation of the *duende* was most clearly articulated by the Spanish poet Federico García Lorca, who collaborated with the composer Manuel de Falla to produce the *Concurso del Conte Jondo* (Festival of the Deep Song) in 1922. The competition, staged in Granada, was intended to showcase and preserve the traditional song forms of Andalusia. Many Spaniards felt that the adaptation of the song forms for commercial flamenco performances threatened to eradicate the non-commercial practice of "true" deep song.

In his essay "Theory and Play of the *Duende,*" García Lorca defines *duende* as "a power, not a work; it is a struggle, not a thought."[33] Though the *duende* can inhabit the arts of any culture, Lorca maintains that "the great artists of the south of Spain, gypsies or flamencos, that sing, dance, play guitar—they know that it is not possible to have any emotion without the arrival of the *duende.*"[34] For Lorca, the *duende* seems always to invoke a sense of loss, a momentary surrender of the self in the moment and the potential eradication of the self through a proximity to death. The transformative power of the *duende* was particularly visible in the dance:

Left: Israel Galván, an experimentalist, often pushes the boundaries of flamenco dance in his highly theatrical work (2006). Photograph by Liliam Dominguez, used with permission. *Right:* Pastora Galván embodies the traditional *sevillano* school of flamenco dance (2006). Photograph by Liliam Dominguez, used with permission.

> The *duende* operates on the body of the dancer like the air on sand. It converts, with magical power, a girl into a lunar paralytic, or fills with adolescent blushes a broken, old man that begs in the wine-shops, it gives a woman's hair the smell of a nocturnal port, and in every moment it works on the arms with expressions that are the mothers of the dance of all time.[35]

During the twentieth century, the poetic metaphors used by Lorca have translated into literal interpretations of the power and meaning of the *duende*. Allen Josephs, a scholar of Andalusian culture, defines it as a "chthonian spirit of inspiration,"[36] a description that resonates with the mythical incarnation of the gypsies captured in several of Lorca's works.[37] For scholars such as Josephs and respected flamencologists like Félix Grande,[38] the romanticism of the gypsies and of the ancient culture of Andalusia endows their narratives with a magical sense of timelessness, mystery, and truth.

Despite the coded inclusion of improvisation and the desired "arrival" of the *duende* within flamenco performance, the innovation of different steps, in some cases, endangers the strict stylistic and formal structures of "true" flamenco. The decisions of the dancer must remain within the traditional conventions for what can be recognized as flamenco. For example, a dancer should never dance outside the *compás,* the rhythmic structure for a specific form. And, although dancers may insert hand and arm gestures into their choreography for comic effect, the pathways for the arms and fingers are very specific, and their variations occur within a certain realm of familiarity. The process of improvisation depends on the negotiation of strict compositional structures—a far cry from the descriptions of the natural, spontaneous movements attributed to flamenco dancers, and gypsies in particular.

The invocation of the *duende* within written narratives of flamenco appears as a phantasmic visitation of what is unrepresentable, the ephemeral dancing body. However, upon closer examination, the *duende* actually functions as a means of representing the complex and intricate decision-making process of the practitioner who operates within the parameters of the tradition. This process is witnessed and applauded by an informed audience. It is precisely this recognition that brings meaning to the performance.

The notion of a "successful" performance of improvisation depends on an evaluative assessment of the event by the performer or spectator, or both. Unless the performance has been introduced as improvisation, through program notes or the context for the gathering, a spectator may assume that the seamless flow from one activity into another is a choreographed piece. Or, as is often the case in flamenco dance improvisations, if the spectator does not recognize the codes that serve as the organizing elements of the performance, it seems as though every movement arrives spontaneously, without reference to a tradition or a system of training. But many times the performers and the audience members who attend improvisational dance events have at least a general idea of what might occur. In these cases, the successful improvisation involves a community interaction in which the codes for the work are cited and manipulated in unique or particularly daring ways.

Does the demystification of the *duende* detract from the enjoyment of improvisation in the continuing traditions of flamenco? Or rather, is improvisation ideally suited to the interventions posed by dialogue among its practitioners and spectators? In fact, the exchange of information is always already at work in improvisation. It is the result of the play within a system of movement, a language. This play happens within specific conventions and is supported by a particular training. An informed community of participants interprets the gleeful citation of these codes and creates or inscribes "meaning" in the performance. When they "read" the "writing," they begin to "translate" the markings into new choreography that constantly refers to the codes of a tradition, yet manipulates them in unexpected ways. Instead of imprisoning the performer, the "intellectual" discussion of improvisation promises the perpetuation of a tradition.

Rising from the Ashes: Spain's Position in the New World Order

Among many contemporary flamenco performers, the constant negotiation of tradition and innovation, improvisation and choreography, has led to new, hybrid forms of flamenco music and dance. Tomasito, a contemporary Gypsy singer and dancer, appeared at the prestigious 2007 Festival Flamenco de Jeréz, rapping *en compás por buleriás*, adding hip hop movements and pedestrian gestures to his dancing. Other artists, like brother and sister Israel and Pastora Galván, perform radical experiments with flamenco structures in works like 2007's *La Francesa*, a critique of the French Romantic stereotypes of flamenco women. Like Carmen Amaya before them, the "new generation" of flamenco artists inhabit and disrupt the stereotypical image of the flamenco dancer to articulate an authorial position that cannot be contained within a single category. However, they remain in dialogue with both purists and tourists, challenging and educating through their use of traditional vocabularies in hybrid productions of flamenco.

The colonial stereotype, a sign of Otherness produced by a narrative desire to penetrate and to know, has been rewritten from the perspective of the Other. She has turned that desire in on itself and, through her performance, insists upon the communal recognition of her self-consciousness. Difference is not erased, but enhanced, in the multiplicity of voices clamoring to be heard in the debates that continue in the international flamenco community. The polarized positions of purist and tourist now represent the ends of a spectrum. Likewise, the positions of the desiring gaze and the object of that gaze shift, exchange places and layer on top of one another. The pattern of those shifts emulates the choreographic decisions of the flamenco dancer. In this moment, dance, previously ignored or dismissed in the history of flamenco, will provide important strategies for the analysis of the complex tensions that have shaped the practice of flamenco, past and future.

The current popularity of flamenco in an international context, and the ability of flamenco performers, Spanish and non–Spanish, to use the flamenco stereotype as a means of articulating an identity informed by the tensions of race, gender, sexuality, and regional or national affiliation should be viewed in the context of recent shifts in power on a global level. Spain's colonial legacy, which faded during the twentieth century and gave way to the emergence of the United States as a world power, shows signs of reassertion in the new millennium, and flamenco tourism plays a key role in the economic health of the nation. The transformation of the flamenco stereotype from a mute to a speaking subject has coincided with Spain's change in status from a de facto Third World country to a new world power. Representation, as Gayatri Spivak reminds us, has not withered away. However, this transition involves a complex renegotiation of the many identities encapsulated by flamenco as a tradition, and as a result has changed the terms of representation for the flamenco exotic. The resilience of the art form attests to the possibility of a dialogue that includes many voices and represents many positions in a continually shifting global context.

7

"Somos Anti-Guapas"—Against Beauty
in Contemporary Flamenco

"¡Guapa!" Shouted at the most difficult moment of a solo, or during the bows following an exceptional performance, to be hailed as "beautiful" is the highest achievement for a female flamenco dancer. "Guapa" is also the name by which girlfriends recognize each other, and female colleagues greet, in the street. "Hola, guapa ... ¿Cómo estás?" However, "beautiful" is not an easy category to inhabit. In any culture, beauty demands conformity to a specifically defined set of constraints. The construction of flamenco beauty borrows many qualities from the stereotype of the Hispanic Other, of Carmen: long hair, restrained but never fully captured, a curvaceous silhouette, shapely legs, tapered fingers, and a supple spine. In contemporary flamenco, the audiences and critics play a key role in determining what is beautiful or desirable in a female dancer's performance. Beauty, more than athleticism or expressiveness, determines the "success" of a dancer. But beauty in flamenco is not merely composed of the features on a face or the proportions of a body. Beyond the attributes of exoticism, there are ideal aesthetic conventions for the female role.

In Cyril Rice's *Dancing in Spain (Argentina and Escudero)* of 1931, La Argentina represents the idealized female dancer, her passionate nature tempered by the refinement of her classical training. By the 1950s, Carmen Amaya had shattered all assumptions about the female role, with her cross-dressed performances of the male dances and appropriation of virtuoso footwork. The films of Gades and Saura feature representations of unruly femininity, expertly danced by Cristina Hoyos and Laura del Sol. During the 1990s, dancers like Eva La Yerbabuena could perform the traditional *bata de cola* dances of their teachers and match the male dancers in their companies with lightning-fast footwork in arrangements that would challenge the late Elvin Jones with their rhythmic complexity. In each of these moments, the boundaries that maintain the female role as feminine and as flamenco stretch, resist, and accommodate innovation. The process of change has been constant

Belén Maya, in an angular pose, displays the elbows her teachers tried so hard to remove from her dancing (2007). Photograph by Paco Sánchez, used with permis-

throughout the history of flamenco, but a curious effect of the representation of tradition is the illusion that "it has always been this way."

The 2008 Festival de Jeréz featured a performance directed by Mario Maya and produced by Miguel Marin Productions called *Mujeres*. The work won the critic's award for the best performance of the festival, a distinction sponsored by the Flamencology Institute of Jeréz. The three featured performers in this production represented three "generations" of flamenco: Merché Esmeralda, Belén Maya, and Rocío Molina. *Mujeres* celebrates traditional femininity as it is deployed in flamenco. *Bata de cola*, fan, castanets, ruffles, shawl, combs, dangling earrings, flowers—no prop was spared in the process. Esmeralda, featured in the films *Flamenco, Sevillanas,* and *Ibéria* with Carlos Saura, has long been hailed as one of the great flamenco artists. Of her *soleá,* danced with a white *bata de cola,* David Fernandez of the *Diario de Jeréz* raved, "We could contemplate how they danced in the old days, with a sharp delivery, full of elegance."[1]

Maya is known for her "minimalist" dancing, a trailblazer in the world of contemporary flamenco, one of the first to manipulate flamenco as a language to express sentiments and emotions beyond the traditional qualities associated with each form. Her angular and sparse *bulerías,* performed in silence, was immortalized and circulated around the world in *Flamenco.* In the same review, Fernandez awards her the moment of the present: "Nobody better than she represents this generation in the current moment of flamenco dance." Molina, the youngest of the three dancers, is a prodigy with a technical virtuosity and speed that astonish no less than her artistry. Of her *seguiyira,* Fernandez says, "She nailed each and every one of her precise *remates* with the fastest, most musical feet that have passed through the theater." *La Voz* hailed the work featuring the three dancers as "A Triumph of the Eternal Feminine."[2] Flamenco festival audiences are notoriously demanding, and the audience at the 2008 Festival de Jeréz performance of *Mujeres* included legends like Manolete and Matilde Coral, as well as students and aficionados from all over the world. At several points during the show, people erupted into applause, shouted *jaleo,* and by the end they clamored for multiple curtain calls. The wave of reviews that followed the next day were like a series of love letters.

Belén Maya

And yet, in an interview the following day, Belén Maya discussed the inconstant nature of such adoring praise. "I'm very happy about the good reviews, but it makes me angry, it's very unjust."[3] Maya explains, "The critics are positive if you do what *they* like. Everything is marvelous, you are marvelous, but it is not objective criticism." The previous year, her more abstract work, *Souvenir,* received lukewarm reviews. Carlos Sanchez of *www.flamenc o-world.com* called it "a staircase that was missing a few steps," and "flamenco in code."[4] Maya shuttles back and forth between the position of the darling of the critics and the misunderstood experimentalist. She describes the process:

Belén Maya rises from the nest of her *bata de cola* (2005). Photograph by Liliam Dominguez, used with permission.

> At times, I "put on the flower" and dance in a very classical way. But it's like a costume I put on. I can do it, or not. The traditional artists, the critics, the festivals, they always want you to enter that space and stay there, because they believe that tradition is more forceful. When I depart from tradition, it has no value to them.

As the daughter of Mario Maya and Carmen Mora, Belén Maya was born into a half-gypsy family to two dancing parents. For many years, she struggled to distinguish herself as an artist in her own right. When asked about her role in flamenco, she replies, "I do not consider myself a flamenco dancer. I do things that are not considered very flamenco. As a language, I find flamenco very limited. When I started, it wasn't like it is today ... the vocabulary was very small, very limited." As a child, she studied many different styles of dance, including classical ballet. Once she became and adult, she studied Indian dance and contemporary dance forms as well as flamenco. "I like to steal steps. I stole a lot of steps from dancers in different styles." These disruptions or inventions characterize her individual, iconoclast style, as well as a sharp, angular quality that her early teachers tried to remove from her dancing. "I have very long arms, and my elbows stick out. When I began, all my teachers told me to get rid of my elbows."

After years of feeling very alone dancing inside and outside the tradition, Maya is pleased to recognize that among contemporary flamenco dancers, there are dancers "stranger than I am." Rocío Molina, for example, is more adventurous in her expansion of the flamenco vocabulary than even Maya has been. "I love it!" she says. "They [the traditionalists] have to accept that flamenco has changed, it is changing and will continue to change." She sees a fundamental shift in the role of women in flamenco:

> In my mother's generation, you danced two or three *palos*. Now we dance them all. We dance them with *bata*, without, with castanets, whatever. The technique of women's footwork is at the same level as the men's. Traditionally, women expressed *el arte*, but now they are just as capable of performing technique as men are.

The most important change in the female role, in her view, is not only the expansion of the vocabulary that is allowed to women of this generation, but the scope of possibilities for the representation of ideas. "In traditional flamenco, you can only express two or three ideas, especially as women. You can't talk about things like loneliness, violence, fear, vulnerability ... not without straying from the realm of the feminine dance. Little by little, women are changing these things." Dancers like Belén Maya, Rafaela Carrasco, Rocío Molina, and others are expanding the content of what can be expressed through their dancing. They are telling their own stories, beyond the traditional *palos* and the gorgeous costumes. Rafaela Carrasco bears significant mention here. A dancer of extraordinary musical complexity and a singular sense of theatrical impact in the design of her choreography, she collaborated with Belén Maya in 2004 on a production that integrated contemporary dance and flamenco called *Fuera de los Límites*, under the direction of Ramón Oller. Maya considers Carrasco a kindred spirit. "We have to renounce beauty. You don't have to be beautiful or marvelous all the time. There are many other things to think, feel and create. We are the anti-guapas."

What, then, is the anti-guapa aesthetic in flamenco? For example, in the first half of *Souvenir*, Maya performs a traditional *tangos* with *bata de cola*. As she reaches the end of the song, she performs a final flourish, a difficult turn that lands the train perfectly beside her. The finish signals the applause of the audience. Then, the singer begins a reprise of the final line of the *letra*. Maya performs the finish exactly as she did only moments before. The audience responds with more applause. The sequence repeats again, and again, and the audience realizes that the song and the dancer are "skipping" like a vinyl record, recalling the old recordings of traditional flamenco. It is this kind of ironic commentary that Maya brings to her more abstract works.

Maya also displaces the flamenco vocabulary outside its traditional context. In the second half of *Souvenir*, the more challenging sections for audiences and critics accustomed to Maya's traditional dancing featured an actor and a contemporary dancer onstage with Maya. She replaced the guitarist and singer with an electronic score. She performed some of the staples of flamenco dancing, like the footwork from an *escobilla*, but in dialogue with the actor's text and the contemporary dancer's more plastic, sculptural movements, not as a developmental section within a codified section of a recognized *palo*. These moments place her outside flamenco. Without the traditional structures to anchor the audience in the development of the composition, traditional audiences get lost. Even familiar steps are unrecognizable if they are combined out of context. As dancers increase their technical speed in footwork, they dance around or atop traditional rhythms, "losing" the familiar auditory "landmarks," like clear *llamadas* (calls) or *remates* (a step that frequently "closes" a phrase).

The displacement of the flamenco vocabulary outside its traditional context for understanding distinguishes many of Maya's choreographic works. In *Dibujos* (2007), she performs a section called *Trémolo* in bare feet. The piece opens with the image of Maya lying nested on top of *bata de cola*. As the music develops, she undulates in and out of the floor, using the train to sweep its surface. She marks rhythmic accents with arm gestures, and makes her way to standing. Employing the traditional use of the *bata*, she performs *brazeo* that reaches up and away from her body as she twists around herself. The train follows the path of her movements, like a trace.

Although the traditional female dancer performs less footwork than the man's role, few flamenco dancers abandon the discursive potential of footwork. Bare feet belong to the world of modern dance. While the *bata de cola* is used to perform many tricks that demonstrate mastery in performance, it is not appropriate to allow the ruffles to fold over, let alone to curl up and fall asleep on them. It is almost shocking to see a *bata* used as a cleaning rag. By reintroducing the circular twisting of the *bata* accompanied by *brazeo*, Maya reframes her experiments within the recognized codes of flamenco.

In addition to the insertion of decidedly un-flamenco gestures within the vocabulary and the use of the traditional vocabulary in unorthodox settings, Belén Maya has also challenged the conventions of the female role through the articulation of queer desire through her collaborations with the cross-dressing singer Mayte Martín. Despite the homoerotic undertones of *Flamenco de camara (Chamber Flamenco)*, the work was celebrated by critics and audiences alike, winning prizes and touring for years following the premiere in 2003. In a review of their performance in Tokyo, flamenco critic Miguel Mora of *El Pais* described them as "friends and accomplices in life and art ... flirting gracefully, so nobody was scandalized."[5] He compares the singer and dancer to la Niña de los Peines and Carmen Amaya, two of the most famous artists in the history of flamenco. The work was globally successful because they performed the traditional *palos* in the most conservative style. Reviews rarely mention the men's suits worn by Martín, but in all of them, Maya appeared quintessentially feminine. She inhabits the role of the "ideal *flamenca*" artfully, drawing on the seductive nature of the stereotype. In a review of a 2005 performance at the London Sadler's Wells Flamenco Festival, Josephine Leask of *The Dance Insider* describes Maya's hypnotic power: "She displays her magnetic force over Martin by ensnaring her, wrapping the material round the singer's feet whenever she tries to walk away."[6]

In the same review, Leask compares the tension between Martín and Maya to the more conventional couplings of flamenco:

> Often in flamenco, the dancer personifies the woman and the singer the man, and they enact a game of conquet and submission which is all too predictably charged with melodramatic lashings of sexual tension. However, with Martín and Maya some of the more commercial and stereotypical passions as well as the inflated egos that are flaunted by many flamenco performers are replaced by modesty, deep mutual respect and understanding. Arriving on a journey from their own personal artistic positions, they join forces rather than battling each other into submission, but still exude plenty of passion and emotion in the process. This is flamenco without its macho baggage, and as a result is highly sophisticated.

Despite her "renunciation" of beauty, Belén Maya manages to maintain her "fixed place in the firmament of flamenco,"[7] by knowing how and when to "put on the flower," expertly. Maya's experiments with language and subject matter in flamenco made it possible for younger dancers, like Rocío Molina and Pastora Galván to dance outside the realm of appropriate femininity with less risk to their careers.

Pastora Galván

Like Belén Maya, Pastora Galván also comes from a half-gypsy "flamenco family." She lives and teaches in the apartment building where her brother, Israel, also lives with his family, in Seville. The two were trained by their parents, José Galván and Eugenia de los Reyes. As adults, they have developed distinct dancing personalities. Israel is known for his highly abstract, experimental work, while Pastora is recognized as an extraordinary traditional dancer. She stunned audiences in 2007 when she performed her brother's choreography in a work called *La Francesa*. The review on *www.flamenco-world.com* by the award-winning flamenco journalist Sylvia Cal-

Pastora Galván, as Silvia Calado describes her, "so classical, so lovely, so Sevillian" (2006). Photograph by Liliam Dominguez, used with permission.

ado sums up the feelings of shock and dismay provoked by Israel Galván's choreography:

> His attachment to distorting and destructuring makes up "La francesa," a show which turns around the pretty bailaora who was seen last year at the Teatro de Guadalcacín, so classical, so lovely, so Sevillian. And it does so to the point of absurdity, ugliness, vulgarity. With no fear of ridicule. Shameless. Pastora Galván experiences a metamorphosis which is not only her own, but that of a generation which can dance wearing high boots or stiletto heels, following a short distance behind the footsteps of the inciting Belén Maya and Rafaela Carrasco.[8]

However, Calado also understood the force of the message the brother-and-sister team were trying to impart. She says "Myths fall. And if they don't fall by themselves, they're given a little push. It must be that 'Carmen' deserved to be taught a lesson, that the flamenco women of the twenty-first century weren't willing to let themselves be tyrannized by the character." *La Francesa* deconstructs the flamenco stereotype of Mérimée and Bizet, then appropriates the French flag, Ravel, Edith Piaf, and even a French soccer star as part of her revenge.

Structured as an opera, with sections like "Carmen Among the Navarres," "Lou Andreas-Salome in Ronda," "Marguerite Duras Becomes a Gypsy," "Rosario Doesn't Regret Anything," and "Alice Becker-Ho is Crying," the Galván duo dismantles the making of the flamenco stereotype. Some of these references are more oblique than others. Lou Andreas-Salome was a feminist contemporary of Rilke, Nietzsche, and Freud. Duras is better known as the prolific postcolonial French artist and intellectual, and Alice Becker-Ho was a scholar of the Romany language. *La Francesa* pits the figure of the female flamenco dancer against the stereotype of Carmen and then re-positions her as feminist scholar. Musically, the composition pieces together flamenco *palos* with songs like Maurice Ravel's *Bolero* or "faux" French songs in the cabaret style. Bizet's "Habanera" from *Carmen* makes an appearance, naturally.

In the section "Carmen Among the Navarres," Pastora Galván appears in a pair of biking shorts, a striped shirt, sport socks, and a pair of white stiletto heels. She layers *zapateado* over the cabaret music, then intentionally teeters on the impossibly high heels as she aggressively moves from one combative stance to another along the front edge of the stage. She sheds her sweat-soaked shirt to reveal the jersey of French soccer star Zinedine Zidane (Zizou). During a moment of flourish in the "Habanera," she head-butts singer David Lagos in the heart, just as Zizou ended his illustrious career. In a display of the "vulgarity" noted by Calado, Galván suggestively grinds against a t-shirt she holds between her legs like the ruffle of a skirt, then cir-

Pastora Galván, sweating furiously and displaying the excess of La Francesa in the 2007 Festival Flamenco de Jeréz. Photograph by Paco Sánchez, used with permission.

cles and shakes her rear end in a "cheeky" display of sexualized irreverence. By the end of the section, she has spun herself in dizzying circles and then ends up pinned against an image of the French flag.

"Rosario Doesn't Regret Anything" combines the music from Ravel's *Bolero* and lyrics from Edith Piaf's "Non, Je Ne Regrette Rien," first in French, then in Spanish. Galván appears in a red silk blouse and *bata de cola*. She uses Ravel's score as a march, traveling along the horizon undulating her hips, windmilling her arms and diving into low backbends. She kicks at her *bata de cola*, castigates it, cajoles it, then switches into the classical "skirt tricks" of the *sevillano* school, suspending the heavy ruffles in the air as she turns. In one vibrant moment, she stands with her back to the audience, train spilling out behind her. As the bass picks up the steady beat of the *Bolero*, the skirt pulses like a great red heart. By the end of the section, she displays her mastery over the skirt by ordering it to move and executing a jump as she catches the skirt on the final note.

Following the premiere of *La Francesa* at the 2006 Bienal in Seville, reviewer Estela Zatania declared, "Aside from the fact that her brother Israel choreographed his new work, last night, Pastora stopped being the 'the sister of' and claimed her rightful place in the elite circle of great flamenco dancers." Of the choreography, she says,

> It's impossible to ignore the fact that "La Francesa" is a feminist declaration, not strident but totally representative of the current social climate ... there is an attempt to recreate the stereotypical femme fatale universally associated with Spain and which Israel Galván exaggerates and ridicules because he knows it's the best way of defusing it.[9]

Silvia Calado also reviewed the premiere of *La Francesa* at the 2006 Bienal, prior to her review of the 2007 Festival of Jeréz, above. Although her review of the Jeréz performance laments the tendencies of the "new generation" of dancers, her assessment of Pastora Galván's performance at the Bienal contrasted her negative review of the choreography:

> To all the dance technique and knowledge she has absorbed since her childhood, she adds guts, internal essences, something physical which rarely comes out on stage. And she dances with mischief, rage, violence, vehemence, eroticism ... to the point of making dance a catharsis of every bailaora and every woman, free at last.[10]

On one level, Calado admires Pastora Galván's ability to transcend the choreography, to go beyond the mere repetition of steps, with her performance. Like Maya, Pastora Galván's "renunciation" of the traditional female role and its conventions of beauty creates anxiety among viewers. On the one hand, she is considered "one of the greats," but her display of ugliness is difficult for audiences and critics to bear. Both dancers hold a kind protected status as children of part-gypsy flamenco families. The "authenticity" of their birthrights, combined with their indisputable talents, allow them "diplomatic immunity," which prevents them from being shunned entirely from the world of flamencos. They are "allowed" to "say" things that other artists would never be able to bring to a stage. However, it is due to their prodigious technical abilities, their ability to conform to the demands of traditionalists, that they maintain their rights and privileged status.

Both artists sacrifice their ability to earn money when they dance outside the realm of the traditional flamenco. "The marketplace," says Galván, "is a cruel reality. *La Francesa* didn't sell. What they want is *guirilandia* (the outsider's stereotype of flamenco). You have to 'put on the flower,' you have to be beautiful."[11] Maya would like to tour her abstract work in places where contemporary dance has more of an audience. "I haven't toured anything modern outside of Spain, they don't sell. The representatives don't want to sell modern work abroad."[12] Although both artists have performed their more experimental work as part of the flamenco circuit, a feat within itself, given how many artists compete for the opportunity to appear in these festivals, there is a problem of perception of flamenco outside of Spain. If a production is flamenco, it has to fall within the realm of the traditional or the highly commercial representations, like the flamenco role in *Riverdance*, originated by Maria Pagés. Experimental flamenco still depends on an understanding of the form and its multiple codes, especially when they are being broken. Contemporary dance presenters and audiences don't necessarily "get it" when a traditionally trained dancer transgresses a boundary or mocks beloved conventions. Ironically, the only place that has a marketplace niche for experimental flamenco is Spain, where it is supported up to a point, but kept at the margins of traditional flamenco.

Rocío Molina

Born in Málaga in 1984, Rocío Molina has, in her young life, already been awarded the prizes of an entire career, most notably the XI Certamen de Coreografía y Danza de Madrid in 2002 prize for the Most Outstanding Dancer, Best Flamenco Dancer in 2006 from the El Madroño and Venencia Flamenca al Mistela, the Critic's Prize for Best Female Flamenco Dancer from *Flamenco de Hoy* in 2007, and the Best Female Flamenco Dancer of 2007 from *www.deflamenco.com*. In addition to performing, she is a prolific choreographer who has been commissioned by the Andalusian Agency for the Development of Flamenco and Málaga in Flamenco, as well as the companies of Maria Pagés and José Porcel.

Rocío Molina dances in *Mujeres* at the 2008 Festival Flamenco de Jeréz. Photograph by Paco Sánchez, used with permission.

Trained at the Real Conservatorio de Danza in Madrid, Molina has the capacity to perform classical Spanish dance and contemporary dance as well as flamenco. However, she doesn't suffer from the prejudices among flamencos about "académia." There is a popular notion that some dancers are born, "natural" dancers, usually from gypsy parents, while other dancers are made, through training. For this reason, flamencos distinguish between *bailarines* and *bailaores*, classically trained dancers and pure flamenco dancers. She is not gypsy, and she was not born into a flamenco family, but she seems to have transcended all the old rules about what makes an extraordinary dancer.

Rocío Molina's ascent to the highest class of flamenco artists occurred in the space of only a few years. Estela Zatania, in 2005, summarized the dancer's astonishing career path:

> Rocío Molina is a young exceptionally talented and intelligent *bailaora*, whose "El eterno retorno," premiered during the Málaga in Flamenco Festival, has staked her claim with imagination and dedication, and must now be judged, as harsh as that sounds. Let's take a step back in time.... Slightly over a year ago, during the prestigious competition held at La Unión, this little lady left

more than one spectator speechless with her original style and talent, but she did not make the finals. Only five months later she figured in the recitals series of the USA Festival with some of the leading names in flamenco such as Sara Baras, Eva Yerbabuena, Enrique Morente, Tomatito, Gerardo Núñez, Belén Maya and others. Two months later, at the Jeréz Festival in March of this year (2005), she debuted with a small group, she alone tackling a different program of long dances, equally long *batas de cola* and with such a high standard that she caused a sensation in the Company's theatre: many of us left with that sensation that rarely overcomes us after having seen something so significant.[13]

Few dancers arrive on the scene and catapult themselves into the inner circle of flamenco artists, but Molina has shown a singular determination to accomplish her vision in a short period of time. Perhaps what is most astonishing about Molina is not her incredible technical abilities, which are truly extraordinary in terms of the speed of her footwork and turns, the plasticity of her torso and the expressiveness of her hands, but the kinds of artistic risks she undertakes at such a young age. When speaking about beauty in flamenco following the success of *Mujeres*, Belén Maya said, "Ugliness doesn't exist in flamenco. Well, except for Israel [Galván]. Can you imagine a woman doing what he does? Rocío will do it. She'll do it because it is in her. She is unique."[14] Although she dances the traditional forms with great artistry, Molina displays the singularity of her vision through her choreography. Her work challenges many conventional ideas of beauty, the body, and desire.

In August of 2006, Rocío Molina and Laura Rozalén Torolé choreographed and produced a work called *Turquesa Como El Limón (Turquoise Like a Lemon)* at Madrid's Pradillo Theatre. The show challenges conventional notions of beauty, intends to "offer the public another kind of beauty, which isn't the kind stipulated by society, but is without a doubt still beauty."[15] In the opening sequence, after snacking on some appetizers, Molina wiggles and gyrates to a samba rhythm, a self-effacing noodling that appears almost Chaplinesque. Then, a voice recorded with an affected, snobbish accent gives "corrections" to the dancer, and Molina moves to the rhythms and meanings of the words. The relentless voice tells her "*manzana, sí, bollicao, no*," meaning "apples, yes, pastries, no." She must eat "apples, *guapa*, apples, *guapa*, apples, *guapa*." At the end of the diatribe, Molina tears down a line of signs that hang from the ceiling. They say things like "Olé, Go on a diet, I'm bitter, Girl, you've got a long way to go, to be able to dance."[16] During the introduction, the dancing body, previously the target of these words, becomes the "voice" of criticism. She ridicules the parsimonious teachers of the past in their assessment of her body and its abilities.

Then, the work changes personality with a musical interlude, and Laura Rozalén emerges from darkness. Her ample figure evokes the images of some

Portrait of Pastora Imperio, the legendary dancer of the Golden Age is attributed to F. Bixio y Cia. of Buenos Aires and was probably taken in the late 1910s. (Jerome Robbins Dance Division, New York Public Library for the Performing Arts, Astor, Lenox and Tilden Foundations).

of the flamenco dancers from the early twentieth century, like Pastora Imperio. Rozalén performs a *garrotín*, a form popularized by La Niña de los Peines, one of the most famous *cantaoras* in history. First, she "enters" with a *salida*. Then she performs the feminine carriage of the arms and body, *marcaje*. Signaling a change of mood with a "call," or *llamada*, she performs more extended footwork in her *escobilla*; the footwork speeds up with a *subida*, followed by more elegant *marcaje*, and a closing. Her dance follows the map of the traditional solo in flamenco. That is, she enters following the guitarist and the singer, interprets the singer's words, then comments on the rhythms with footwork so as not to detract from his singing. Only when he finishes singing a verse does she insert building phrases of footwork, but nothing pyrotechnic, not like contemporary dancers. The pacing is slower, reminiscent of the tempo from another age.

Trading solos, Molina enters in a man's costume from the 19th century and performs a *zapateado* that features constant commentary through rapid footwork. She dances like a percussionist, matching the work of the *cajón*. However, from the waist up, she is pure flamenco *postura*, with turns that halt and change direction in a millisecond. The traditional development of the solo dance is discarded in favor of a dialogue between musicians. The distinction is that one of them dances.

Rozalén enters singing a *jota*, in a long *bata de cola*, comb, shawl, all the trappings of the Golden Age, while Molina bounds around her, partnering her with boyish enthusiasm, playing castanets. As Rozalén descends into a seat, Molina first performs footwork before her, then circles her, tickling the back of her neck, an intimate, flirtatious gesture. Molina circles again, then initiates the movement of one of Rozalén's graceful arms, and departs. The musicians change time signatures, and Rozalén strikes a regal pose from the early twentieth century as she begins her *alegrías*. This is a love affair of opposites, a postcard matched with a text message, *lo puro con el futuro* ... purism with futurism.

The concert culminates in a tight spotlight on Molina's face. The audience becomes her mirror. She makes faces, squeezes pimples, until Rozalén pushes her out of the way, playfully fighting for space, grooming herself in the gaze of the audience. The final image of the two women in the space of a bathroom mirror, pressed cheek-to-cheek, cements their connection, their alliance against the criticism of the world. Juan Vergillos of *www.deflamenco. com* describes the evening as an effortless achievement: "And everything without grinding an axe, as easy as breathing in and out."[17]

Turquesa como el limón challenges the ideal body of the dancer from Molina's opening solo. Her technical abilities suggest that the constraints of the ideal body are inadequate to her capabilities as a dancer. Her body exceeds the limits of the conventional female role in performance. Further, the work offers up a deferential, almost worshipful positioning of Laura Rozalén's body in performance, and it does so by reminding flamencos of their nostalgic past. Like Maya and Martín, Molina and Rozalén use the unassailable conventions of the Golden Age to represent unconventional desire.

The "queering" of the flamenco body through the choreographic representations of the "anti-guapas" is not merely the articulation of desire outside the boundaries of heteronormativity, although *Turquesa como el limón* makes a few pointed allusions to the intimacy between the partners. The two made stronger statements about their relationship when, for example, on February 8, 2008, Laura Rozalén accepted the "Flamenco Hoy" Critic's Award for Best Female Dancer of 2007 on behalf of Rocío Molina, directly from the hands of the queen of the *sevillano* school, Matilde Coral.[18] In their deconstruction of the ideal female body, they manage to "queer" their representation of themselves within flamenco in the way that Juana María Rodriguez defines the term:

> "Queer" is not simply an umbrella term that encompasses lesbians, bisexuals, gay men, two-spirited people and transsexuals; it is a challenge to constructions of heteronormativity. It need not subsume the particularities of these other definitions of identity; instead it creates an opportunity to call into question the systems of categorization that have served to define sexuality.[19]

The flamenco stereotype is always sexualized; further, it is always heterosexualized according to the dynamics of domination in an Orientalist fantasy. The gendered conventions of traditional male and female dancing support the underlying narrative of heterosexual seduction. The assumption that the female body must always be displayed at its most "beautiful," conforming to a very specific definition of "beauty," reveals the hetereonormative, socializing function of flamenco as a cultural practice. "Queering" the flamenco body allows for a destabilization of the categories of gender, desire and subjectivity, and expands the possibilities for what can be represented in flamenco. In that space, ideas beyond beauty emerge.

In 2007, Molina choreographed a solo evening called *Almario*, which debuted at the Jerez Festival. The premise of the piece is a journey through Molina's "soul-closet," with several changes of costume and mood. Words painted in lipstick on a mirror admonish the dancer (and the audience?) to "be yourself." She opens with a *taranto*, dressed in a leather dress and jacket and what were very likely the high-heeled boots that Silvia Calado lamented in her review of *La francesa* with Pastora Galván: "a generation which can dance wearing high boots or stiletto heels, following a short distance behind the footsteps of the inciting Belén Maya and Rafaela Carrasco."[20] Molina plays finger-cymbals in counterpoint to her rapid footwork, adding multiple "broken turns" (*vueltas quebradas*), to her sequences of movement.

In her costume change between pieces, Molina converts from a leather-clad fireball to a contemporary dancer in a unitard. Rappelling off a box that serves as a pedestal and a weight to be dragged, she leaps over the multiple ruffles on an elaborate *bata de cola*. Poised on top of the pedestal, she transforms once again into a traditional flamenco dancer. Accompanying herself on castanets, she performs a *seguirilla*, one of the deep song forms, desolate in its overall feeling. The fierce creature of the opening sequence softens and yields into the body of one of the *cantaores*, leaning back in a posture of complete vulnerability. Then she reasserts herself, and performs elaborate sequences of footwork and turns with the *bata de cola*.

Changing personality again, she appears as a Chaplinesque character in "*Garrotín* Feo," an ugly version of the *garrotín*. She exaggerates postures, pulls faces, shimmies her shoulders, all in perfect *compás*, commenting on every note of the scratchy old recording. Doll-like, she is stripped and reconstituted in a red silk dress, then drapes herself in a floor-length shawl for her bambera. Leaving behind the extended displays of footwork of the other *palos*, she focuses on the mastery of the shawl in its swinging motion, and sculptural positioning of the body. Throwing off the shawl, surrounded by *palmeros*, she switches into an impossibly fast *bulerías*. She improvises over the rhythms, combining permutations of intricate footwork patterns. In a final deconstruction, "*Mentiras* (Lies)," Molina peels off her red dress and adds contemporary dance vocabulary to her movements. Eventually she removes her shoes, switching in and out of the flamenco idiom, dressed only in her unitard.

Program notes, written by Miguel Serrano, describe *Almario* as a journey inward:

> Inside us all, there are both remnants of our ancestors as well as the immediate reality, reflections of the age in which we live, invading our inner selves, in a continuous confrontation between old and new. That's human, and that's how we grow into a person, defining and differentiating ourselves from others.[21]

Rocío Molina's performance suggests the excavation of an internal landscape, revealing layers of history and, with each one, the mastery of certain techniques. The solos of *Armario* portray the contemporary *flamenca* as tethered to the past and buoyed by the future. The song forms of the Golden Age, with their attendant skill sets (*mantón, bata de cola*), Spanish classical structures like castanets, and the quirky expressiveness of a contemporary dance vocabulary combine to produce this generation of dancer, hellbent on transcending limitations, but most at home in dialogue with structures, taking ownership of the riches from the past. Nothing is discarded, just added, recombined and redefined.

The transgressions of the "anti-guapas," from the theatrical commentary of Belén Maya's *Souvenir* to the "shameless" coarseness of Pastora Galván's performance of *La francesa* and the "queering" of the flamenco body in *Turquesa como el Limón* challenge the exotic flamenco stereotype as well as the conventions of appropriate femininity within the flamenco tradition. In *The Cantaoras*, Loren Chuse provides a history of the development of the dichotomy of the morally pure idealized image of femininity and the anti-heroine in flamenco and Spanish culture. Since the early twentieth century, flamenco historians, almost always men, have pitted these two narrow characterizations against one another. However, with the establishment of major companies under the artistic director of women, Cristina Hoyos, Eva La Yerbabuena, Sara Baras, Rafaela Carrasco, and more, within the past ten years, the roles for women in flamenco have multiplied. These women have maintained the conventions of the feminine role, often "rescuing" song and dance forms forgotten in the *tablaos*, but they have also expanded what subjects may be addressed in flamenco dance. They have changed flamenco's subjectivity. The dancing gypsy girl is no longer subaltern. She speaks. In fact, the half-gypsy dancer (Maya) performs alongside the *paya* (Molina) in the presence of a diva (Esmeralda), in a self-conscious spectacle of femininity in the case of *Mujeres* at the 2008 Festival de Jerez.

Make no mistake: the stereotypes still resonate with power and meaning. At least two exist in within the convenient reference of conversation: the limited archetype of femininity valorized by traditionalists (La Guapa) and the commercial caricature celebrated by tourists (Carmen). However, they no longer maintain the same power and meaning that they had in previous historical contexts. The historic dualities, like tourism and purism, tradition and innovation, Gypsy and *payo*, Spaniard and foreigner, continue to exist, but they no longer hold the same oppositional tension. New "local" tensions, specific to the individual community where flamenco is practiced, fray at the old debates concerning origins and authenticity, adding to their complexity. Rafaela Carrasco addressed the state of flamenco in an interview with Silvia Calado of *www.flamenco-world.com* in June of 2004. She said,

> I think that right now the dancing is being done better than ever, but there are also a lot of mistakes, obviously. There's a lot of information about everything, a lot of ability, a lot of training and you have the freedom to choose. You have to allow yourself the freedom to choose the road you want to take, in the more traditional and more flamenco way, or in the way more.... It's your choice and it's great. For us to be allowed the freedom to choose the opposite, for us to be allowed to make mistakes because that's where the wealth and learning lie, in being able to make mistakes and in being able to get it right.[22]

Carrasco, and her *comadres,* indeed the entire generation of new flamenco artists, by virtue of their mastery of existing forms and the play of the expressive possibilities in new recombinations, play a key role in the perpetuation of flamenco as a tradition. They "speak" lovingly from a desiring subjectivity, one that articulates the need for and means by which they honor the past as they construct the future. Even as they question assumptions about the rigidity of purism or the commercial demands of a global marketplace, they revere the legacy they inherit and treat their experimentation as a means of cultivating a field of meaning in which their work is intelligible. Like their forebears, they face the challenges of constantly renegotiating flamenco's identity across the lines of racial difference, ethnic categories, class positioning, gender construction, regional tensions, national affiliations, and international politics. However, as these chapters hopefully demonstrate, flamenco's divergent histories reveal its capacity for continual reinvention even in the most stultifying of circumstances. The re/territorialism of flamenco in the context of the world-wide web and new networks for successful international touring, paralleled by the unprecedented support for the proliferation of flamenco within Spain, suggest new landscapes of possibility for flamenco's future. Although critics and certain audiences may despair at the liberties contemporary artists take with the structures of tradition, their experimentation shows a deep reverence for the past; they are not impoverished in terms of their vocabulary and its seemingly infinite iterations. Flamenco dance instills in its practitioners certain skills: flexibility, an attentiveness to line, sensitivity to melody, rhythmic acumen, astonishing strength, dynamic range of motion, and the rigorous ability to spontaneously compose in a moment of improvisation. Equipped with these skills, *bailaoras* possess all the tools they require to preserve their traditions while renewing them through innovation. *Qué rico, de verdad!* How rich, indeed.

Chapter Notes

Introduction

1. Creators Celia Ipiotis and Jeff Bush went on to create an expanded series called *Eye on Dance and the Arts* through their non-profit corporation Arts Resources in Collaboration, which now has several divisions, including the television series, video archive, and electronic and print commentary. More information is available on their website: *www.eyeondance.org*.

2. Sander L. Gilman, *Difference and Pathology: Stereotypes of Sexuality, Race and Madness* (Ithaca and London: Cornell University Press, 1985), pp. 17–18.

3. Gilman, p. 20.

4. Gayatri Chakravorty Spivak, "Can the Subaltern Speak?" *Marxism and the Interpretation of Culture*, ed. Cary Nelson and Lauren Grossberg (Urbana: University of Illinois Press, 1988), p. 308.

5. See Jacques Derrida's "The Violence of the Letter," *Of Grammatology*, tr. Gayatri Spivak (Baltimore and London: Johns Hopkins University Press, 1976), pp. 101–140.

6. Bill Nichols, *Ideology and the Image* (Bloomington: Indiana University Press, 1981), p. 43.

7. Judith Butler, *Bodies That Matter: On the Discursive Limits of "Sex"* (New York: Routledge, 1993), p. 10.

8. Peter Robinson, "Merimee's Carmen," in *Georges Bizet: Carmen*, ed. Susan McClary (New York: Cambridge University Press, 1992), p. 1.

9. Robinson, p. 1.

10. Robinson, p. 4.

11. Susan McClary, "Images of Race, Class and Gender in Nineteenth-Century French Culture," in *Georges Bizet: Carmen*, ed. Susan McClary (New York: University of Cambridge, 1992), p. 31.

12. McClary, p. 18.

13. James Woodall, *In Search of the Firedance* (London: Sinclair-Stevenson, 1992), p. 132.

14. Alfred Charles Richard, Jr., *The Hispanic Image on the Silver Screen* (New York: Greenwood Press, 1992), p. 144.

15. "Introduction: A World in Motion," *The Anthropology of Globalization: A Reader* (Malden, MA: Blackwell Publishing, 2002), p. 12.

Chapter 1

1. For a detailed discussion of tensions between Gypsies and Andalusians, see "Gypsy Jokes and the Andalusian Self-Image," in Stanley Brandes's *Metaphors of Masculinity: Sex and Status in Andalusian Folklore* (Pittsburgh: University of Pennsylvania Press, 1980), pp. 53–73.

2. William Washabaugh's "The Histories of Flamenco," in *Flamenco: Passion, Politics and Popular Culture* (Oxford and Washington, D.C.: Berg, 1996) presents an overview of the scholarly discussions concerning the gypsy invention of flamenco, including the theories of Antonio Mairena, Ángel Álvarez Caballero, José Caballero Bonáld, and Félix Grande, p. 31.

3. The term *payo* is often but not always used negatively in flamenco circles. Literally, it defines an outsider, a non-gypsy.

4. The 1993 film *Latcho Drom* displays the variety of cultural influences in contemporary gypsy communities in splendid visual and audio detail.

5. James Woodall provides a poetic exploration of Muslim culture in Andalusia in "The Gilded Triangle," from *In Search of the Firedance: Spain through Flamenco* (London: Sinclair-Stevenson, 1992), pp. 31–68. The comparison between the *zajal* and the *copla* appears on p. 41.

6. Jane S. Gerber, *The Jews of Spain* (New York: The Free Press, 1992), p. 2.

7. Alain Gobin, *Le Flamenco* (n.p. 1975), p. 62.

8. Allen Josephs, "Dancer of Gades," *White Wall of Spain* (Pensacola: University of West Florida Press, 1990), p. 69.

9. Donn E. Pohren, *Lives and Legends of Flamenco: A Biographical History* (Madrid: Society of Spanish Studies, 1964), p. 173. See also Félix Grande, *Memoria del Flamenco I: Raices y Prehistoria del Cante* (Madrid: Espasa-Calpe, S.A., 1979), p. 43, and José M. Caballero-Bonald, *Andalusian Dances* (Barcelona: Editorial Noguer, S.A., 1959), p. 55.

10. Pohren, p. 174.

11. B. Morar, et al., "Mutation History of the Roma/Gypsies," *American Journal of Human Genetics*, Vol. 75, Issue 4 (2004): 604.

12. Shovana Narayan, *Rhythmic Echoes and Reflections: Kathak* (New Delhi: Lotus Collection, Roli Books Pvt. Ltd., 1998), p. 9.

13. Narayan, pp. 14–15.

14. The complexity of this transformation is discussed in Avanthi Meduri's "Bharatha Natyam, What Are You?" *Asian Theatre Journal* 5 (Spring 1988), pp. 1–22.

15. Miriam S. Phillips, "A Shared Technique/Shared Roots?: A Comparison of Kathak and Flamenco Dance History," *Proceedings of the Fourteenth Annual Conference of the Society of Dance History Scholars, February 8–10, 1991: Dance in Hispanic Cultures* (Riverside, CA: Society of Dance History Scholars, 1991), p. 47.

16. Richard Ford, *Gatherings from Spain* (London: J.M. Dent & Co., 1906), p. 354.

17. Woodall, p. 129.

18. Woodall, p. 129.

19. José Blás Vega, *Los Cafés Cantantes de Sevilla* (Madrid: Cinterco, c. 1982), p. 40.

20. Though Lorca wrote these works in the years I have attributed to them above, the poems were not published until the years 1928 and 1929 by Revista Occidente of Madrid.

21. Félix Grande, *Memoria del Flamenco II: Desde el Café Cantante a Nuestros Días* (Madrid: Espasa-Calpe, S.A., 1979), p. 500. My translation.

22. J.L. Gili, *Selected Poems* (Harmondsworth: Penguin, 1960), p. 127.

23. Madeleine Claus, "Baile Flamenco," in *Flamenco: Gypsy Dance and Music from Andalusia*, ed. Claus Schreiner (Portland, OR: Amadeus Press, 1985), p. 97.

24. Woodall, p. 213.

25. Susan Cashion discusses the standards for an "authentic" performance at a *peña*, which involves the arrival of the *duende*, in "The *Duende* of Spanish Cante Flamenco,"

ANGF Journal (Asociación Nacional de Grupos Folklóricos) 4, no. 1 (1969), pp. 1–12 .

26. Madeleine Claus, "Baile Flamenco," in *Flamenco: Gypsy Dance and Music from Andalusia*, ed. Claus Schreiner (Portland, OR: Amadeus Press, 1985), p. 97.

27. Walter Benjamin, "Theses on the Philosophy of History," *Illuminations*, ed. Hannah Arendt, trans. Harry Zohn (New York: Schocken Books, 1969), p. 261. The editor's note on this quotation indicates that Benjamin's use of "Jetztzeit" should not be translated as the "present," but instead as the "mystical *nunc stans*."

28. Louis Althusser, in "Ideology and Ideological State Apparatuses," *Lenin and Philosophy and Other Essays*, trans. Ben Brewster (New York: Monthly Review Press, 1971). Reprinted in *Critical Theory Since 1965*, ed. Hazard Adams and Leroy Searle (Tallahassee: University of Florida Press, 1986), p. 244.

29. Adams and Searle, p. 240.

30. Adams and Searle, p. 239.

31. This quote is attributed to "Leopold von Ranke (1795–1886), German historian," in Adams and Searle, p. 681.

32. Benjamin in Adams and Searle, p. 681.

33. Susan McClary, "Images of Race, Class and Gender in Nineteenth-Century French Culture," in *Georges Bizet: Carmen*, ed. Susan McClary (New York: University of Cambridge, 1992) p. 47.

34. Hayden White, "Narrativity in the Representation of Reality," *The Content of the Form: Narrative Discourse and Historical Representation* (Baltimore and London: Johns Hopkins University Press, 1987), p. 20.

35. White, p. 21.

36. White, p. 5.

37. Bill Nichols, *Ideology and the Image: Social Representation in the Cinema and Other Media* (Bloomington: Indiana University Press, 1981), p. 10.

38. Nichols, p. 30.

39. Nichols, p. 34.

40. Marvin D'Lugo, *The Films of Carlos Saura* (Princeton: Princeton University Press, 1991), p. 193.

41. José Ortega y Gasset, "Teoría de Andalucía," *Obras Completas*. 5a. edición. (Madrid: Revista de Occidente, 1961), p. 112.

Chapter 2

1. For a contemporary discussion of the gypsies in Europe, see Isabel Fonseca's *Bury Me Standing: The Gypsies and Their Journey* (London: Chatto and Windus, 1995).

2. The concept of a "classical" body that

can be compared to its exact opposite, a "grotesque" body, is developed in Mikhail Bakhtin's theory of the carnivalesque in *Rabelais and His World*, tr. H. Iswolsky (Bloomington: Indiana University Press, 1965).

3. Rice does not assign this performance a date or a location. It is interesting to note that his example of the gitana comes, once again, from a Spanish classical composition, not a traditional flamenco performance.

4. The use of "the spectatorial gaze" in this discussion is informed by Laura Mulvey's work in film theory. For a discussion of "the gaze" and the structures of gender and power that produce it, see " Visual Pleasure and Narrative Cinema" and "Afterthoughts on Visual Pleasure and Narrative Cinema Inspired by Duel in the Sun," *Feminism and Film Theory*, ed. Constance Penley (New York: Routledge, 1988), pp. 57–79.

5. For a discussion of homoerotic tension and homosocial bonding between men across the body of a woman, see Eve Sedgewick's *Between Men: English Literature and Male Homosocial Desire* (New York: Columbia University Press, 1985).

6. Marta Savigliano, *Tango and the Political Economy of Passion* (Boulder: Westview Press, 1995), p. 74.

7. Rice attributes this quote to A. Levinson in Argentina (Paris: n.p., 1928).

8. Madeleine Claus in *Flamenco: Gypsy Dance and Music from Andalusia*, ed. Claus Schreiner, tr. Mollie Comerford Peters (Portland, OR: Amadeus Press, 1985), pp. 89–120.

9. Madeleine Claus cites, within her text, Alain Gobin's *Le Flamenco* (Paris: n.p., 1975); Roger Mindling's *Spanischer Tanz* (Olten: n.p., 1966); Jose Udaeta's *Flamenco* (Hamburg: n.p., 1964); Ilsa Meudtner's *Flamenco Showgeschaft und Wurlichkeit* (Merian 5: n.p., XXX/C); and Félix Grande's *Memoria del Flamenco II: Desde el Café Cantante a Nuestros Días* (Madrid: Espasa-Calpe, S.A., 1979).

10. José Blas Vega, *Los Cafés Cantantes de Sevilla* (Madrid: Editorial Cinterco, 1987), p. 25.

11. For a more elaborate discussion of the concept of essence and the threat of reproduction, see Walter Benjamin's "The Work of Art in the Age of Mechanical Reproduction," *Illuminations*, ed. Hannah Arendt, tr. Harry Zohn (New York: Schocken Books, 1968), pp. 217–251.

12. Cathexis here is used in the sense that Sigmund Freud defines it in his writings on the formation of the object-libido in *Three Essays on the Theory of Sexuality*, tr. James Strachey (New York: Harper Collins, 1962), p. 83.

13. For example, the music group Ketama

is composed of members from the Habichuela family. Although they come from a gypsy line, their performance of flamenco is informed by jazz fusion and other contemporary world music forms.

14. Greco spares no details in the account of his many seductions in *The Gypsy in My Soul: The Autobiography of José Greco* (New York: Doubleday & Company, 1977). His self-portrait would offer interesting material for an analysis of the self-conscious performance of the male Latin Lover.

Chapter 3

1. Richard Ford, *Gatherings from Spain* (London: J.M. Dent & Co., 1906), p. 315.

2. Edward W. Said, *Orientalism* (New York: Random House, 1994), p. 6.

3. Savigliano, p. 77.

4. Gayatri Chakravorty Spivak, "Can the Subaltern Speak?" *Marxism and the Interpretation of Culture*, ed. Cary Nelson and Lauren Grossberg (Urbana: University of Illinois Press, 1988), p. 308.

5. For a more developed discussion of "archeviolence" and "arche-writing," see "The Violence of the Letter," in Derrida, *Of Grammatology*, tr. Gayatri Chakravorty Spivak (Baltimore and London: Johns Hopkins University Press, 1976), pp. 101–140.

6. Michel de Certeau, *The Writing of History*, tr. Tom Conley (New York: Columbia University Press, 1988), p. 2.

7. Edward W. Said, *Culture and Imperialism* (New York: Random House, 1993), p. 16.

8. de Certeau, p. 2.

9. José Blás Vega, and Manuel Rios Ruiz, *Diccionario Enciclopedico Ilustrado del Flamenco.* (Madrid: Editorio Cinterco, 1988), p. 129.

Chapter 4

1. Mary Ann Doane, "Film and Masquerade: Theorizing the Female Spectator, Mary Ann Doane on the Woman's Gaze," *Screen* 25, 3–4, (1982): 82.

2. This choreographic process can be likened to the signification of a text as discussed by Jacques Derrida: "And if a text always gives itself a certain representation of its own roots, those roots live only by that representation, by never touching the soil, so to speak. Which undoubtedly destroys their *radical essence*, but not the necessity of their *racinating function*." From *Of Grammatology*, tr. Gayatri Chakravorty Spivak (Baltimore and

London: Johns Hopkins University Press, 1974), p. 101.

3. Sarah Kofman, *The Enigma of Woman* (Ithaca and London: Cornell University Press, 1985), p. 53.

4. From "The Mechanics of Fluids," in *This Sex Which is Not One*, tr. Catherine Porter (Ithaca: Cornell University Press, 1985), p. 111.

5. In previous chapters, I have discussed the means by which subjects are constituted within ideology. In this particular instance, the character of the bride is located within a patriarchal structure where masculinity and authority are synonymous. For this reason, I use the term "phallogocentric" as Luce Irigaray does, to describe a system of law and meaning that focuses on the role of the phallus in the hierarchy of power.

6. Laura Mulvey. "Visual Pleasure and Narrative Cinema," in *Feminism and Film Theory*, ed. Constance Penley (New York: Routledge, 1988), p. 58.

7. Irigaray, p. 113.

8. Catherine Clement, *Opera, or the Undoing of Women* (Minneapolis: University of Minnesota Press, 1988), p. 47.

9. Donna Haraway, "A Manifesto for Cyborgs," *Simians, Cyborgs and Women: The Reinvention of Nature* (New York: Routledge, 1991), p. 149.

10. Teresa de Lauretis, *Technologies of Gender* (Bloomington and Indianapolis: Indiana University Press, 1987), p. 108.

11. Susan McClary, "Images of Race, Class and Gender in Nineteenth-Century French Culture," in *Georges Bizet: Carmen*, ed. Susan McClary (New York: University of Cambridge, 1992), p. 135.

12. Savigliano, p. 46.

13. Savigliano, p. 47.

14. Laura Mulvey, "Visual Pleasure and Narrative Cinema," *Feminism and Film Theory*, ed. Constance Penley (New York: Routledge, 1988), p. 62. Mulvey further develops her theory of female spectatorship in a second article, "Afterthoughts on 'Visual Pleasure and Narrative Cinema,' Inspired by *Duel in the Sun*," printed in the same volume, pp. 69–79.

15. Mulvey, p. 124–25.

16. Claus Schreiner, ed. *Flamenco: Gypsy Dance and Music from Andalusia* (Portland, OR: Amadeus Press, 1990), p. 31.

Chapter 5

1. Although I do not include it in this discussion, Saura's film *Ay, Carmela!* (1992) contains a principal character who is a cabaret dancer. Also, the 2005 *Iberia* and 2006 *Salome* focus on flamenco.

2. Marvin D'Lugo, *The Films of Carlos Saura* (Princeton: Princeton University Press, 1991), p. 193.

3. William Washabaugh devotes the final chapter of *Flamenco: Passion, Politics and Popular Culture* (Oxford and Washington, D.C.: Berg, 1996) to a detailed analysis of the *Rito* series. Although he focuses on the political analysis of the *cante* in this section, his arguments are useful as a foundation for the consideration of the dance.

4. Anna Kisselgoff, "A Provocateur at Large in the World of Flamenco," *New York Times*, September 16, 1996, C 12: 2.

5. James Woodall, *In Search of the Firedance* (London: Sinclair-Stevenson, 1992), pp. 299–300.

6. "Viva Sevilla," "Mi novio es un cartujano," "Rosa de pitimirí," "Tiene una cinturita," and "Lo tiré al pozo," five *coplas* in all.

7. D'Lugo, p. 193.

8. Woodall, p. 109.

9. Eva La Yerbuena in an interview with Jenny Gilbert published in *The Independent on Sunday*, December 26, 2004.

Chapter 6

1. Reprinted in Samuel Flagg Bemis' *The Latin American Policy of the United States* (New York: Harcourt, Brace and World, 1943), p. 257

2. Bemis, p. 258.

3. Carlos Cortés, "Chicanos in Film: History of an Image," in *Chicano Cinema: Research, Reviews and Resources*, ed. Gary D. Keller (Binghamton, NY: Bilingual Review/Press, 1985), p. 99.

4. Allen Woll, *The Latin Image in American Film* (Los Angeles: Latin American Center, University of California, 1977), pp. 34–5, 54–6.

5. Cortés, p. 99.

6. Cynthia Enloe, *Bananas, Beaches and Bases: Making Feminist Sense of International Politics* (Berkeley and Los Angeles: University of California Press, 1990), p. 127.

7. Cortés, p. 100.

8. Tom O'Sullivan, "The South American Way," *Boston Traveler*, 17 June 1941. Carmen Amaya clippings file, microfilm, Dance Collection, New York Public Library.

9. "Latin Americans' Torrid Music All the Rage on Broadway," *New York Post*, 6 April 1941. Carmen Amaya clippings file, microfilm, Dance Collection, New York Public Library.

10. Robert Bagar, *The New York World Telegram*, 14 January 1942. Carmen Amaya

clippings file, microfilm, Dance Collection, New York Public Library.

11. "Gypsy Tornado," *Cue*, 10 January 1942. Carmen Amaya clippings file, microfilm, Dance Collection, New York Public Library.

12. Virginia Mishnun, "Flamenco, Spanish and Spanish-American," *The Nation*, 16 May 1942, 154. Carmen Amaya clippings file, microfilm, Dance Collection, New York Public Library.

13. Bill Butler, "The Legend of Carmen Amaya," *Dance Magazine* (April 1954), p. 25.

14. Butler, p. 24.

15. Meira Goldberg, "A 'Heart of Darkness' in the New World: Carmen Amaya's Flamenco Dance in South American Vaudeville," *Dance in Hispanic Cultures. Proceedings of the 14th Annual Conference of the Society of Dance History Scholars, February 8–10, 1991* (Riverside: Society of Dance History Scholars, 1991), pp. 191–192.

16. *Time*. 17 February 1941. Carmen Amaya clippings file. Dance Collection. New York Public Library.

17. Danton Walker, "Broadway," *New York Daily News*, 10 April 1941. Carmen Amaya clippings file, microfilm, Dance Collection, New York Public Library.

18. Gertrude Bailey, "Smart Costumes Cost Under $20," *New York World-Telegram*, May 14, 1941. Carmen Amaya clippings file, microfilm, Dance Collection, New York Public Library.

19. Vicente Romero, *Dance Magazine* (November 1963), p. 47.

20. Meira Goldberg, "Carmen Amaya Wore Pants: Flamenco as a Forum for Cross-Gender Identification Within Spanish Gypsy Culture" (paper presented at the Congress on Research and Dance, Performance and Possibilities, Los Angeles, October 1987), p. 281.

21. Goldberg, p. 282.

22. Goldberg, p. 283.

23. Donn Pohren, *Lives and Legends of Flamenco* (Madrid: Society of Spanish Studies, 1964), p. 231.

24. Pohren, pp. 231–2.

25. La Meri, "Encounters with Dance Immortals: La Argentinita and Carmen Amaya," *Arabesque* (Jan.-Feb. 1985), p. 9.

26. James Woodall, *In Search of the Firedance* (London: Sinclair-Stevenson, 1992), p. 250.

27. For a discussion of prostitution and military bases, see Cynthia Enloe's "Base Women," in *Bananas, Beaches and Bases: Making Feminist Sense of International Politics* (Berkeley and Los Angeles: University of California Press, 1990), pp. 65–92.

28. Woodall, p. 252. .

29. Eduoard de Blaye, tr. Brian Pearce, *Franco and the Politics of Spain* (New York: Penguin Books, 1976), p. 197.

30. Woodall, p. 254.

31. Antonia Rojas no longer lives in Southern California. Currently she and her guitarist husband, Joel Kabokov, live in the Pacific Northwest. She enjoys the "choreographies of nature" she witnesses there on a daily basis.

32. "El Duende," *Dance Perspectives* 27 (Autumn 1966): 47.

33. Federico García Lorca, "Teoria y juego del duende," *Obras Completas* (Madrid: Aguilar, S.A. 1967), p. 110.

34. Lorca, p. 112. My translation.

35. Lorca, p. 118. My translation.

36. The concept of the *duende* is integral to Josephs's study of Andalusian culture. He includes, in his book *White Wall of Spain: The Mysteries of Andalusian Culture* (Pensacola: University of West Florida Press, 1990), a chapter devoted to flamenco, titled "Dancer of Gades." This particular quotation appears on page 97.

37. See "Poema del Cante Jondo," and "Romancero Gitano" in the above cited edition of Lorca's complete works, pp. 295–318, and pp. 425–457.

38. Grande has produced two exhaustive volumes of flamenco history: *Memoria del Flamenco I: Raices y Prehistoria del Cante* and *Memoria del Flamenco 2: Desde el Cafe Cantante a Nuestros Dias*. Madrid: Espasa-Calpe, S.A., 1979.

Chapter 7

1. David Fernandez, "Tres estrellas iluminan el Villamarta," *Diario de Jeréz*. Saturday, March 1, 2008, p. 3.

2. José María Castaño, "Triunfo del eterno feminino." *La Voz*. Saturday, March 1, 2008, No. 8, Supplement, p. 2.

3. Belén Maya, interview with the author, Jeréz, Spain, Saturday, March 1, 2008. Translation by the author.

4. Carlos Sánchez, online review of *Souvenir*, April 12, 2007. *www.flamenco-world com*.

5. Miguel Mora, "Mayte Martín y Belén Maya llenan de dulzura y buen gusto el Festival de Tokio," May 14, 2005. *www.elpais.com*. Translation by the author.

6. Josephine Leask, "Long Train Running: Maya and Martín Wrap It Up," February 2005, *www.thedancesider.com*.

7. Fernandez, p. 3.

8. Silvia Calado, Review of *La francesa*, Jeréz, March 1, 2007. www.flamenco-world. com.

9. Estela Zatania, Review of *La francesa*, September 16, 2006. *www.deflamenco.com*.

10. Silvia Calado, Review of *La francesa*, September 16, 2006. *www.flamenco-world.com*. Translation Joseph Kopec.

11. Pastora Galván, interview with the author, Seville, Tuesday, March 4, 2008. Translation by the author.

12. Maya, interview with the author, Jeréz, Saturday, March 1, 2008. Translation by the author.

13. Estela Zatania, Review of *El eterno retorno*, September 18, 2005. *www.deflamenco.com*.

14. Maya, interview with the author, Jeréz, Saturday, March 1, 2008. Translation by the author.

15. Program notes, *Turquesa Como El Limón*, *www.rociomolina.com*.

16. "Hey, what do you say she needs?" Silvia Calado. Seville, November 22, 2007. *www.flamenco-world.com*.

17. Juan Vergillos, "Stripping down to basics as easily as breathing, Rocío Molina, Laura Rozalén, *Turquesa como el limón*," November 22, 2007. *www.deflamenco.com*.

18. "9th Edition Flamenco Hoy Awards of Flamenco Critics 2007," February 6, 2008. wwww.deflamenco.com.

19. Juana María Rodriguez, *Queer Latinidad, Identity Practices, Discursive Spaces* (New York: NYU Press, 2003), p. 24.

20. Silvia Calado, Review of *La francesa*, Jeréz, March 1, 2007. *www.flamenco-world.com*.

21. Miguel Serrano, program notes for Almario, *www.rociomolina.com*.

22. Rafaela Carrasco, interview with Silvia Calado, Jeréz, June 2004. *www.flamenco-world.com*. Translation Joseph Kopec.

Bibliography

Adams, Bryan. "Have You Ever Really Loved a Woman?" *Don Juan de Marco*. A&M Records, 1995.

Adams, Hazard, and Leroy Searle, eds. *Critical Theory Since 1965*. Tallahassee: University of Florida Press, 1986.

Alba, Victor. *Transition in Spain: From Franco to Democracy*. Tr. Barbara Lotito. New Brunswick, NJ: Transaction Books, 1978.

Althusser, Louis. *Lenin and Philosophy and Other Essays*. Tr. Ben Brewster. New York: Monthly Review Press, 1971.

Alvarez Caballero, Angel. *El baile flamenco*. Madrid: Alianza Editorial, 1989.

_____. *Historia del Cante Flamenco*. Madrid: Alianza Editorial, 1981.

Amaya, Carmen. Scrapbook, clippings and programs, 1940–44. Microfilm, Dance Collection, New York City Library.

El Amor Brujo. Director Carlos Saura and choreographer Antonio Gades. Emiliano Piedra, 1986.

¡Ay, Carmela! Director Carlos Saura. Juan Lebron, 1992.

Bakhtin, Mikhail. *Rabelais and His World*. Tr. H. Iswolsky. Bloomington: Indiana University Press, 1965.

Baudrillard, Jean. *Simulations*. Tr. Paul Foss, Paul Patton, Philip Beitchman. New York: Semiotext(e), Inc., 1983.

Bemis, Samuel Flagg. *The Latin American Policy of the United States: An Historical Interpretation*. New York: Harcourt, Brace & World, Inc., 1943.

Benjamin, Walter. *Illuminations*. Ed. Hannah Arendt. Tr. Harry Zohn. New York: Schocken Books, 1969.

Bennahum, Ninotchka Devorah. "Old Spain or New? Divided They Dance." *New York Times*, 15 February 1998.

Binding, Paul. *Lorca: The Gay Imagination*. London: GMP Publishers, 1985.

Bhabha, Homi K., ed. *Nation and Narration*. New York: Routledge, 1990.

Blás Vega, José. *Los Cafés Cantantes de Sevilla*. Madrid: Editorial Cinterco, S.A., 1987.

Blaye, Edouard de. *Franco and the Politics of Spain*. Tr. Brian Pearce. New York: Penguin Books, 1976.

Bodas de Sangre. Director Carlos Saura and choreographer Antonio Gades. Emiliano Piedra, 1981.

Bongie, Chris. *Exotic Memories: Literature, Colonialism and the Fin de Siecle*. Stanford: Stanford University Press, 1991.

Brandes, Stanley. *Metaphors of Masculinity: Sex and Status in Andalusian Folklore*. Pittsburgh: University of Pennsylvania Press, 1980.

Butler, Bill. "The Legend of Carmen Amaya." *Dance Magazine* (April 1954).

Butler, Judith. *Bodies That Matter: On the Discursive Limits of "Sex."* New York: Routledge, 1983.

Caballero Bonald, José Manuel. *Andalusian Dances*. Barcelona: Editorial Noguer, S.A., 1959.

Carmen. Director Carlos Saura and choreographer Antonio Gades. Emiliano Piedra, 1983.

Cashion, Susan. "The *Duende* of Spanish Cante Flamenco." ANGF Journal (Asociación Nacional de Grupos Foclóricos) 4: 1 (1969).

Certeau, Michel de. *The Writing of History*. Tr. Tom Conley. New York: Columbia University Press, 1988.

Charnon-Deutsch, Lou. *The Spanish Gypsy: The History of a European Obsession*. University Park: The Pennsylvania State University Press, 2004.

Chuse, Loren. *The Cantaoras: Music, Gender and Identity in Flamenco Song*. New York and London: Routledge, 2003

Clement, Catherine. *Opera, Or the Undoing of Women*. Minneapolis: University of Minnesota Press, 1988.

Cortés, Carlos. "Chicanas in Film: History of an Image." *Chicano Cinema: Research, Reviews and Resources*. Ed. Gary D. Keller.

Binghamton, NY: Bilingual Review/Press, 1985.

Coverdale, John F. *The Political Transformation of Spain after Franco.* New York: Praeger Publishers, 1979.

Cruces Roldán, Cristina. *Más Alla de la Música: Antropología y Flamenco (I).* Seville: Signatura Ediciones, 2006.

_____. *Más Alla de la Música: Antropología y Flamenco (II).* Seville: Signatura Ediciones, 2006.

Derrida, Jacques. "The Violence of the Letter." *Of Grammatology.* Tr. Gayatri Chakravorty Spivak. Baltimore and London: Johns Hopkins University Press, 1976.

D'Lugo, Marvin. *The Films of Carlos Saura.* Princeton: Princeton University Press, 1991.

Doane, Mary Ann. *Femme Fatales: Feminism, Film Theory, Psychoanalysis.* New York: Routledge, 1991.

_____. "Film and Masquerade: Theorizing the Female Spectator, Mary Ann Doane on the Woman's Gaze." *Screen 25,* no. 3–4 (1982): 54–97.

Don Juan de Marco. Director Jeremy Leven. American Zoetrope/New Line Cinema, 1995.

Down Argentine Way. Director Irving Cummings, producer Darryl Zanuck. Twentieth Century Fox, 1940.

Enloe, Cynthia. *Bananas, Beaches and Bases: Making Feminist Sense of International Politics.* Berkeley and Los Angeles: University of California Press, 1990.

Flamenco. Director Carlos Saura. Juan Lebron Productions, 1995.

Fonseca, Isabel. *Bury Me Standing: The Gypsies and Their Journey.* London: Chatto and Windus, 1995.

Ford, Richard. *Gatherings from Spain.* London: J.M. Dent & Co., 1906.

Freud, Sigmund. "Writings on the Formation of the Object-Libido." *Three Essays on the Theory of Sexuality.* Tr. James Strachey. New York: Harper Collins, 1962.

García Lorca, Federico. *Bodas de Sangre and Yerma.* Madrid: Espasa-Calpe, S.A., 1971.

_____. *Obras Completas.* Madrid: Aguilar, S.A., 1967.

_____. *Poem of the Deep Song.* Tr. Carlos Bauer. San Francisco: City Lights, 1987.

Gerber, Jane. *The Jews of Spain.* New York: The Free Press, 1992.

Gili, J.L. *Selected Poems.* Harmondsworth: Penguin, 1960.

Gilman, Sander L. *Difference and Pathology: Stereotypes of Sexuality, Race and Madness.* Ithaca and London: Cornell University Press, 1985.

Gilmour, David. *The Transformation of Spain:* *From Franco to Constitutional Monarchy.* New York: Quartet Books, 1985.

Goldberg, Meira [Weinzweig]. "Carmen Amaya Wore Pants: Flamenco as a Forum for Cross-Gendered Identification Within Spanish Gypsy Culture." Paper presented at the Congress on Research and Dance: Performance and Possibilities, Los Angeles, October 1987.

_____. "A 'Heart of Darkness' in the New World: Carmen Amaya's Flamenco Dance in South American Vaudeville." *Dance in Hispanic Cultures. Proceedings of the Fourteenth Annual Conference of the Society of Dance History Scholars, February 8–10, 1991.* Riverside: Society of Dance History Scholars, 1991.

Grande, Félix. *García Lorca y el Flamenco.* Madrid: Mondadori España, S.A., 1992.

_____. *Memoria del Flamenco I: Raíces y Prehistoria del Cante.* Madrid: Espasa-Calpe, S.A., 1979.

_____. *Memoria del Flamenco II: Desde el Café Cantante a Nuestros Días.* Madrid: Espasa-Calpe, S.A., 1979.

Greco, José. *The Gypsy in My Soul: The Autobiography of José Greco.* New York: Doubleday and Co., 1977.

Guerrant, Edward O. *Roosevelt's Good Neighbor Policy.* Albuquerque: University of New Mexico, 1950.

Hamilton, Thomas J. *Appeasement's Child: The Franco Regime in Spain.* New York: Alfred A. Knopf, 1943.

Haraway, Donna. "A Manifesto for Cyborgs." *Simians, Cyborgs and Women: the Reinvention of Nature.* New York: Routledge, 1991.

Irigaray, Luce. "The Mechanics of Fluids." *This Sex Which is Not One.* Tr. Catherine Porter. Ithaca: Cornell University Press, 1985.

Jiménez, José Cenizo. *La madre y la compañera en las coplas flamencas.* Seville: Signatura Ediciones de Andalucía, 2005.

Josephs, Allen. *White Wall of Spain: The Mysteries of Andalusian Culture.* Pensacola: University of West Florida, 1983.

Keller, Gary D. *Hispanics and United States Film: An Overview and Handbook.* Tempe: Bilingual Press, 1994.

Klein, Dennis A. *Blood Wedding, Yerma, and The House of Bernarda Alba.* Boston: Twayne Publishers, 1991.

Kofman, Sarah. *The Enigma of Woman.* Ithaca and London: Cornell University Press, 1985.

Lacan, Jacques. "Function and Field of Speech and Language." *Ecrits: A Selection.* Tr. Alan Sheridan. New York and London: W. W. Norton and Co., 1977.

Lafuente, Rafael. *Los gitanos, el flamenco y los*

flamencos. Seville: Signatura Ediciones de Andalucía, 2006.

Latcho Drom. Director Tony Gatliff. Michele Ray: 1993.

Lauretis, Teresa de. *Technologies of Gender.* Bloomington: Indiana University Press, 1987.

Lavaur, Luis. *Teoría romántica del cante flamenco: Raíces flamencas en la coreografía romántica europea.* Seville: Signatura Ediciones de Andalucía, 1999.

McClary, Susan, ed. *Georges Bizet: Carmen.* Cambridge: Cambridge University, 1992.

Meduri, Avanthi. "Bharatha Natyam, What Are You?" *Asian Theatre Journal 5* (Spring 1998): 1–22.

Melgar Reina, Luis, and Angel Marín Rújula. *Arte, Genio y Duende: Notas Flamencas.* Córdoba: Publicaciónes del Monte de Piedad y Caja de Ahorros de Córdoba, 1988.

Meri, La. "Encounters with Dance Immortals: La Argentinita and Carmen Amaya." *Arabesque* (Jan.-Feb. 1985).

Mitchell, Timothy. *Flamenco Deep Song.* New Haven: Yale University Press, 1994.

Morar, B., D. Gresham, D. Angelicheva, I. Tournev, R. Gooding, V. Guergueltcheva, C. Schmidt, A. Abicht, H. Lochmüller, A. Tordai. "Mutation History of the Roma/ Gypsies." *American Journal of Human Genetics,* Volume 75, Issue 4 (2004).

Mulvey, Laura. "Afterthoughts on Visual Pleasure and Narrative Cinema, Inspired by *Duel in the Sun.*" *Feminism and Film Theory.* Ed. Constance Penley. New York: Routledge, 1988.

_____. "Visual Pleasure and Narrative Cinema." *Feminism and Film Theory.* Ed. Constance Penley. New York: Routledge, 1988.

Narayan, Shovana. *Kathak: Rhythmic Echoes and Reflections.* New Delhi: The Lotus Collection, 1989.

Nichols, Bill. *Ideology and the Image.* Bloomington: Indiana University Press, 1981.

Niles, Doris. "El *Duende.*" *Dance Perspectives 27* (Autumn 1966): 43–57.

Ortega y Gassett, José. *Obras Completas.* 5a. edición. Madrid: Revista de Occidente, 1961.

Payne, Stanley. *A History of Spanish Fascism.* Stanford: Stanford University, 1961.

Phillips, Miriam S. "A Shared Technique/ Shared Roots?: A Comparison of Kathak and Flamenco Dance History." *Proceedings of the Fourteenth Annual Conference of the Society of Dance History Scholars, February 8–10, 1991: Dance in Hispanic Cultures.* Riverside, CA: Society of Dance History Scholars, 1991.

Pike, Frederick B. *The United States and Latin America: Myths and Stereotypes of Civilization and Nature.* Austin: University of Texas, 1992.

Pohren, D.E. *Lives and Legends of Flamenco: A Biographical History.* Seville: Society of Spanish Studies, 1964.

_____. *A Way of Life.* Madrid: Society of Spanish Studies, 1980.

Quintana, Bertha B., and Lois Gray Floyd. *¡Que Gitano! Gypsies of Southern Spain.* New York: Holt, Rinehart and Winston, 1972.

Rice, Cyril. *Dancing in Spain: Argentina and Escudero.* London: British Continental Press, 1931.

Richard, Alfred Charles, Jr. *Censorship and Hollywood's Hispanic Image, An Interpretive Filmography.* Westport, CT: Greenwood Press, 1993.

_____. *The Hispanic Image on the Silver Screen: An Interpretive Filmography from Silents into Sound, 1898–1935.* Westport, CT: Greenwood Press, 1992.

Rodriguez, Juana Maria. *Queer Latinidad: Identity Practices, Discursive Spaces.* New York and London: New York University Press, 2003.

Romero, Vicente. "To Carmen Amaya." *Dancemagazine* (November 1963).

Rother, Larry. "Forget the Maine. Spain is Back," *New York Times,* 15 February 1998.

Savigliano, Marta. *Tango and the Political Economy of Passion.* Boulder: Westview Press, 1995.

Schreiner, Claus, ed. *Flamenco: Gypsy Dance and Music from Andalusia.* Tr. Mollie Comerford Peters. Portland, OR: Amadeus Press, 1985.

Sedgewick, Eve. *Between Men: English Literature and Male Homosocial Desire.* New York: Columbia University Press, 1985.

Sevillanas. Director Carlos Saura. Juan Lebron Productions, 1992.

"Spanish Dance." *Eye on Dance.* Producers Celia Ipiotis and Jeff Bush. ARC Videodance, 1991.

Spivak, Gayatri Chakravorty. "Can the Subaltern Speak?" *Marxism and the Interpretation of Culture.* Ed. Cary Nelson and Lauren Grossberg. Urbana: University of Illinois Press, 1988.

Steingress, Gerhard. *... Y Carmen se fue a París: un estudio sobre la construcción artística de género flamenco* (1833–1865). Córdoba: Editorial Almuzara, 2006.

_____. *Flamenco postmoderno: entre tradición y heterodoxia: un diagnóstico sociomusicólogo (escritos 1989–2006).* Seville: Signatura Ediciones de Andalucía, 2007.

_____, and Enrique Baltanás, eds. *Flamenco y*

nacionalismo: aportaciones para una sociología política del flamenco. Seville: Fundación Machado/Universidad de Sevilla/Fundación El Monte, 1998.

That Obscure Object of Desire. Director Luis Buñuel. Greenwich Film Production, 1977.

Vargas, Manuel Ríos. *Antología del baile flamenco.* Seville: Signatura Ediciones de Andalucía, 2006.

Vittucci, Matteo Marcellus, with Carola Goya. *The Language of Spanish Dance.* Norman: University of Oklahoma, 1990.

Washabaugh, William. *Flamenco: Passion, Politics and Popular Culture.* Oxford and Washington, D.C.: Berg, 1996.

White, Hayden. *The Content of the Form: Narrative Discourse and Historical Representation.* Baltimore: Johns Hopkins University, 1987.

Woll, Allen. *The Latin Image in American Film.* Los Angeles: Latin American Center, University of California, 1977.

Woodall, James. *In Search of the Firedance: Spain through Flamenco.* London: Sinclair-Stevenson, 1992.

La Yerbabuena, Eva. Interview with Jenny Gilbert. *The Independent on Sunday.* December 26, 2004.

Index

Page numbers in **bold italics** indicate photographs.

197